TOBACCO ADVERTISING
THE GREAT SEDUCTION

GERARD S. PETRONE, M.D

Schiffer Publishing Ltd

77 Lower Valley Road, Atglen, PA 19310

Library of Congress Cataloging-in-Publication Data

Petrone, Gerard S.
    Tobacco advertising : the great seduction with
values/ Gerard S. Petrone.
        p. cm. (A Schiffer book for collectors)
    Includes index
    ISBN 0-88740-972-5 (hard)
     1. Advertising--Tobacco--United States--History.
    2. Advertising--Cigarettes--United States--History. I. Title.
II. Series
    HF6161.T6P48 1996
    659.1'967973'0973--dc20   96-6405
                                      CIP

Printed in China

ISBN: 0-88740-972-5

Published by Schiffer Publishing Ltd.
77 Lower Valley Road
Atglen, PA 19310
Please write for a free catalog.
This book may be purchased from the publisher.
Please include $2.95 for shipping.
Try your bookstore first.

We are interested in hearing from authors
with book ideas on related subjects.

I dedicate this book to my sweetheart, Pam, and our "babies," Bentley and China.

ACKNOWLEDGMENTS

I am indebted to the following people whose lending of images and advertising artifacts helped make this book possible: fellow collector Joseph Hudgins of Greensboro, NC, who shared rarities of his vast cigarette advertising collection; Sid Emerson of Escondido, CA; Bill Enniss of Everett, WA; and Jim Shaw of Guerneville, CA. I give special thanks to fellow author Ron Barlow who edited this material and stressed the value of short sentences.

I also appreciate the cooperation of auction house James D. Julia, Inc. of Fairfield, Maine, and photographer David Beane; Dunbar Gallery of Milford, Massachusetts; Witherill's Americana Auctions of Sacramento, California; and Guernsey's Auction house, New York City.

CONTENTS

*"**No particular ability is required** to sell meat or flour or shoes. Elemental necessity compels the purchase of these things without effort on the part of the salesman. But to sell a man something he doesn't even know he wants is a very different thing."*
- U.S. Tobacco Journal (1913)

INTRODUCTION

This book tells the story of America's early romance and repulsion with tobacco. It covers a period of time, 1830 to 1930, that saw the nation become lured into and eventually hooked by the nicotine habit. This seduction was in large part aided by a specialized form of advertising that came to mark the hand of the tobacco merchant.

Ever since 1789 when the first tobacco ad appeared, tobacco manufacturers, imbued with long-range vision and an innate power of persuasion, pioneered selling techniques that literally stood conventional advertising on its ear and revolutionized the American way of doing business. They were good at what they did.

The strength of tobacco advertising lay in imagery and the power of suggestion. It began in the 1880s with alluring poster art that blossomed in full force during the Victorian age. Customers lounging in tobacco shops came eye to eye with the fair face of "the American girl," the smiling, young enchantress who, in her delicate, lily-white hand, extended brands of cigars and cigarettes.

The folksy, familiar and innocent-looking images portrayed in tobacco advertising were part of the new wave of product promotion - tin tags, cigar and tobacco labels, insert cards (including the first baseball cards) – that helped transform America into a nation of smokers by 1900.

Using illustrations of antique artifacts, old photographs and contemporary advertising, the onward march of tobacco is chronicled on these pages. It takes the reader through the rapid growth of the tobacco industry following the Civil War, introduction of the cigarette, early newspaper advertising, and passing consumer preferences for snuff, chewing and pipe tobacco and cigars.

Also covered are wide-ranging promotional ploys and gimmickry that evolved in this century: tobacco tins, cigarette pack art, and outdoor advertising (painted barns, billboards, and electric signs). Additionally there were the cute little things pressed into advertising service such as lapel buttons, pocket mirrors, postcards, watch fobs, pocketknives, envelope stickers and the like.

The tobacco industry also introduced and perfected the most powerful sales device ever invented, premium-giving, and drove it to unprecedented heights of success.

However, the most dramatic change in consumer preferences for tobacco, assisted materially by advertising, occurred with cigarettes. Introduced shortly after the Civil War, their mildness, convenience, low cost, and attractiveness of packaging mesmerized and tantalized a nation of men, women and children.

Demand for the dainty white rolls eventually went on to dwarf other forms of tobacco. By 1930, America had become addicted to them and today cigarette sales comprise 98 percent of the entire tobacco industry's business.

But this book tells other stories dealing with the social aspects of smoking. It shows how women took up smoking, the unfounded medical hysteria that surrounded tobacco in early times, the problem of juvenile smoking, the adulteration of tobacco and attempts to "de-nicotinize" it, and a chapter on old-time tobacco cures.

Most importantly, this volume recounts the growing public hostility directed toward the evils of tobacco and specifically cigarettes. Documented is the great anti-tobacco reform movement that panicked the United States at the beginning of this century and culminated in the nationwide passage of discriminatory anti-cigarette laws.

This extreme and extraordinary social experiment, while laudable in its purpose, failed miserably, but from it important lessons were learned that are readily applicable to the smoking problem facing the country today.

"The greatest symbol in American advertising was, is, and always will be, the face of a beautiful woman: it is used to sell everything except municipal bonds and steam locomotives." Fortune Magazine (1947)

PART I
TOBACCO ROMANCES THE WORLD

Tobacco and America were discovered at the same time. The boat crew Columbus sent forth from his caravels in 1492 to explore the island of Guahani (later renamed San Salvador) saw some of the native islanders carrying small lighted "firebrands" in which they burned a "strange herb" and inhaled the smoke from time to time.

To persons unacquainted with the practice, the sight of men smoking was misinterpreted as a means of perfuming themselves. Much amazed, the sailors returned to give their captain the first recorded tidings of a practice that was to overcome the world.

Indians smoking. This illustration of 1575 is believed to be one of the first prints depicting the use of tobacco.

The "strange herb" was first taken to Europe in 1559, over a half century later, by Francis Hernandez de Toledo, a physician, who had been dispatched by the Spanish king Philip II to Mexico to investigate the products of that rich country. He brought the plant back to Spain and cultivated it for medicinal and ornamental purposes.

From Spain, tobacco made its way to other countries in Europe. Jean Nicot, French ambassador at the High Court in Lisbon, purchased leaves and seed from a sailor and sent them to France as an "herb of peculiarly pleasant taste and good medicinality." Nicot presented some to Catherine de Medici, dowager queen of his sovereign, Francis II.

The exotic tobacco took the queen's fancy in the form of snuff, or *tabac en poudre*, as it was first termed, afterwards and still, *tabac a priser*. Snuff, from the verb, "to sniff," seemed a less roundabout label.

Queen Catherine's passion for snuff procured for its source the proud title of "herbe de la reine," or "the queen's weed." This name, however, soon fell out of favor. Among connoisseurs of the weed it was known simply as tobacco, *tabac, tabak, tabacco, tabaco,* and *tombeki,* in the vernacular of England, France, Germany, Italy, Spain, and Turkey.

Tobacco was introduced into the Old World from the New soon after Columbus' discovery of America. Deemed as one of the wonders of the world and credited with magical virtues and extraordinary medicinal qualities (which were greatly exaggerated), it was greeted with a chorus of enthusiastic praise and became an article of luxury.

We read that in 1589, the Pope's nuncio, Cardinal Santa Croce, returned from the court of Lisbon to Rome with a packet of tobacco in his portmanteau. This event inspired some poet of the age to pen the following lofty strain:

> *"Herb of undying fame,*
> *Which hither first with Santa Croce came,*
> *When he, his time of nunciature expired,*
> *Back from the court of Portugal retired,*
> *E'en as his predecessor, great and good,*
> *From Palestine brought back the Holy Rood."*

In the early 1600s, Sir Walter Raleigh obtained from Queen Elizabeth a grant of land in Virginia, which she gave him readily enough since it belonged to the Indians. He fitted out an expedition and planted a succession of colonies on the banks of a river named in honor of King James.

Elizabeth's death left Raleigh out of a job as his colonization scheme did not find favor with Elizabeth's successor, James I. But, before he was beheaded by his monarch, Raleigh introduced tobacco to England, raising the curtain on the Elizabethan age.

Ever since the redoubtable sea captain strolled down London's Pall Mall one fine day smoking the first corn-cob pipe, tobacco has since become, according to many, the "solace of mankind."

For the next 50 years, pipe smoking not only became popular among all classes of people, but a thing of high fashion, held by some in the light of an art. In less than a generation, there were 7,000 shops vending tobacco in London. In those days, it was not said that a man smoked tobacco but that he "drank" or "sucked" it, and the smoker was termed a "tobacconist." The gallant of society had no hesitation about smoking in the presence of women.

One "On" Sir Walter Raleigh.

This woodcut portrays the famous scene in which Raleigh's servant, seeing him smoking, thought he was on fire and doused him with a bucket of beer.

POETS' DELIGHT

From the first, literature in England became inextricably linked with tobacco. Whereas the effect of inhaling the smoke by the Indians was an inclination to sleep, by the Englishman it was an urge to express himself.

One of the strange things about Shakespeare's works is that the great bard never mentioned the word "tobacco." While the conclusion is drawn that he did not care for it, many of his contemporaries did.

Spenser, in his *Faerie Queene,* written soon after the introduction of the plant in England, called it "sovereign weede, divine tobacco," and from Ben Jonson's comedies can be gathered a perfect compendium of "tobacco drinking" as one of the most important social phenomena of the age. Carlyle was a confirmed pipe smoker. Charles Lamb remarked that he hoped that his last breath would be inhaled through a pipe and exhaled in a pun.

Ben Jonson

Alfred Lord Tennyson

Since their day most literary men became addicted to the soothing pipe of tobacco and, in measured verse and prose, sung its praises. It aided them in concentrating nervous energy into intellectual labor, they said, by allaying all extraneous irritation. Some who used tobacco even lived to a great age.

"The pipe," wrote Bulwer Lytton, "is a great soother, a pleasant comforter. It ripens the brain, it opens the heart, and the man who smokes thinks like a sage and acts like a Samaritan." Thackeray found his cigar one of the greatest creature comforts of his life – "a kind companion, a gentle stimulant, an amiable anodyne, a cementer of friendship."

Tennyson's passion for a long clay was well known; mild birds'-eye was his favorite tobacco. His devotion to the herb became so intense that he literally could not exist without it. On one occasion at an evening soiree of the Royal Society, he announced that he must have a pipeful. Told that he could either smoke inside the large fireplace in the library or on the roof, Tennyson chose the latter. With his body thrust half-way through the skylight, he puffed away in peace, descending in quarter of an hour greatly refreshed.

Tobacco sellers were mostly apothecaries in Elizabethan England. Some of them took in pupils. These professors of the art of smoking taught students the "slights," as tricks with the pipes were called then, which included inhaling and blowing out smoke in the form of globes and rings.

"Taking the whiff" was what Swift, a professor of the smoking art in Jonson's "Every Man Out of His Humor," had in mind when he posted a bill in St. Paul's offering to teach any young gentleman newly come into an inheritance "to entertain the most gentlemanlike use of tobacco."

One contemporary instructor in smoking professed to able to teach the secret of emitting smoke not only from the nose but also the ears. A healthy skepticism was permitted in this case.

The rich young swell of Merry Olde England carried about him an elaborate tobacco kit, often made of gold or silver. It contained a tobacco box, a pair of tongs with which to lift a live coal to light his pipe, a ladle "for the cold snuffle into the nosthrill," a priming iron, and as large a collection of pipes as his means could afford and his pockets could hold.

Occasionally the tobacco box was of ivory with a mirror set in the lid to allow the dandy, upon opening it, to bask in the glory of his handsome countenance.

There is a tradition that Queen Elizabeth herself once smoked - with unpleasant results. Campbell, in his "History of Virginia," stated that Raleigh offered Her Majesty some tobacco to smoke and she was seized with nausea "after two or three whiffs." Any disfavor Elizabeth may have heaped upon tobacco was more than undone by her court. Its use soon became of such vogue that "some of the great ladies, as well as the noblemen, would not scruple sometimes to take a pipe very sociably."

THE SMOKING KING OF HOLLAND

No one ever disputed the right of Mynheer Van Klaes of 17th century Holland to be called the "king of smokers." His den was a museum of nicotine relics, containing specimens of every kind of tobacco smoked in the world and every kind of pipe through which nations drew inspiration. Here he smoked constantly and incessantly. His life's consumption of tobacco was conservatively estimated at four tons, or ten pounds every week of his 60 smoking years.

Van Klaes died at the age of 81, having devoted his entire adulthood to the smoking of tobacco. His funeral was in harmony with his life. By his express instructions, his coffin was lined with the wood of old cigar boxes. At his feet was placed a bladder of the finest Dutch golden leaf and a packet of caporal. By his sides were laid his china-bowled pipe and his steel, flint and tinder.

In accordance with his will, all smokers of Rotterdam were invited to the funeral and instead of the traditional mourning rings, each attendee was presented ten pounds of good tobacco and two pipes bearing the Van Klaes coat-of-arms. All the mourners smoked during the funeral service, and at the words, "Ashes to ashes, dust to dust," shook out the contents of their pipes onto the coffin lid.

TOBACCO IN COLONIAL AMERICA

England was the first country in Europe to adopt smoking. The practice grew so rapidly and demand was so great that attention was turned to the new colonies for the growing of tobacco.

The history of tobacco cultivation in America began in 1607 with the colonial settlement at Jamestown, Virginia. John Rolfe was the first white man to cultivate tobacco systematically. He made it the principal crop of the new plantation, Varina, on the James River, to which he took his bride, Pocohontas, the daughter of Chief Powhatan.

The first settlers in Virginia saw at once that the Indians regarded the cultivation of tobacco second in importance only to the corn crop. Gifts of tobacco invariably accompanied the native's overtures of friendship. In all councils and consultations between Indian chief and Indian chief and between Indian chief and pale-faced captain, the pipe of peace was passed around in the manner of a loving cup.

Smoking also played a prominent part in religious rites of the natives, and while the cigarette was as yet unknown, the tobacco pouch, ornamented in crude fashion, was as much a part of the regular equipment of these earliest American warriors as the bow and arrow.

Rolfe began his tobacco-growing operation in 1611. Its success assured the permanence of Virginia as a colony and provided the basis of a necessary exchange between the new land and the mother country.

Throughout the colonial period, tobacco was established as the premier cash crop of America and this nation's first major export. Every Virginia planter raised the "strange herb" which had so captivated men, doing his part to satisfy the demand which neither king nor priest could control in the motherland of England. There the exile's typical American product was traded for the greatest desire of his heart's wildest imagination – good English merchandise with which to feed and clothe himself and his family.

The planter's four-poster bed, his silver tankard, his flashing sword and shoe buckles, his coach and harness, his lady's spinet, her lute, her gown, her "frills and falls" of choice lace and other things "fashionable to London," as well as the rougher clothing of the owner of a few acres, were "brought out of England," in exchange for hogsheads of tobacco which little white-sailed ships constantly bore across the Atlantic.

For many years tobacco was currency in the colony of Virginia, and with the Virginians of the day the "tobacco note" served the purpose which the gold and silver certificate served later. It was honored in all local shops. Taxes and parish levies, fines and gambling debts, wedding fees, the cost of mail order brides from England, and funeral expenses were paid in tobacco. Officials of the Established Church were salaried regularly with the weed. "Every minister...of Virginia shall have an annual salary of 16,000 pounds of tobacco" decreed King George I of England in 1748.

Tobacco paid for two shiploads of maidens dispatched from England to pair up with colonists and become the mothers of young Virginians. Tobacco built mansions and bought slaves from Africa. It brought candles and books and, from the Continent, the minuet.

Parishes were rated and known according to the quality of tobacco produced in them; an "Orinoko" parish was considered less desirable than a "sweet-scented" one.

In the course of time, the fascination that the Virginia weed had created for itself had so far overcome objections to its presence and consumption in England. Toward the close of the seventeenth century, Virginians were pleading with Mother England to give the colony a college, "for the sake of their souls."

The Attorney-General is said to have replied, "Damn your souls, plant tobacco!"

DRAWING ENEMIES

Strong opposition to tobacco developed soon after it was introduced in England in the Seventeenth Century. The weed was denounced by Church and state and its use forbidden upon pain of whipping, excommunication and, in some instances, death at the stake.

In 1604, His Majesty James I composed a "Counterblaste" against tobacco and Charles I continued the verbal attack in 1633 by claiming that tobacco provoked users "to drinking and other inconvenience to the great impairing of their healths and depraving of their manners."

Several Popes, Urban VIII and Innocent XI among them, launched against tobacco the thunders of the Roman Church. The priests and sultans of Turkey also denounced smoking as a crime. Murad, a ruthless Ottoman ruler - after whom an American brand of cigarettes was named in the early 1900s – blamed an uprising in 1633 on smokers who congregated in dens where contrary political views were aired.

STYGIAN SMOAKE.

"A custome loathsome to the eye, harmful to the brain, dangerous to the lungs and in the black stinking fume thereof, nearest resembling the horrible Stygian smoake of the pit that is bottomless." So wrote King James in his famous diatribe against tobacco, a rambling, ranting and biased attempt to curb a habit that he personally found detestable. The monarch, citing lurid but unfounded medical details, hoped to strike fear in the hearts of those who used the weed. Printed anonymously in 1604 and constituting the world's first piece of anti-tobacco literature, the tract provoked much public comment but, in the end, its message was ignored.

Murad consequently declared smoking punishable by death and the sadistic sultan kept his word; he beheaded 25,000 victims in the last five years of his reign. Another sultan had the pipes of smokers thrust horizontally through their noses as a reminder of the weed's pernicious hazard.

All these condemnations, penalties and punishments were in vain. The use of tobacco spread rapidly over the continents of Europe and Asia and returned to the civilized portions of the New World.

SCOURGE OF SOCIETY: EARLY ANTI-TOBACCO SENTIMENTS IN AMERICA

"Tobacco surely was designed
To poison and destroy mankind."
- Philip Freneau

added, and tended to promote idleness. Rush also maintained that its use led to a desire for alcohol, a belief that persisted for many years.

As late as the 1840s, smoking was prohibited on the streets of Boston. Violators were arrested. Even lighting up a pipe on the Boston Common was not allowed, except on top of an earthen mound southwest of the music field; it came to be known as "Smokers' Circle."

In pre-Civil War days, a group of educators, physicians, clergymen, and the famous P.T. Barnum banded together to fight the evil weed. They were joined by John Hartwell Cocke, co-founder of the University of Virginia, who disseminated anti-nicotine tracts and awarded no-tobacco medals to young boys.

Opposition to tobacco has existed in America since colonial days. It was temporarily sidetracked during the great reform era preceding the Civil War when alcohol and slavery were far more pressing issues of the day.

The earliest tobacco prohibitionists were the Puritans. No tobacco was permitted on ships leaving their colony and its use was strictly limited to medicinal purposes. However, smoking continued.

Eventually, in 1638, the Puritan leaders relented and passed a law prohibiting smoking in barns, fields, forests, inns, and public houses (except in private rooms, or by soldiers in time of training). Violators were fined two shillings, six pence for every offense and the new law became a steady source of revenue.

Later, smoking in public was permitted if done on a journey of five miles or more. Cotton Mather, flexible on the issue of tobacco, suggested moderation in its use.

Dr. Benjamin Rush, who affixed his signature to the Declaration of Independence, wrote a stinging attack on tobacco and enumerated some of its ruinous effects on the human system. Tobacco was expensive anyway, he

Blue laws of the State of Connecticut *in 1650 punished transgressors who chose to chew tobacco and decorate the floors of cable cars. The statute read: "It is ordered that no man...shall take any tobacco publiquely, in the street, highwayes, or any barnyardes, or uppon training days, in any open places under penalty of six-pence for each offense against this order."*

Chewing tobacco came under sharp attack by an authority of eugenics and phrenology, Reverend Orson S. Fowler, who clearly saw in the weed the cause of insanity, impotency, sexual perversion, and cancer of the mouth. "No man can be virtuous as a companion who eats tobacco," he said, "for, although he may not violate

THE

TOBACCO SCOURGE.

BY

D. W. C. HUNTINGTON, D.I

NEW YORK.
PHILLIPS & H
CINCINNATI:
CRANSTON & S

New Series.]

[No. 171.

THE TOBACCO-SCOURGE.

A SCOURGE it is, and it is every-where in shameless profusion. Old men, sallow and meatless, consuming the last ounce of their vitality in smoking and chewing tobacco; laborers going to and from their work, with pipes or cigars in their mouths; idlers and loungers, cursing rich men and corporations and consuming more for cigars than would be required to furnish them bread; mere boys, dissipating with pipes, cigarettes, and stumps of cigars, their faces flushed with tobacco-intoxication, or pallid from tobacco-exhaustion; every other man you meet is puffing or chewing this baneful commodity.

Tobacco, scourge of society. Anti-tobacco tracts could be found circulating in America around the time of the Civil War, many composed by Bible-thumping clergymen like Dr. Huntington.

for "the building of an institution on the banks of the Connecticut River to house poor invalids, made such by Spanish cigars."

Trask was best known for a widely circulated tract published in 1852 entitled "Thoughts and Stories for American Lads," subtitled "Uncle Toby's Anti-Tobacco Advice to his Nephew Billy Bruce."

Also active in the antebellum period was Dr. Joel Shew. He carefully itemized a long list of ailments, 87 in number (the first being insanity), caused by using tobacco. Shew, agreeing with Fowler, also warned tobacco users that their habit caused impotency.

Anti-tobacco tracts circulated widely in the United States before and after the Civil War. Some were illustrated and covered a wide variety of other subjects and social issues. One, published in 1860, touched on smoking in prison, the use of snuff, discipline of the church, and "your first cigar."

Some who railed against liquor also found time to take a shot at the evils of tobacco. John B. Gough, a temperance lecturer and former drunkard, used to pull a plug of chaw from his pocket and inhale its fragrance deeply, yelling out, "Ah, you black devil, I love you" – and then throw it away.

*"Tobacco is a filthy weed,
The Devil he doth sow the seed."*

the seventh commandment, yet the feverish state of the system which it produces necessarily causes a craving and lustful exercise of amativeness...You, who would be pure in your love-instinct, cast this sensualizing fire from you."

Perhaps the most ardent and vociferous reformer of antebellum days was the "anti-tobacco apostle," Reverend George Trask of Massachusetts, a prolific writer of religious tracts and capable of penning some of the longest sentences in the English language.

"Tobacco is a poison," he said, "it injures health and abridges life." To use it was not only immoral but a sin because it trampled down the laws of nature, inflicting illness and death. Trask also poured vehemence on those who cultivated tobacco in his native state. It ruined soil and destroyed the Christian character of his fellow man. He also went so far as to call

The Mexican War, the California gold rush and the prosperity of the 1850s created a popular demand for cigars and chewing tobacco. Soon the voices of the anti-tobacco forces began to fall on deaf ears. Dr. William Alcott pronounced in 1849 that: "From one end of the commonwealth to the other – temperance or no temperance – it is, as it were, one mighty puff, puff, puff."

Dr. R.T. Trall, a prominent critic of tobacco and alcohol, reported sadly in 1854 that America had attained the highest per capita use of tobacco in the world. Street urchins of New York City between the ages of three to six were now smoking cigars and their older companions chewing tobacco.

The worst news he saved for last: "Some of the *ladies* of this refined and fashion-forming metropolis are aping the silly ways of some pseudo-accomplished foreigners, in smoking Tobacco through a weaker and more *feminine* article, which has been most delicately denominated *cigarette*."

THE FICKLE PRESS

Newspapermen in America did not always take kindly to things said by the early tobacco warriors. When provoked, they fired off editorial broadsides in rebuttal, some serious and some in half-jest.

In 1876, an editor of the New York Times became angered after reading of a citizen in Philadelphia who proudly refused to rent rooms to visitors "addicted to tobacco" during the busy tourist season of the nation's Centennial celebration. No money could "induce him to admit a commoner of tobacco beneath his roof."

That was it. The newsman unleashed a vitriolic attack on self-righteous "enemies of the weed" who were responsible for the unhappy state of affairs facing "victims of the anti-tobacco habit." They were prohibited from enjoying their smokes on streetcars, ferry boats, trains, and in theaters because of a minority's "atrocious opinions" being imposed on the rights of the majority.

Another blow was suffered by the anti-tobacco forces when, in 1879, a regulation barring the use of tobacco by midshipmen at the Naval Academy in Annapolis was lifted. The respite was given as a reward. The middies helped extinguish a fire that threatened the city by hauling fire hoses down to the river after the municipal fire hydrant system broke down.

The action outraged the fickle press and civic groups. Charging the government with encouraging the youths to follow the "lamentable evils" of smoking and chewing the weed, the crusaders let loose a verbal barrage aimed at the Superintendent, Commodore Parker.

"The chances of our ever receiving from the Academy at Annapolis any sailors of the pattern of Truxton, Bainbridge, Paul Jones, Decatur, Lawrence, and Perry are not good," they bemoaned.

In 1882, another editor of the New York Times authored a piece entitled "Selfishness in Public." The journalist pointed out the injustices suffered by America's legions of smokers at the hands of the non-tobacco community.

Examples were given: "Designated smoking rooms on ferryboats and railway trains are often crowded with nonsmokers who monopolize valuable seating space and read their newspapers in defiance and utter carelessness of the fact that they are interfering with the rights and destroying the comfort of the other men, the smokers.

"Things are made worse by these nonsmoking space usurpers who inflict unwanted conversation on smokers, disrupting the peace they need to enjoy their smokes. By far though, the most reprehensible attribute of the nonsmoker is his blatant flirting with ladies. This vulgar spectacle, to be sure, is never witnessed in a smoking car."

The newsman went on to say that 99 ladies out of 100 who had unwelcome attentions thrust upon them while traveling by rail or car would testify that in every case the transgressor was a man who was not smoking.

Nothing could more forcibly show the demoralizing effects exhibited by those "malicious fanatics who abstained from tobacco," the editor concluded.

PART TWO
TOOLS OF PERSUASION

ANTEBELLUM ADVERTISING

Little history is recorded of our nation's early tobacco enterprises except those that survived the years. The Lorillard Company, still in business today, is the oldest tobacco company in the United States. It was started in 1760 by a French Huguenot, Pierre Lorillard, in a small house on Chatham Street in New York City. Lorillard, finishing his apprenticeship as a snuffmaker, packed his product in bladders and entered business for himself, selling snuff to wholesalers. The company went on to become one of the largest in the country.

Title as the oldest tobacconists' store in the United States is claimed by the Demuth Tobacco Shop of Lancaster, Pennsylvania. It was founded in 1770 by Christopher Demuth, a Moravian immigrant. Here early patriots gathered as much to pass the time of day in trivial conversation as to enjoy Demuth's Golden Lion cigars and fine rappee snuff made in a small factory in back of the shop.

George Washington himself, father of our country, though not a consistent smoker, was one of the leading tobacco growers and exporters of precolonial times. Tobacco was replaced by cotton as the nation's chief export around 1800, but the weed played a vital role in financing the Revolutionary War. In 1776, Benjamin Franklin arranged the exchange of 5,000 hogsheads of Virginia leaf for a French loan of two million pounds of silver.

Publicizing tobacco in the early days of America re-

Tobacco & Snuff of the best quality & flavor,
At the Manufactory, No. 4. Chatham street, near the Gaol
By Peter and George Lorillard,
Where may be had as follows :

Cut tobacco,	Prig or carrot do.
Common kitefoot do.	Maccuba snuff,
Common smoaking do.	Rappee do.
Segars do.	Strasburgh do.
Ladies twist do.	Common rappee do.
Pigtail do. in small rolls,	Scented rappee do. of dif-
Plug do.	ferent kinds,
Hogtail do.	Scotch do.

The above Tobacco and Snuff will be sold reasonable, and warranted as good as any on the continent. If not found to prove good, any part of it may be returned, if not damaged.

N. B. Proper allowance will be made to those that purchase a quantity. May 27—1m.

*(Above). **America's first tobacco advertisement**. Run by the Lorillard brothers, it appeared in the New York Daily Advertiser on May 27, 1789.*

__Formal tobacco advertising__ of the 1830-1860 period was graphically threadbare. This woodcut broadside (ca 1840s) announcing Mt. Vernon cigars would have been considered quite extravagant in its day.

flected the casual pace of doing business. Flyers, notices, business cards, and broadside posters answered the promotional needs of a fledgling industry. Little or no artistic flair was expended in designs and renditions; their existence and purpose was strictly utilitarian.

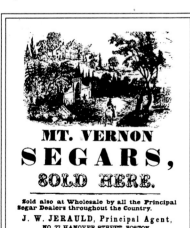

MT. VERNON
SEGARS,
SOLD HERE.

Sold also at Wholesale by all the Principal Segar Dealers throughout the Country.

J. W. JERAULD, Principal Agent,
NO. 77 HANOVER STREET, BOSTON.

LORILLARDS BRANCH OUT IN BUSINESS

There were business entrepreneurs in this era. The Lorillard brothers, Peter and George, were the first to achieve direct mail order advertising as early as the 1830s. Without the convenience of mailing lists, their solution to reach out was a simple and effective one. The brothers made up broadsides listing all their products and mailed them to postmasters all over the country.

Knowing that the keeper of the post was a vital member of the community, they banked on his getting out the word. What resulted was nothing short of a business bonanza. Not only was the Lorillard name spread widely and response overwhelming, but many keepers of the post requested sales franchises.

The Lorillards, in essence, established America's first mail order business. It was to signal a new trend in business as the postal employees later became agents for a host of other companies peddling articles ranging from pianos to farm machinery.

The Lorillard mail order enterprise soon took on a new and unexpected direction. Agents in the field began asking for smoking and chewing tobacco to sell as private brands. This request for specialized service was honored by the Lorillards who, in the process, pioneered tobaccodom's first private label service which later become a standard practice in the industry.

AN INFANT INDUSTRY

From the 1800s to the Civil War, the use of tobacco, chiefly cigars, snuff and chewing plug, was limited and with it the numbers of those involved in its manufacture, distribution and sale.

Tobacco warehouses, established in the 1790-1810 period in Virginia, led to the development of factories. Consequently, Richmond, Lynchburg and Petersburg became the primary antebellum sites of tobacco manufacture in the nation.

Lacking means of national merchandising, manufacturers were concerned only with meeting the local or, at best, regional demands for their products. Retail dealers in tobacco were uncommon, the need not being sufficient in many areas to support the vending of tobacco as a primary occupation.

Consumers found their favorite brands in the stores of grocers, saloon keepers, news vendors, druggists, stationers, and liquor merchants, where they were carried more as a convenience to established clientele than as a profitable side business. In fact, some merchants deliberately undersold tobacco wares to attract foot traffic.

The Planter's Tobacco Warehouse, built in 1839 and the largest in St. Louis, was located at the corner of Laurel and Second streets, near the steamboat landing. The spacious structure was capable of storing 5,000 hogsheads of tobacco and helped establish the city as the nation's leading manufacturer of plug chewing tobacco.

NEW IDEAS AND NEW LOOKS

Prior to the 1860s, tobacco men bought little or no advertising space, often relying more on indirect means of reaching the editorial or news columns. When a manufacturer happened to pay an outrageous price for a shipment of leaf tobacco, he also "bought" newspaper space in the deal when wind of the transaction was caught by the local newspaperman.

No less subtle - but no less successful - was the giving of samples to the editorial citadel. Manufacturers often extended generous presents of chewing brands to newspaper owners or editors, hoping for favorable comment in the press.

"Good – very good!" were the words printed by P. D. Bernard, owner of the Southern Planter and veteran chewer of some 30 summers, upon tasting samples given him by the Richmond firm of Gilliam and Mathews. The editor of the Daily Dispatch in Richmond was also complimentary of a box of Winfree's Rock Candy quid which he described as "an excellent article, admirably adapted to our taste."

Printed advertisements were primitive. A typical notice placed in a periodical was usually small in size and inserted by retail establishments, not manufacturers. They announced without fanfare whatever goods a tobacconist or general merchant had for sale. Brand names were rarely mentioned.

The presumption was that people already knew what tobacco had to offer, and that no effort was needed to educate them, or to portray the products as being especially desirable or better than any others. This manner of doing business was plain and simple – so were the goods.

Posters, as a means of advertising, came into use slowly. They were nothing new to the public. Letterpress and woodcut handbills were common wall-hanging fare as early as the 1700s, but the development of colored printing techniques opened up a new means of promotion in the form of posters and signs.

SMOKING TOBACCO,
MANUFACTURED by John Turel & Co., Baltimore, and for sale by the single paper or dozen at the CENTRAL RETREAT.
April 28, 1838.

Beginning in the 1830s, tobacco companies like these arose in America, forming the nucleus of an industry that was to expand rapidly after the Civil War.

ST. LOUIS
Tobacco Manufactory

HUGH RICHARDS
&
TRACY & WAHRENDORFF,

INFORM the public, that they have entered into Co-Partnership, under the firm of
HUGH RICHARDS & CO.
For the purpose of carrying on the Manufacturing of Tobacco, Snuff and Segars, in the town of St. Louis.

H. RICHARDS being well acquainted with the above business, and the subscribers' intending to Manufacture Tobacco of the growth of this state, they hope for the support of their fellow-citizens. They intend to enlarge their establishment so as to manufacture a large proportion of the Leaf-Tobacco, raised in this state, and will either barter, or otherwise contract for the same.——They offer for sale at the Factory, opposite the stone house of colonel Easton, or at the store of Tracy & Wahrendorff.

PIG-TAIL, TWIST and
PLUG TOBACCO,
SEGARS, MACCOUBA and
RAPPEE SNUFF.
HUGH RICHARDS & Co.
St. Louis, Jan. 1st 1822—87 3m

Stone lithography, later to play a vital role in tobacco advertising imagery, was in its infancy when, in 1840, the first colored print was made in Boston by an English immigrant, William Sharp. The event was followed shortly by "chromos," produced by a small group of European-born printers in New York City and Philadelphia whose firms numbered around 60 on the eve of the Civil War.

These lithographic houses hired staffs of artists and engravers to meet the growing needs of clients. The demand was vigorous. Businessmen and merchants, including specialized interests as theater companies, circus owners and political organizations, as well as the ubiquitous tobacco men, found posters uncommonly effective as trade stimulators.

It was not long before large colorful images printed on paper, wood or tin became standard background trappings in cigar, tobacco and pipe shops all over the country. Branding of tobacco products was a newly acquired practice; customers were still in the habit of simply asking for "a good cigar" or "a good chew," not a brand name.

The first company to start giving its products names was Lorillard. Equally perceptive tobacco men also discovered the advantages of a distinctive brand label, thereby freeing their products from the mundane name of the manufacturer. Goods were christened instead with words containing a dash of imagination and allure.

Black's Plug gave way to Golden Slipper, Brown's Twist to Sweet Mash Twist and Smith's Leaf to Speckled Beauty. The trend caught on quickly and makers of chewing and smoking tobacco went on to establish a rich legacy of colorful and glamorous brand appellations that filled volumes.

Early labelling of tobacco containers was rudimentary. Brand names were literally branded on wooden containers with a red-hot iron or stencilled with commercial ink.

The Lorillard company is credited *with producing America's first metal tobacco container. Around 1860, a small, hand-soldered unit held a chunk of Century chewing tobacco, a brand named in honor of the firm's one-hundredth year in business. To push sales, a $100 bill was placed in random tins. The promotion was a huge success until the government stepped in and shut it down, claiming it was a lottery and hence unlawful. The use of tin containers was a novel idea but it would be another two decades before tin-making technology would advance enough to exploit this far-sighted promotional concept.*

THE NATIVE AMERICAN

"Americans are the only civilized people who habitually chew tobacco...having, it is to be regretted, a monopoly of the most unwholesome and obnoxious of practices...To see a landsman chewing tobacco anywhere abroad is to know him for an American, native or adopted."

- *New York Times (1878)*

An advertising flyer of the Pimlico Tobacco Works*, a Baltimore manufactory of snuff and smoking tobacco. It was a notable exception to the typically drab and unimaginative style of tobacco advertising in antebellum America. Circa 1850s, the piece was well ahead of its time with bold and vivid colors, a rare, extravagant and technically difficult luxury back then. Courtesy Maryland Historical Society, Baltimore, Maryland.*

THE SNUFFING HABIT

Snuff is a powdered form of tobacco, often perfumed, that became a favorite of the French and English royal courts of the Eighteenth Century. Its use also reached quite a fashionable level in America after the Revolution and was accepted into all classes of society, by men and women alike.

Snuff was originally packaged in dried animal bladders, and later in barrels, tins and special glass jars. Snuff was either inhaled into the nostrils, the most common means of enjoying the habit, or placed between the gum and teeth. It was dipped out in small quantities with a stick or tiny spoon, a technique that gave rise to the term "snuff dipping." Some users, especially in the Southern states, preferred to chew a wooden stick into a mop-like consistency and then dip it into the snuff.

There were several classes of the product. They included Maccoboy, a strong, moist, and coarse variety scented with attar of roses, and the dry, coffee brown Scotch types, salted or unsalted to suit individual tastes. Rappee, made of dark tobacco, was the most pungent of the lot.

Snuff was believed to possess high antiseptic and detergent qualities and for these reasons, it was frequently rubbed onto the teeth and gums.

The taking of snuff has a proud and interesting past. The day was when the ceremony of snuffing was the most important of all social customs. In Elizabethan times it was an elaborate and practiced art and it

was absolutely necessary to perform a set ritual.

Holding the snuff box in the right hand, it was tapped and opened. After it had made the rounds of the human company, its owner gathered up the snuff in the box by striking the side with the middle and forefingers, and then took a pinch with the right hand.

It was held two or three moments between the fingers and carried to the nose. It was then sniffed in with precision by both nostrils. This done, the box was closed, the performance concluding with a sneeze and a vigorous application of an enormous bandanna handkerchief to the nose, made necessary by the habit and originated for it as well.

Of course, in refined company, this was the prescribed routine; in informal settings, however, snuff was taken haphazardly.

The consumption of snuff at the great gaming tables of Europe was considerable as players believed that it cleared their heads, stimulated their intellects and soothed their nerves, attributes that largely accounted for its almost universal use.

Napoleon was a great believer in the virtues of a few pinches of snuff repeated often, though they failed him at Waterloo where it is said that he applied himself assiduously to his snuffbox.

The common foot soldier, too, was also addicted to a pinch amid the roar of battle. For instance, during a battle in Holland, a general was generously offered a snuffbox by one of his officers. At the very moment the latter was presenting the box, he was carried off by a cannon ball. Not in the least disconcerted, the general turned to his other side and asked quietly of another officer, "Well, sir, then you must give me a pinch."

The sight of gentlemen gracefully lifting a pinch of snuff from a small jewelled box in America gradually passed from the social scene. Except for colonies of displaced foreigners – Swedish laborers in Kansas and French coal miners in Missouri, for instance – the snuffing habit, by the 1890s, was on the way out, displaced by the cigar and chewing tobacco.

A calculation was once made showing that, during 40 years of consumption, a snuff user occupied no less than 24 months in taking pinches, based on one pinch taken every ten minutes. It gives some idea of the great popularity of snuff in the olden days.

THE COMFORTING CHEW

Twisting Plug Tobacco.

In the early 1800s, a new form of the weed gained wide popularity in America: chewing tobacco. Its origins are attributed to New World sailors who, aboard wooden vessels where smoking lamps were lit with great trepidation, chewed tobacco instead of firing it in their pipes as a safe, practical and satisfying alternative. It was also relished by pioneers and frontiersmen who found cigars and pipes too unhandy.

Chewing tobacco was originally prepared by moistening dried tobacco leaves with licorice and sugar, then molding them into lumps which were carried about in the user's pockets. Pieces were bitten, cut or chewed off as needed.

Later, the manufacturing process became more refined. "Flat goods," as chewing tobacco came to be called, were flavored by a wide range of agents, wrapped with an outer layer of tobacco leaf and pressed into long, rectangular bricks. In shops, this bulk form was lopped off into convenient pocket-sized pieces with large cast iron tobacco cutters.

Most of the leaf for chewing tobacco used east of the Appalachians was grown in Henry County, Virginia, while two districts in Kentucky and Missouri furnished the bulk of plug goods consumed beyond the Divide.

Four types of chewing tobacco were made:

1. loose leaf: made of sweet or semi-sweet tobacco leaf;
2. plug, or pressed leaf: a type originally made by plugging fine tobacco soaked in wild honey into green hickory or maple logs;
3. fine cut: a granulated variety similar to moist snuff that could also be smoked in pipes; and
4. twist: made by curling cured leaves into the shape of a pigtail.

The high point of chewing tobacco use in the United States ranged from the mid-1800s through the early 1900s. Regional preferences existed. The New Englander, it was said, preferred fine cut, while the man south of the Potomac chewed nothing but three-ply twist. Later he turned to flat plug.

Unlike snuff taking, the chewing of tobacco was never regarded as a mark of social grace; many people considered it a disgusting personal habit. A lumpy jaw and telltale amber-colored stains on mustache, beard or spattered down shirt fronts gave away this particular connoisseur of the weed.

In some parts of America, however, notably the South, a quid of plug was no bar to social prestige and leadership and was actually favored by sires and scions of prominent families. But, in general, tobacco chewing was the consolation of those "in the trades" who gained their livelihood through hard work out-of-doors, a prime requisite being a convenient place to spit.

At one time in history, strong-jawed chewers had their pick of over 12,000 different brands on the market going by such imaginative labels as My Wife's Hat, Wiggletail Twist, Sweet Buy & Buy, and Scalping Knife.

Cuspidors, those much maligned articles of necessity, became standard floor appurtenances wherever men congregated, from the privacy of living room parlors to the floors of Congress where three stand today at the feet of tobacco-chewing senators.

THE CIGAR STORE INDIAN
SIDEWALK SENTINEL
OF BUSINESS

In the early days, tobacco was regarded as a gift of the native American to civilization, and it was quite natural to mark the location of a tobacconist's shop with a carved figure of an Indian. For many years no symbol was more representative of the old-time tobacco shop than this stalwart figure which was wheeled out to stand in the shadow of the doorways.

There he looked out upon a world that saw the passing of his contemporaries and of an age in which he was as familiar a figure as was the striped pole of the barber shop and the three balls of the pawnbroker. Trade stimulator, he was called.

Wooden Indians hold an important and secure place in the field of advertising American art and native traditions. In their approximate 30-year period of peak popularity (between 1850 and 1880), it is estimated that from 80,000 to 100,000 cigar store figures were cast or carved in the United States.

Of these numbers, less than 3,000 survive today in museums and in a handful of private collections. They have achieved a collector status and value that would shock those carvers in wood who made them so long ago.

EARLY HISTORY

Cigar store Indians evolved from a 5,000-year-old tradition of signboard art. Trade signs were first used by ancient Egyptians and carved figureheads have adorned the bowsprits of wooden sailing vessels since Cleopatra's time.

Aristotle refers to tradesman's signs displayed in Greek towns and it is recorded that the Romans had so many signboards hanging about that they began to name city streets after them.

Most of these early advertising symbols were polychromed cut-outs made from wooden boards, but many survived the ages as three-dimensional figures. A sculpted vase or bunch of grapes was displayed by the wine vendor and purveyors of milk often hung out a carved goat to mark their shops on crowded streets.

Cigar store Indian. Made by an unidentified sculptor and painted by Ezra Ames, ca 1823. Courtesy of Albany Institute of History and Art, Albany, New York.

AMERICA ADOPTS THE INDIAN

A tobacconist's shop in the time of James I (from a reprint of Brathwait's "Smoaking Age," published in 1617). It established the early use of the Indian figure as a tobacco shop trade sign.

The sign-making tradition passed from Rome to England and the rest of the European continent, then on to America. Wooden Indians were not the first advertising symbols utilized by tobacco merchants. Diminutive countertop blackamoors were the favorite trade signs of the 17th and 18th century European tobacco shops, coffee houses and tax collectors.

An Amsterdam tobacconist is known to have used such a figure before 1600. These ubiquitous 24-inch-tall negro boys, in their tobacco-leaf skirts and feathered headdresses, were still popular in Great Britain well into the late 19th century.

One has to remember that few, if any, of the early European woodcarvers had ever seen an actual native American Indian. Squaws resembled figures portrayed on 18th Century German porcelain figurines. Braves recalled images on early Dutch tobacco jars, or costumes worn by men who toured with "Indian medicine shows." Most artisans of the period relied upon mapmakers' vignettes and other fanciful engravings which portrayed the New World aborigines in a multitude of threatening configurations and poses.

Legend has it that Boston, in 1730, boasted of a Cupid-like Pocohontas outside a tobacconist's doorway on Hancock Street. Documented beyond question was a cigar store figure carved in 1770 for a Lancaster, Pennsylvania, tobacco shop owner, Christopher Demuth. Since his stock-in-trade was snuff, the Moravian immigrant chose the delicate image of a colonial gentleman with a snuff box in hand to announce Demuth's wares.

In the 1850s, New York City's first wooden Indian stood in front of Chichester's cigar store in the Bowery between Bayard and Canal streets and acted as a beacon to those wishing to sample his well-known "cinnamon cigars," costing three coppers apiece. The figure was followed by two others, one holding a box of snuff at Lorillard's retail snuff store on Chambers Street and another standing guard at McAlpin's shop on Catherine Street.

Baltimore had a few carved Indians on display before 1780, but it was not until after the Civil War that they became widely distributed in America.

Some dealers specialized in the cigar store Indian trade. The best known was an eccentric and reclusive Alsatian immigrant and tobacconist named Edward Hen. In the 1870s, Hen assembled the largest accumulation of carved wooden Indians the world has ever known; hundreds of them in brand-new war paint and crowding the dilapidated five-story brick building Hen called home in New York City.

After two years of test marketing, William Demuth & Co. of New York City (no relation to Demuth of Lancaster), a large wholesale vendor of pipes and tobacco accessories including Indians, announced in the spring of 1871 the manufacture of a complete line of metal show figures.

They were designed to supplement existing stock and, as Demuth remarked in his catalog, "thus prevent the cracking which sometimes occurs in wooden figures, especially when exposed to the climate of our Southern States." Some were 13-inch models intended for window or counter display.

Most of these figures were cast in zinc and bear a copyright date of 1875, along with Demuth's name. Moritz J. Seeling, a German immigrant and owner of The Art Establishment of Brooklyn, cast many fine sculptures for both William Demuth and J.W. Fiske.

Other signatures found on metal Indians of the time are Miller, Dubrul & Peters Mfg. Co. of Cincinnati, and Henry Dibblee of Chicago.

Left: This chief, armed with a musket, stood guard outside a Fort Smith, Arkansas, cigar store until well into the 1920s.

S. Hoene's cigar emporium, Lawrence, Kansas. Courtesy of University of Kansas Libraries (Kansas Collection).

Cigar store Indians ranged in size from about three to six feet. Replacement parts were easy to obtain from factories which were producing them at a rate of 200-300 a year. As late as the 1910s, New York City claimed the only repair shop of wooden figures in the country.

THE ORIGINAL CARVERS

Commercial carvers of wooden Indians in America fell into three categories: old-time carvers of ships' figureheads who had gradually turned to the tobacco trade for work when shipyards closed, skilled Swiss and German immigrants who could carve anything out of wood, from cuckoo clocks to classical Greek figures, and students and apprentices of both camps who churned out countless models for bargain-hunters and merchants with thin pocketbooks.

Some carvers established factories and employed a small staff of woodworkers, turning out pieces on an assembly line basis. Most, however, preferred to work alone.

The names of these early master carvers are unfamiliar to most people today, save those students of the ancient art of wood carving: Samuel Robb, Thomas Brooks and Charles Dodge of New York City; William Rush and Fritz Decker of Philadelphia; Theodore Crongeyer of Detroit; and Herman Matzen of Cleveland, to name a few.

Even from the first, most Indians were carved by hand out of clear pine and usually from one piece, most often a salvaged ship's mast or spar. Sometimes extra wooden blocks were glued on. One Indian is known that was made entirely of small blocks of wood.

Logs were blocked out with an ax for the body after which the hands and arms were attached with screws and the features marked out by chisel. Finer carving tools produced the finishing touches. Then they were painted and mounted on wheeled wooden pedestals for delivery.

Master carver Julius Melchers of Detroit was hired in 1852 to carve his first cigar store Indian for a local tobacconist, Isaac Miller. The 22-year-old artist's work was greeted with success and was soon followed by many prestigious commissions.

Melchers was interviewed in 1899 by a Detroit newspaper at the age of 69. He reminisced:

"We don't know how long the Indian has been used as a tobacco sign. Before I left Germany in 1849, pictures of Indians were hung in tobacco shops and were also pasted on packages of tobacco. The first wooden Indians I saw were just profiles, sawed out of flat board and painted in several colors. When I first came to Detroit, a few crudely carved and painted signs were found in stores.

"I hired a real Indian to model for my first carving, a chief about five feet tall. It was no trouble to get an Indian to model in those days (1850s). Give him a lunch and a glass of beer and he was happy to pose all day, if necessary. I received $55 for the image.

"As time went on...I was commissioned to do all kinds of Indians – big, little, chiefs and queens. Some were modeled after real people but most often ideal interpretations.

"I did Blackhawks, Pontiacs, Hiawathas, and Pocohontases...I received from $5 to $150 for (run-of-the-mill) figures. (Melchers' finer works eventually fetched from $300 to $700 apiece)."

FAMOUS FIGURES

Designs of carved figures fell into four groups: Indian chiefs; Indian squaws (also called Pocohontases); blackamoors, or Pompeys; and "white men." This last group included a wide variety of forms: Turks, Lord Dundrearys, Punches, Sir Walter Raleighs, Champagne Charleys, and scores of female figures, some naughty ones lifting their skirts to provocatively show an ankle, or smoking cigarettes.

Melchers recalled:

"...sometimes a cigar dealer wanted a classical figure instead of an Indian – a statue of Pomona with cigars instead of apples in his hand, Ceres holding tobacco leaves instead of wheat. Sometimes a patriotic merchant wanted a Goddess of Liberty or an Uncle Sam. I have made several Brother Jonathans for customers with strong Yankee sentiments."

***Not all Indians were Indians.** Very early figures were often embellished with Roman shields, spears and tunics, like this carved statue of Mercury, the Roman god of commerce. This particular figure stood for many years in the editorial rooms of the trade organ, the Tobacco Leaf.*

These young boys don't know *quite what to make of the funny wooden princess outside a Cincinnati tobacco shop. Was mischief on their minds? Many Indians bore scars of rough treatment at the hands of pranksters.* Courtesy of the Cincinnati Historical Society.

The most popular figure of the 1870s was a fancy one known as "The Girl of the Period." She was dressed in the style of the decade, wearing high-heeled shoes and a spicy little hat with a squirrel perched on top.

There was also the Dandy Dude, his legs spread wide apart and top hat set at a rakish angle, enjoying a smoke. A Negro minstrel invited viewers with a wide grin to try the weed. In some places, a tall Highlander decked out in Black Watch regalia tendered the contents of an extended snuffbox to curious passersby.

Powhatan and his brother chieftains found great popularity in America – Pocohontases and other squaws became rivals and eventually surpassed them in favor. Unlike the fierce postures of warriors brandishing an upraised tomahawk, the wooden ladies instead held out a tempting bunch of cigars in their hands.

Prices for Indians varied; small ones went for $20 to $30 in the 1880s. Canal Street in New York City soon became the official bargain mart for full-sized Indians, but most were trade-ins or reconditioned chiefs and they could be purchased for $25.

Demuth's models sold for $50 to $75. More elegant ones went for as much as $100. Hen had them cheaper and in a larger stock.

The Brooklyn cigar store of Morris Hirsh was fronted by the carved figure of a man, cigar in his mouth, who stood with his hands clasped to the sides of his head and a medicinal plaster applied to his back.

"Oh, how hard the cigar draws!" proclaimed a sign behind him. People came from all over the country to look at Hirsh's Indian and laugh.

A Seminole chief standing guard outside Samuel Willard's tobacco shop in Washington, D. C., was so lifelike that he frightened women and small children. Willard was ordered by the police to saw off the barrel of the chief's musket and to eventually remove the Indian altogether.

An Indian with the longest continuous record of sidewalk service was a wooden red man posted outside a tobacco shop in Reading, Pennsylvania. Purchased by owner Charles Maltzberger in 1847, he stood faithfully at attention well into the 1920s, except on Sundays and the day he was kidnapped and carried in a parade by members of the Order of the Red Men.

A story was once told by an aged tobacconist of a Yankee skipper who bought up as many of the wooden effigies as he could when they lost favor and sailed them to heathen lands. There he bartered them for gold and ivory and, in so doing, the cast-off Highlanders, Dandy Dudes, Uncle Sams, and Forty Niners became worshipped gods in Polynesia and other far-off countries.

PASSING OF THE INDIAN

The demise of cigar store Indians came slowly, as much by accident as by design. To many tobacconists, the figures simply became nuisances. Shop owners grew tired of lugging and pushing the heavy figures on cast iron wheels outside every morning, and inside every evening, chaining and unchaining them to iron posts or window grates to prevent theft.

Many figures were taken to the city dump and discarded; others were thrown into rivers to float away or were burned as firewood. The rest were vandalized, smashed by runaway horses and carts or were stolen. Being placed outdoors, they tended to weather and rot, despite periodically pouring linseed oil down a special hole drilled in the figure's head.

The great fires that swept Chicago, Baltimore and San Francisco also claimed many wooden victims.

The "Longfellow" Indian, so named because the great American poet, Henry Wadsworth Longfellow, was said to have been infatuated by this elegant figure of Hiawatha. It graced the lobby of the Fifth Avenue headquarters of the American Tobacco Company in New York City and was the only known example cast in bronze.

This wooden turbaned Turk was an abbreviated model who greeted customers from tobacco shop counters.

It's off to the junkyard with this old squaw – her days are through. The use of wooden Indian trade figures lingered on into the new century but, by the 1920s, their numbers had dwindled drastically.

Election nights in New York City held great hazard for Indians when they were snatched up and thrown on spectacular celebratory bonfires then permitted.

By 1911, only 150 out of 2,000 tobacco shops in Baltimore, for example, still retained the services of wooden Indians. It was no longer fashionable to use them.

Julius Melchers put the blame on "Yankee thrift." Shrewd tobacco men rented the valuable space outside their shops for fruit stands, newsstands, and other sidewalk businesses, thereby replacing their Indians for much-needed cash.

Unfortunately, these financial arrangements led indirectly to the real deathblow of the cigar store figure. Sidewalks became so choked with merchants and dangerous to foot traffic that local ordinances were passed, prohibiting obstruction. Many wooden Indians were thus sacrificed in the name of legal compliance.

The passing of the Indian figure as a symbol of the tobacco trade was of more than sentimental interest. It really marked a significant and permanent change in the philosophy of retail merchandising of tobacco products.

By 1900, the appearance, internal trappings, and management of tobacco shops in this country lagged far behind the progress made in most other lines of business. Cigar and tobacco establishments underwent modernization and, within a few short years, vast improvements in merchandising brought the tobacconist's shop up to the very last word in modern shopkeeping. This new business look was materially accelerated by the appearance of the first chain stores such as United Cigar Stands and Schulte Cigar Stores.

By the 1920s, most Indians had been discarded in the name of progress, vilified by modern businessmen who looked upon them as symbolic of an inferior grade of quality and service.

Their usefulness had passed into history.

THE VANISHED TRIBE
LAST OF THE CIGAR STORE INDIANS

THE CIVIL WAR
BIRTH OF THE "BULL"

Tobacco, next to food and clothing, was the greatest morale builders a Southern or Yankee foot soldier could lay his hands on. Sutlers were the major source of supply in camps until late in the war when tobacco rations were formally authorized on both sides.

It was not until December 17, 1863, for instance, that the Confederate House of Representatives formally declared that "a ration of tobacco, of one half pound per week, be allowed to all officers, non-commissioned officers, musicians and privates of the land and naval forces of the Confederate States."

Pipe smoking came into favor during the Civil War. Before that time the only pipes in common use were those made of clay, meerschaum and German porcelain. Northern and Southern troops found cigars too expensive and too hard to carry, and pipes too fragile for accidents likely to happen on long marches or in battle. Wooden pipes, therefore, became the preference of all soldiers.

A celebrated event in tobacco history occurred in the waning hours of the Civil War. The locale was Durham Station (later, Durham), North Carolina. In April of 1865, some 80,000 fighting men of both sides camped idly by, awaiting arrangement of peace terms between General Johnston and General Sherman.

Occupying neutral ground between the two armies during the armistice, sat John Ruffin Green's small tobacco factory, home of his special smoking tobacco made from local bright leaf which he prepared for sale to students at the nearby University of North Carolina. As fate would have it, the foraging soldiers, enjoying one of the few perks of wartime, plundered the premises and relieved Green of his entire stock. Filling their tobacco pouches, they marched homeward after the surrender.

Green would hardly have considered that his fortune had just been made – but it had. Within a short time, letters from as far away as Maine and Texas inundated the tiny post office in Durham Station, addressed to the likes of "mayor," "peace officer" and "baggage master," all inquiring how they might obtain more of that elegant tobacco for which they were now willing to part with money.

Trade was revived with a rush in response to the avalanche of orders. The raiders, in the end, proved to be Green's best customers and advertisers.

The rest became the substance of legends. Green's business took off like a skyrocket and along the way he renamed his tobacco and added a bull for a logo, copied from the Colman mustard trademark of England. Thus, in 1868, "Bull" Durham was born.

Green's factory, employing 10 hands in 1865, had grown to 800 by 1884 and the "Bull" would eventually become the world's largest selling tobacco.

The popularity of the "Bull" also gave impetus to the growing national trend for smoking tobacco and the hand-rolling of cigarettes.

During lulls in fighting and in defiance of strict orders to the contrary, enemy soldiers often met secretly at picket lines to swap Southern tobacco for Northern coffee, an event memorialized on this tobacco trade card of the 1880s.

THE 1870S
GETTING BACK TO BUSINESS

The decade following the Civil War was marked by growth and expansion of the Northern tobacco industry, and a complete rebuilding of that in the South decimated by long years of the war.

Heavy taxes imposed by the Confederate government on Southern tobacco manufacturers made the recovery a slow one. Tobacco factories in Virginia, standing at 252 before the war in 1860, fell to 131 in 1870, before rebounding to over 500 by 1880.

The manufacture of tobacco products before and immediately after the Civil War was primarily performed by hand, a primitive, labor-intensive process. In the making of smoking tobacco, young blacks flailed dried tobacco with sticks until the leaves were pulverized, sifted it, weighed it, and then packed it into small cloth bags.

In spite of this cumbersome method, George Washington Duke's modest firm in Durham, in 1866, was able to turn out nearly 500 pounds of tobacco a day, a remarkable achievement under the circumstances.

The Southern flat-goods chewing tobacco industry took a long time in recovering. Factories in the 1870s typically operated on a seasonal basis, open four months to manufacture tobacco and closed the rest of the year to grow and sell it.

Local distribution was carried out in primitive fashion by country peddlers (often the manufacturers themselves) who became familiar sights on rural byways. With their wagons filled with tobacco and hitched to a team of mules, they wandered from town to town. Times, however, were still hard, money was scarce and sales difficult to make.

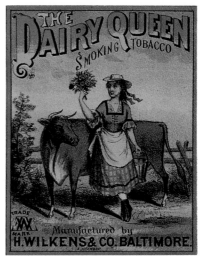

In the end, the itinerant salesmen bartered their tobacco for food or other necessities of life, or for just about anything that could be resold or retraded at a profit. Conditions were made worse by unscrupulous competitors who made the evasion of government tax on tobacco a religious pastime; their bargain prices on illegal wares were hard to beat.

NEW ERA OF TOBACCO ADVERTISING

As America shifted into the industrial revolution taking shape after the Civil War, a new-found prosperity began to grip the nation. Money was now at hand to afford some of life's simpler pleasures in the form of a fine Havana cigar, a plug of Virginia chew or a pinch of Scotch snuff.

Demand for tobacco surged and companies engaged in its manufacture and sale enjoyed unprecedented sales and income. Factories by the score sprang up in many large-sized cities of the Midwest and East Coast, and even a few in seemingly out-of-the-way places like Quincy, Illinois, and Middletown, Ohio.

They spewed forth a multitude of chewing, smoking and snuffing brands. Hand-rolling factories, many small backroom operations, sprouted like weeds across the American landscape to maintain a plentiful supply of that Victorian barometer of prosperity, the cigar.

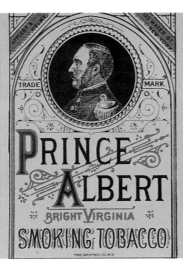

With the expansion of tobacco goods into the marketplace, there arose a need for new methods of merchandising. Tobacco entrepreneurs not only had to learn how to properly introduce a new product to the public, but how to create and sustain demand for it in an increasingly competitive market.

Certain business failure awaited those manufacturers too lazy or too outdated in marketing philosophy to change their ways. Things were different now.

A new element entered the tobacco business, salesmanship, and with it, a different approach to advertising. It could no longer be assumed that people knew what they wanted to buy and, indeed, there was a driving need for tobacco men to create a demand where none had existed before.

Advertising accomplished these goals. Hand-in-hand with improved printing techniques, chiefly the ability to print in color, messages were sent by tobacco manufacturers to consumers by way of powerful but pleasing images that enveloped every phase of the industry. No stone was left unturned – from large signs painted on billboards and the sides of buildings, to wrappers and packages that held the products.

Out of this period of business competition came a flood of printed ephemeral material that identified, communicated, instructed, promoted, and always encouraged thousands of brands of tobacco.

Colorful trade cards, brochures, pamphlets, flyers, posters, stickers, banners, and catalogs entered the tobacco business scene, even down to little things such as office stationery. They brightened the day of the consumer and prospects of success for the seller.

A few tobacco companies began to flex their advertising muscles. Late in the 1870s, major manufacturers of smoking and chewing goods such as Duke and Blackwell in Durham, Pioneer in Brooklyn, Marburg in Baltimore, Pace in Richmond, and Jackson in Petersburg, reached out to customers nationwide by testing a new and unproven medium, newspapers; small and simple ads were placed in country weeklies and big city dailies. Likewise, wholesale cigar houses on the East Coast advertised bulk sales to dealers, jobbers and anyone else who cared to buy.

The new age of tobacco advertising had arrived and was here to stay.

EARLY NEWSPAPER ADVERTISING
(1860-1880)

The advertising of tobacco products in American newspapers was slow to develop; means of promotion were centered primarily at the point of purchase. Ads began to appear sporadically in the late 1870s for the mainstay articles–cigars, smoking and chewing brands. With few exceptions, ads were virtually devoid of graphic decoration and some still retained the old line-by-line broadside format.

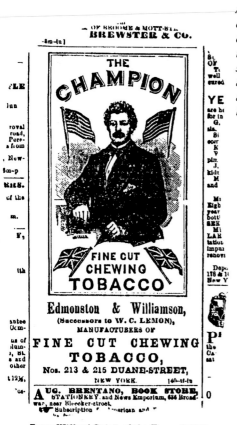

From Wilkes' Spirit of the Times (1860)

From Harper's Weekly (1876)

TRADE CARDS
(1870-1890)

Trade cards were America's first major advertising medium. What had formerly existed as simple and unimaginative black-and-white advertising cards made from engraved copper plates or wooden blocks exploded in a blaze of color as chromolithography revolutionized the printing art.

While this curious but fascinating form of promotional ephemera came to life in the 1870s, its highest peak of commercial use occurred over the next decade or two. The low cost of trade cards placed them within the means of every merchant in America who had a product to sell or service to offer; their business use was prolific.

These colorful pieces of paper also captivated many Americans, young and old, who pasted them up in Victorian scrapbooks, thereby preserving for posterity precious records of the life, habits and dress of a past generation.

The aim of trade cards was to attract attention. Many of them depicted themes typically that had little or nothing to do with the business promoted; the reverse side of these stock images identified the advertiser.

The majority of trade cards were distributed at the place of business. Merchants piled cards high in baskets or trays on the counter and handed them out with purchases, or gave them out free for the asking. Others were enclosed with orders and a few were mailed out as advertising pieces.

Tobacco companies capitalized on the pass-along merchandising value of trade cards and issued many of them advertising brands of smoking and chewing tobacco – and a few for cigarettes.

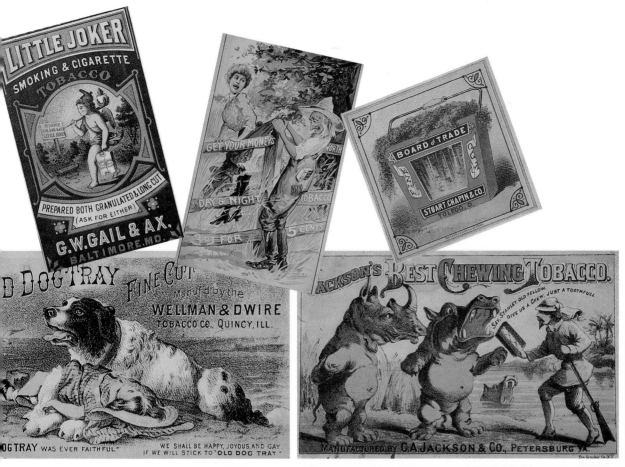

Tobacco trade cards. *They were an early and important means of promotion and formed a Who's Who list of major manufacturers. Designs ranged from the quaint and whimsical to the silly and naughty; quality from plain black-and-white cheapies to gaudy ones in rich, lithoed colors; and from one-sided cards to "metamorphic" models that folded out to tell a story in rhyme. Wealthier merchants could afford more elaborate, customized cards; the less well-off chose from a wide selection of stock images and filled in brand names in blank spaces provided.*

America's first cigarette advertisements appeared on trade cards. Makers such as Kimball, Kinney, Marburg and Allen & Ginter released a flood of large-sized cards in the 1870s and 1880s. All themes were utilized; demure young maidens and smiling children were favored.

MY CARD!

Out of the trade card craze of the 1870s came the tobacconists' first business cards–cute, colorful and, typical of the times, incorporating fanciful but unrelated imagery. The cards came in various sizes; some reached that of postcards.

HITTING THE SHOWS

The American public has always turned out for parades, fairs and expositions; they were major social events of the day. The shows also served as a healthy stimulus to the country's industrial and business progress and had a particularly beneficial effect on the growth of advertising and the pictorial arts.

It started in 1876 with the Philadelphia Centennial Exposition. Scattered throughout the halls of the show were colorful handbills, trade cards, folders, and announcements. It marked the first time that such a large number of people, an estimated ten million strong over the exposition's six-month stand, came face to face with the force of advertising.

For those who made tobacco products, these occasions provided unique opportunities for manufacturers to show off their goods and their participation became almost a religious devotion for years to come. It was an easy, effective and relatively cheap way to promote products.

Agricultural Hall of the 1876 Centennial Exposition was crowded with exhibits of tobacco products. These trade cards prove that Blackwell and Kimball were there. Kimball's message that Vanity Fair cigarettes did not bite the tongue was translated into seven languages on the back of the card for the benefit of foreign visitors.

Attracting a great deal of attention at the Philadelphia show in 1876 was this posh 18-foot-tall exhibit by Kerbs & Spiess, cigar makers of New York City. Made of ebony, brass railings and crowned with ornate bronze cherubs, the display featured boxes of cigars placed on satin-lined shelves.

A rare early stereoscopic view of a booth set up by Toledo, Ohio, tobacco king Charles Messenger (ca 1880s). Even in this relatively primitive era of advertising, tobacco men had learned the value of patriotic flags, stacking of tobacco boxes and an excess of posters in forming an impressive display.

TOBACCO TAGS
ADVERTISING IN TIN

Discovered by accident, tin tags were originally used to label chewing tobacco brands, but oddly, by the 1890s, they had evolved into the nation's first large-scale system of premium-giving.

Tobacco tags were first employed in the mid-1870s and reached peak commercial use between 1880 and 1920. Purely out of tradition, a few firms continued to utilize tags up to the days of World War II.

Tags were small flat pieces of tin, die cut and fitted with prongs, one for twist and two for plug, which were pressed into compressed bars or rolls of tobacco before they were sealed.

Tin was chosen because of its non-corrosive property, critical when dealing with moist weed. While most tags were made of metal, many were also made of paper and, rarely, wood. Most tin tags were decorated on one side with a lithographed design; others were cut out into various configurations of bare metal.

Initially tobacco tags were not intended as promotional devices. They arose out of a dire need to prevent illegal substitution of inferior grades of tobacco, not an uncommon practice with unscrupulous dealers.

The invention of tin tags is historically credited to Pierre Lorillard III, successor captain of the tobacco company bearing his grandfather's name, and the circumstances are the subject of a well-known story.

One day in 1875, Mr. Lorillard, inspecting a day's run of chewing tobacco, spotted an odd bit of tin accidentally packaged in a plug of chaw. At first angered, a thought came to him. If that piece of tin carried the name of his company, might it not serve as an effective deterrent to brand switching?

He then ordered some flattened discs stamped out and embossed with the Lorillard name, and thus was born the tobacco tin tag. Lorillard was so enthused over his invention that he named one of his chewing brands, Tin Tag.

Tags, like ornately designed cigar labels, lent individuality to chewing tobacco brands. Despite Lorillard's patent, their popularity spread like wildfire and rival firms rushed to copy the idea. A flood of personalized versions hit the market, much to the consternation of Lorillard who went to court to protect his patent. He lost. Judges ruled that specific tag designs could be patented, but not the general idea.

Tags were not a business success at first. The metal pieces were originally placed under the tobacco leaf

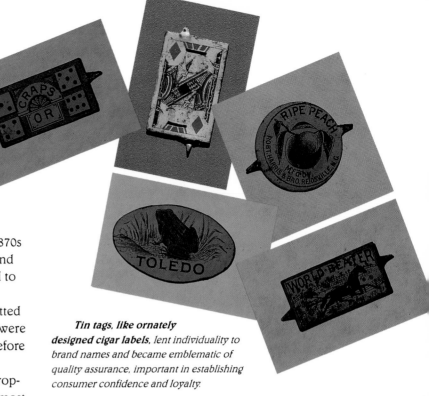

Tin tags, like ornately designed cigar labels, lent individuality to brand names and became emblematic of quality assurance, important in establishing consumer confidence and loyalty.

wrapper, hidden inside the plug. A rash of broken teeth and lacerated gums soon gave Lorillard's brands a bad reputation until the tin pieces were attached outside the wrapper, an improvement attributed to tobacco man Ben Finzer of Louisville.

The tedious chore of affixing tin tags to tobacco was initially performed by hand, usually by teams of boys or young ladies. By the early 1880s, hand labor was replaced by automatic tagging machines.

A BETTER APPLICATION

The original tin tags of the 1870s were plain and unadorned. In the next decade, the advent of chromolithography allowed tinmakers to embellish the tags with colored designs and the business took on a new flavor and direction. Attention was now paid to appearances. Manufacturers, by this time, had come to recognize the remarkable promotional appeal offered by these brightly colored bits of tin.

The novelty, beauty and small size of tin tags, like those of trade cards and postage stamps, started a wild collector craze. The hobby grew so large that, in 1886, a national collecting society was formed, served by a newsletter, The Tag World, published in Cleveland.

Tin tags eventually grew into a relatively inexpensive but highly effective means of advertising. They fit the thriftiest of corporate budgets, no matter how large or small the firm.

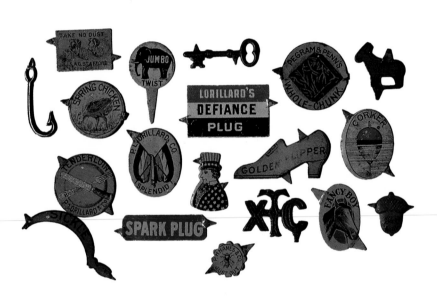

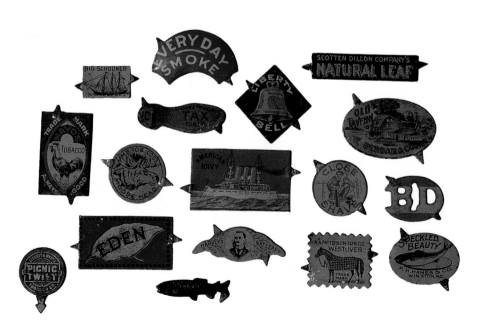

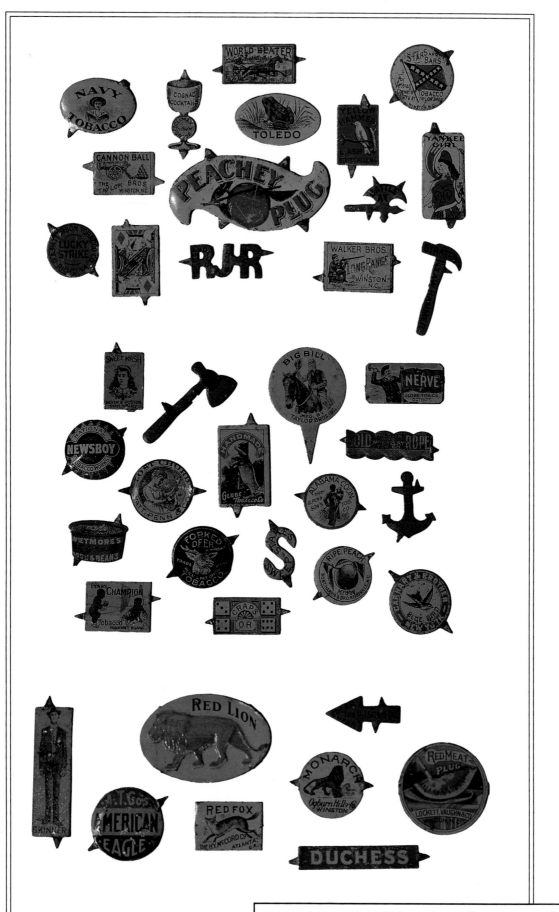

An assemblage of tobacco tin tags. *They were cute and came in a kaleidoscopic array of colors, sizes and shapes. Tags were utilized by almost every plug maker in America in the 1880s and 1890s, large and small, and aided brand promotion immeasurably.*

Look! Look!

GOLD ROPE
HAPPY THOUGHT
KINGBOLT
AND NO TAX

TAGS

are worth

from

2¢ TO 75¢ EACH

for securing any of the Articles

IN THIS CATALOGUE.

THE WINTERS CO., SPRINGFIELD, O.

GET A FARM!

One of the first tobacco companies to utilize tin tags for promotional purposes was the Sorg firm of Middletown, Ohio. In 1884, the company offered a variety of prizes to consumers mailing in the most Spear Head tags. First prize was deed to 160 acres of raw land in the Great Plains. "Chew Spear Head and Get a Farm," newspaper ads shouted.

Later the same year, the Sorg company sponsored a guessing contest, awarding cash prizes for those coming closest to the exact number of popular votes cast in the Presidential election. Spear Head tin tags were required with each entry. "Chew Spear Head and Acquire Wealth," the manufacturer proclaimed this time.

By the 1890s, making tags redeemable for cash, prizes or more tobacco turned into a marketing brainstorm. The enthusiastic response of the nation's quid-chewing populace turned the tin tag redemption scheme into America's first large-scale premium system.

A typical tin tag premium catalog of the Wilson & McCallay company of Middletown, Ohio (ca 1895). To receive gifts, tags were not enough in themselves—a little cash was required on the side. Customers were kindly reminded to flatten the prongs before mailing, a detail appreciated by clerks who had to handle the shipments.

To facilitate redemption of tags, some companies, like Drummond in St. Louis, provided customers with handy pre-punched cards to attach the tags.

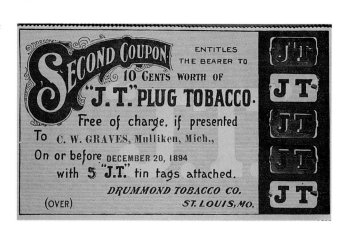

SECOND COUPON ENTITLES THE BEARER TO 10 CENTS WORTH OF "J.T." PLUG TOBACCO. Free of charge, if presented To C. W. GRAVES, Mulliken, Mich., On or before DECEMBER 20, 1894 with 5 "J.T." tin tags attached. DRUMMOND TOBACCO CO. ST. LOUIS, MO. (OVER)

VICTORIAN CHEESECAKE, WOODEN BUCKETS, AND POKER CHIPS

Postmasters in the 1870s were treated to a big surprise when they received brightly colored posters in the mail promoting chewing brands. Made of cloth and rolled up in cardboard tubes, the posters featured maidenly, down-home themes and spiced up many a dull wall in rural post offices throughout America.

Advertising poker chips made of clay circulated in the 1870s, as well as large wooden buckets of fine cut chewing tobacco decorated with oversized labels in striking hues.

CADDY LABELS
HANDS ACROSS THE SEA

Extremely colorful labels were attached to caddies (large wooden boxes) of Virginia plug tobacco shipped to markets in England, South Africa, Australia, and other foreign ports. Themes typifying the country of destination were utilized, as well as traditional American scenes. The use of caddy labels extended from the 1860s through the 1950s.

THE 1880S

PROSPERITY, COMPETITION AND NEW MEANS OF PROMOTION

The 1880s witnessed the rapid industrialization and growth of the tobacco industry. The processing, manufacture and packaging of tobacco products was made more efficient through improvement of prototypical machines of the previous decade and invention of new ones.

Driving this growth was a rising demand for tobacco. The nation, with a population fixed at 63 million in 1880, had more than doubled since the outbreak of the Civil War.

The amount of tobacco produced in the United States between 1870 and 1880 almost doubled and in 1880 alone, over 567 million cigarettes were consumed, 10 times that in 1875 and 1000 times more than in 1870. The consumption of cigars and chewing tobacco was also on the rise. Business was booming.

The greatest movement of manufactured tobacco ever recorded in the history of Lynchburg, Virginia, took place on May 1, 1883, when 38 boxcars filled with the leaf, representing more than 800,000 pounds, were shipped to distribution points. If it were not for a strike among factory workers, the amount would have been greater.

As manufacturers modernized and expanded their production facilities, their merchandising sights shifted to targets far beyond local markets. Transcontinental railroads allowed access to new cities out West which represented tempting fields for eastern and southern tobacco companies. Manufacturers contracted with trade merchants in far-off cities and towns who, acting as "sole agents," became exclusive distributors.

This was an especially popular business set-up with the manufacturing of cigars, an industry virtually unknown west of the Mississippi in 1870. Market penetration with this smoking product was met with flattering success. A real Marlboro Country existed back then. In the rugged mining camps and lawless cattle towns, men who were men chewed tobacco and smoked cigars. Lowly cigarettes marked the genuine dude, fresh,

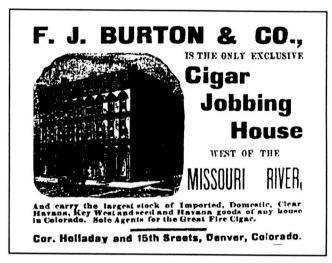
fragrant and newly arrived from the East.

Dependency on jobbers to distribute tobacco was eased when the first company salesmen were sent out on the road to call on tobacconists and establish brand footholds. Sales spurted and drummers became a permanent fixture in the trade.

Companies instituted sales inducements which proved vital in securing orders in the field, especially as competition stiffened. Rebates, free samples and prepaid freight were perks generally offered to wholesalers and retailers.

The Morten Bros. of Cincinnati offered a free tobacco scale with each order of Summit fine cut, an $8 value, and both Cotterill, Fenner of Dayton and McAlpin of New York City threw in alarm clocks. Samples of Jackson's Best plug were mailed out free to those responding to newspaper ads.

PICTURE CRAZY

Enormous strides in promotional techniques took place. Improved methods of color lithography were used to combine fine art imagery with consumer products, conferring an air of dignity, confidence and a highly visible profile to whatever was being sold to the public.

Lithography had ways of promoting goods that were alien to the letterpress. Artists and printers, not bound by trays of type metal or strict two-inch column rules, experienced a newfound freedom of expression. Their designs could run wild in style, size and direction – and often did. Stodgy traditionalists gasped as lettering and scrollwork took on an intricate and ornate form.

This new and exciting style was quickly applied to advertising; better and more striking images in color were quickly applied to tobacco labels, trade cards, posters, and signs. Similarly, cigarette insert cards left their drab, sepia-toned likenesses behind them and progressed to lifelike colors.

A New York City lithographer summed it all up: "People in these days seem to have gone picture-crazy. There never has been such a demand as there is now. They do not care so much for black and white as they used to – they want color."

Elaborately detailed steel engravings found their way onto envelopes, letterheads and billheads as tobacco companies, joining the printing rage underway across the country, embellished these everyday articles of commerce with a touch of class. Commercial artwork was thus born in America.

Tinmakers were busy, too. Chromolithography, coupled with major advances in metal box construction, led to the industry's first mass-produced commercial line of tobacco tins. Typically decorated in two colors and covered with fancy Victorian scrollwork, they ushered in a new age of containerization that would last for the better part of a century.

Businessmen were also waking up to the power of newspaper advertising. The number of tabloids and periodicals in print, standing at over 6,000 in 1871, nearly doubled by 1880, and tripled in 1890. Scores of successful merchants bore testimony to the fact that a first class newspaper ad was unquestionably the best method yet devised to gain patronage of those who had money to extend.

Some old-fashioned promotional methods slowly faded into history – broadcast circulars, clocks covered with business cards, public mirrors with advertisements carried on the frames, handbills of all sizes, banners stretched across streets, and men and boys covered by collapsible wooden signs who pounded miles of city boardwalks in the interests of promotion.

THE VIRGINIA
TOBACCO AND CIGAR STORE.

I have just opened a Tobacco and Cigar House in this place. Having had long experience in the sale of Tobacco, and having peculiar advantages for the manufacture of Cigars, I wish to call the particular attention of consumers to my FINE Stock of genuine old Virginia Smoking and Chewing Tobacco, and to the large assortment of select Cigars which I have constantly on hand

All my own make.

My stock comprises the following brands of choice Virginia Tobacco:

New Idea, Puzzle, Paper Tag, Spun Roll, Rough and Ready,
and the Celebrated

SILVER COIN.

I can recommend this Tobacco and feel sure it will give entire satisfaction.

I manufacture the following brands of fine Cigars.

El Carino, XLCR, Oscar Y. Amanda, El Campeon, La Pluma, Penelope, Four in Hand,
and look out for

KENO
ON THE TOP LINE.

Try the Hiawathia Smoking Tobacco,
YOU WILL FIND IT CHEAP AND GOOD.

A nice assortment of Pipes and Smokers' Articles.

Remember the SILVER COIN, and don't you forget it.
97 Santa Fe Ave., two doors south of the Baltimore Clothing House.

Respectfully,
A. A. WISE.

Starting up. In June, 1880, tobacconist A. A. Wise opened his doors to business in Salina, Kansas. He was one of many thousands of Americans rushing to enter a new and rapidly growing profession.

HORDES OF NEW PLAYERS

Competition in the '80s was fierce. New businesses shot up all over the land in cities and towns ranging in size from tiny, cubbyhole cigar stands in hotel lobbies to large, well-appointed smoking emporiums on busy downtown street corners. In 1880, in New York City alone, more than 9,000 dealers in tobacco could be counted.

The business of selling tobacco held great appeal to the common man. College degrees did not count in this trade. More important were grit, determination and a strong desire to succeed.

Fluency in the English language was not a prerequisite. Tobacco sold itself in any language. Vending it as a business offered a ready-made occupation to immigrants stepping off a boat at Ellis Island and many new citizens started their lives in this country as tobacconists.

Although many tobacco retailers carved out a living that paid well, many operated on a shoestring. This group was particularly vulnerable to sudden downturns in business conditions, even small ones.

It was worse – even catastrophic – in times of national economic calamity. Financial crises, like the one that hit in 1891, caused many tobacconists and cigar makers to close up shop.

There were few lines of business in the United States during the 1880s that experienced the degree and intensity of business rivalry that the tobacco trade knew. There was just so much room and it was a situation that would worsen by the next decade.

THE DRIVING FORCE OF ADVERTISING

The demand for tobacco was created and maintained through the medium of advertising. Simply put, those companies that believed in advertising and possessed the means to afford it were the ones that benefitted the most. The risk was usually worth the taking. It would become an infallible rule in the industry: advertising was the essential means of achieving success.

Naturally the cost of promotion had to be considered in setting prices for new tobacco issues. It was expensive in those days, for instance, for major producers to introduce a cigarette. In 1889, this cost was estimated at $250,000, most of which was earmarked for promotion. This excessive amount was usually beyond the means of the financially strapped or business-shy company.

The root of the problem lay in the tobacco-consuming public. They had become quite a spoiled bunch as they eagerly awaited each new brand with all the promotional hoopla that accompanied it.

Notwithstanding the promotional antics of the trade's market leaders, other manufacturers were not exactly standing still, either. They could not afford to. In order to maintain their business edge, they were forced to keep up a steady release of advertising, particularly giveaways. The public loved them.

This was especially true with those who made cigarettes. Allen & Ginter used the nation's newspapers to push the Richmond Gem brand as early as 1879 and Pet cigarettes later in the 1880s. The Kimball company, countering Duke's intrusion in the cigarette field, sponsored cash lotteries and packaged smokes in small cardboard boxes simulating Thackeray novels.

The Kinney Bros. of New York City added cork mouthpieces to Sweet Caporal cigarettes, claiming that they "absorbed nicotine and rendered a cooling sensation to the smoke." The company also enamelled the ends of Sultana cigarettes for smokers fearful of the contact of their lips with the paper wrapper. The coddling of consumers was underway.

Operators of large businesses had larger goals in mind. Before newspaper and magazine advertising held sway in the industry, other imaginative promotional tactics were devised. For their inventors, they paid off well. The full force of advertising was just around the corner.

SEEDS OF TROUBLE

In 1884, a bill was introduced in the New York State Assembly prohibiting the sale of cigarettes and tobacco to minors under the age of 16; a similar law was already on the books in New Jersey.

Later, in 1889, the Kansas and Pennsylvania state legislatures, pressured hard by health officials, passed laws making it unlawful to sell tobacco in any form to minors and empowering police to arrest and fine guilty shop owners. The idea caught on; the District of Columbia followed suit in 1892.

The new statutes caused little social comment at the time except to give heart to growing numbers of Americans who feared that the lives and moral fiber of young people in this country were being corrupted by tobacco, chiefly cigarettes. Though the laws were generally ignored and poorly enforced, they constituted the first ripples of a giant tidal wave of anti-cigarette reform that, within a decade, would hit the shores of the United States.

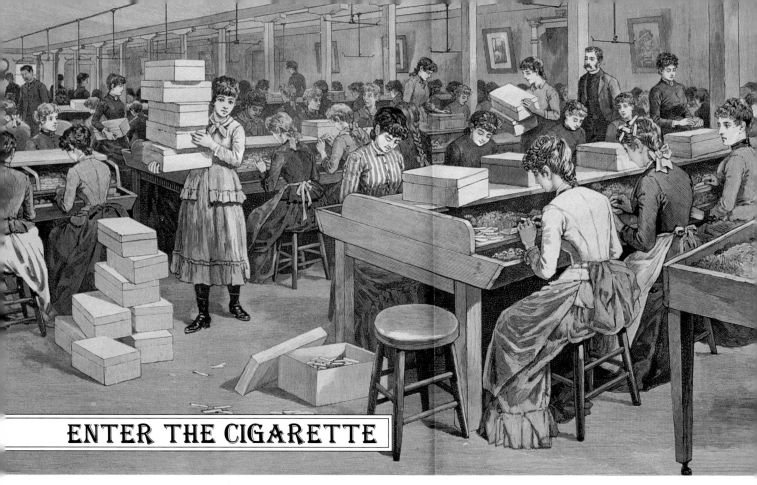

ENTER THE CIGARETTE

In 1883, the tobacco factory of Allen & Ginter was one of the nation's largest. Here 650 hands were employed, 500 of them Richmond's finest young ladies carefully screened for their "good moral character." In the cigarette room, 450 women rolled, cut and bundled packages of cigarettes carrying such enticing labels as Opera Puffs, Pets and Little Beauties. An efficient roller could turn out 18,000 smokes a week. She earned $18 a month and took her breaks in a private library provided on the premises.

Cigarettes first attracted attention in England following the Crimean War of 1845-46. British soldiers returning home brought with them a smoking novelty picked up from allied troops, chiefly the Turks. British officers, idols of the day, rolled and smoked cigarettes made from fragrant Turkish tobacco and their examples were copied by the swells and dandies of high society. The fad soon spread to the United States.

The cigarette in America, in the 1860s, was strictly a big city smoking article. To satisfy those curious enough to try the new form of smoking, many of notoriously inferior quality were imported from Cuba and Germany. A shop in New York City, operated by the Bedrossian brothers, was one of the first to make cigarettes in the early 1860s using bright tobacco from the South. This caught the attention of a rival in town, Francis S. Kinney who, in 1869, brought in rollers from Europe to instruct his female staff in the fine art of making cigarettes by hand.

The commercial birth of the American cigarette is generally attributed to John F. Allen of Richmond. Among the boxes of fine cut and smoking goods displayed at the Philadelphia Exposition in 1876 was Allen's small supply of cigarettes packed specially for the trade.

They attracted inordinate attention and were quickly bought up by a ravenous public.

Recognizing the importance of what he had just witnessed, Allen, upon his return to Richmond, joined business forces with a former merchant, importer and Confederate army major, Lewis Ginter. The newly established firm, Allen & Ginter, concentrated on the manufacture of the slender rolls of tobacco.

William S. Kimball resigned his mechanic's position in the Union Navy in 1863 and returned home to Rochester, New York, where he established the Peerless Tobacco Works. In 1876, he began making cigarettes, turning out 15 million the first year. Two years later the Kimball firm with its cigarette brands – Fragrant Vanity Fair, Satin, Four-in-Hand, Cupid, and Superlative – was awarded a medal at the Paris Exposition.

Cigarettes came of age in the 1880s. Their rising popularity challenged the longstanding market domination held by chewing tobacco and cigars, largely due to the determined efforts of a small group of energetic companies who were taking chances with this newfangled product: Kimball in Rochester; Kinney and Goodwin in New York City; Allen & Ginter in Richmond; and the Marburgs and Felgner in Baltimore.

Joining this exclusive pioneering club in the mid-1880s was a brash, young upstart from the South, James Buchanan Duke, now running his father's business in Durham, W. Duke, & Sons.

The making of cigarettes in the early 1880s was performed by hand. Each company employing armies of rollers, chiefly young women, and the most skilled worker could turn out about four cigarettes a minute. It was a system desperately in need of mechanization.

The Allen & Ginter firm stepped forward and offered a prize, $75,000, to anyone inventing a machine that could make a completely rolled cigarette. The challenge was undertaken by many but the first to succeed was a most unlikely prospect, the 22-year-old son of a Virginia wool manufacturer named James Bonsack.

After painstaking experimentation, Bonsack patented his machine in 1881. However, the device only worked sporadically and major manufacturers refused to take a chance on it – except one.

James Duke, entering the cigarette business that year, saw the vast potential of Bonsack's invention. In a bold gamble, Duke leased the machine. His engineers overcame a host of mechanical imperfections and perfected a machine that really worked.

The Bonsack cigarette-making machine was the tobacco industry's most important invention of the 19th century; it revolutionized the making of cigarettes overnight. One machine was capable of turning out smokes at the staggering rate of 120,000 per day, equivalent to 40 rollers.

For Duke, the gamble paid off handsomely. In 1886, his factories were pouring out 4 million cigarettes a day, and, by 1888, he had cornered 40 percent of the cigarette market. The Bonsack machine had disproved the long-held belief among manufacturers that consumers preferred hand-rolled articles.

Production of cigarettes was no longer a problem; it only remained to sell them. In this area Duke proved himself a master and, in so doing, thrust the cigarette into national prominence, a market position it would never lose.

Cigarette Making by Machinery.

INSERT CARD MANIA
(1880-1900)

Insert cards constituted the tobacco industry's most ambitious and successful advertising venture of last century. Small rectangular pieces of cardboard, originally placed inside boxes and packages of tobacco products (chiefly cigarettes) to help stiffen the contents, soon found a better application – that of brand promotion. They caught the fancy of smokers and helped fuel the explosive popularity of cigarettes taking place in the 1880s.

The first card dates to 1879 and was used with the Marquis of Lorne brand of cigarettes manufactured by the American News Company of New York City. Others followed in short order. The "Big Five" of the cigarette industry in the '80s, W. Duke & Sons, Allen & Ginter, Kimball, Goodwin, and Kinney, vied mightily in a tumultuous race to furnish the nation's smokers with a profusion of these novel advertising pieces.

The format of early insert cards was generally alike, a real photograph mounted on the front of a piece of heavy cardboard and advertising text printed on the reverse side. Smokers looked forward to finding these cute and fascinating cards tucked inside their favorite brands as the craze swept the country. Their popularity was enhanced when cards carrying illustrations in color appeared in the late 1880s.

As with tin tags, cards were collected and traded by everyone, men and women of all ages and especially children. Many cards were issued in serially numbered sets, 25 or 50 being customary, but the record went to Duke's Sweet Caporal set portraying actors and actresses where almost 2,000 different cards have been identified.

Dimensions of cards varied. Most cards were designed to fit in packs of ten cigarettes; they measured approximately 1-1/2 by 3 inches. Larger cards reached a size of 3 by 4-1/2 inches.

Themes ran a full spectrum. No topic was overlooked if it could be transformed pictorially into something of interest. Thick-thighed actresses scantily clad in tights and striking a variety of stage poses were the most popular subjects.

Cards like these offended many people who considered them bawdy and in poor taste, including the deeply religious George Washington Duke, James Duke's father. He implored his son to stop using the "lascivious photographs." The old man's plea, however, was ignored in the pursuit of business.

Depiction of sports figures was extremely popular. The list went on and on: military uniforms, ships, coats-of-arms, dog breeds, flags, world rulers, birds and animals, jokes, pirates, generals, Indian chiefs, race horses, Dickensian characters, postage stamps, and coins.

Some unusual series appeared: a directory of New York City merchants, trick bicycle riders, types of flirtation, savage chiefs of the world, police inspectors, jockeys, and "Terrors of America," the Duke company's tribute to mischievous children.

A Careful Father.

Customer—Give me two packages of cigarettes, please.
Dealer (wishing to offer inducements)—This is the best brand. In each package you will find one of those very spicy photographs—
Customer (horrified)—Heavens, man! Give me some other kind. These are for my daughter!

America's first pin-up queens. *Posterity was captured forever in a camera lens as budding stage actresses, as well as reigning beauties like Lillian Russell and Julia Marlowe, lent their forms to promote cigarettes, cigars and chewing tobacco. These promotional cards of the '80s incidentally form the largest portraiture of actresses of the Victorian stage.*

Typical insert cards of the 1880s and 1890s. They made no pretense to art or culture; their job was to be pretty or interesting. The Kinney company, for variety's sake, issued die-cut paper inserts in the form of plates, purses, fans, goblets, and other objects.

CASHING IN ON THE NATIONAL GAME: AMERICA'S FIRST BASEBALL CARDS

Of all sports themes utilized in tobacco company giveaways the most popular and most sought after by the public were those devoted to baseball, which, by 1890, was well on its way to achieving status as America's favorite pastime.

While a few cigar and tobacco companies issued short sets of insert cards featuring big league ball players as early as 1886, it was over a two-year period, 1887-88, that a record-busting series was released by the Goodwin company of New York City, a major manufacturer of cigarettes. Over 2,000 different brown-toned real photographs mounted on stiff cardboard were included in packages of Old Judge and Gypsy Queen cigarettes.

Uniformed athletes, standing in front of stock background sets, assumed a variety of exaggerated poses simulating action, such as catching baseballs suspended on strings (which also happened to be visible). Large cabinet photos were made available for 35 coupons. The same gallery portraits also appeared on the covers of give-away scorecards prepared for certain National League games.

In like fashion, Allen & Ginter of Richmond issued a small group of diamond stars but rendered them in color, upstaging their Northern business rivals.

The association was beneficial to both parties. The card promotions helped popularize baseball, and tobacco companies enjoyed much warm publicity. More importantly, the relationship set the stage for future business arrangements when players were paid for product endorsements and started a new baseball card collecting frenzy that continues today.

INSERT CARD ALBUMS

Of all the captivating advertising imagery employed by tobacco men before 1900, little exceeded the magnificent graphics that graced insert card albums released in the 1888-1895 period. These portfolios, some loose-leaf and bound by string, were pictorial knockouts – page after page of finely detailed engravings done up in lavish colors. They were truly a crowning touch to the tobacco insert card mania.

Initially the albums contained complete sets of card issues, thereby sparing collectors the trouble of running down all the individual units. Later, in response to overwhelming demand, other albums were printed that had no card counterparts. Albums were obtained in exchange for special paper coupons packed in cigarette boxes and packs, requiring 50 to 100 for each album.

Most insert card albums were produced by major tobacco companies. Allen & Ginter of Richmond was the leader with 25 separate editions to their credit, followed closely by the Kimball and Duke firms. A few were issued by smaller tobacco houses such as Kinney, Hess, Camerons & Sizer, and Pilkinton.

BAD INFLUENCE

Children were drawn to the beauty of insert card albums. Gangs of kids could be found every Saturday afternoon crowding the front doors of cigarette factories, eager to exchange vouchers for books. These scenes alarmed some tobacco dealers in New York City who questioned the wisdom of albums as giveaways which, in their minds, contributed to the rising problem of juvenile smoking.

Allen & Ginter's "Our Navy" album captured in splendorous color and detail the Navy's transformation from wooden-masted man-of-wars to the new age of iron-hulled warships.

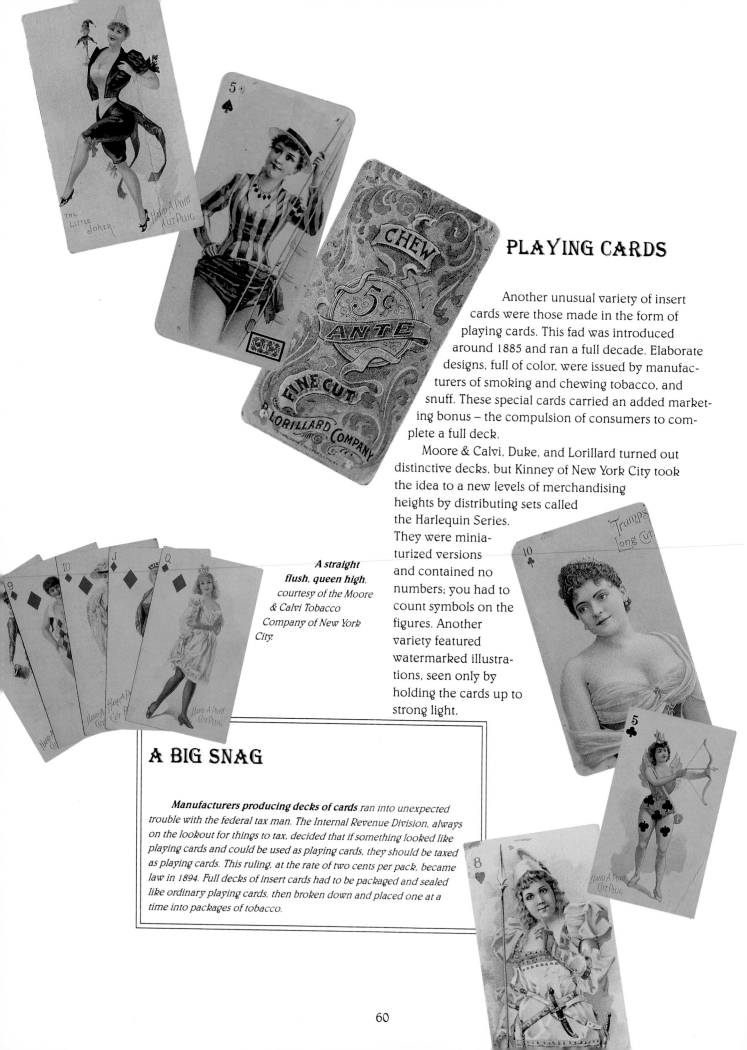

PLAYING CARDS

Another unusual variety of insert cards were those made in the form of playing cards. This fad was introduced around 1885 and ran a full decade. Elaborate designs, full of color, were issued by manufacturers of smoking and chewing tobacco, and snuff. These special cards carried an added marketing bonus – the compulsion of consumers to complete a full deck.

Moore & Calvi, Duke, and Lorillard turned out distinctive decks, but Kinney of New York City took the idea to a new levels of merchandising heights by distributing sets called the Harlequin Series. They were miniaturized versions and contained no numbers; you had to count symbols on the figures. Another variety featured watermarked illustrations, seen only by holding the cards up to strong light.

A straight flush, queen high, courtesy of the Moore & Calvi Tobacco Company of New York City.

A BIG SNAG

Manufacturers producing decks of cards ran into unexpected trouble with the federal tax man. The Internal Revenue Division, always on the lookout for things to tax, decided that if something looked like playing cards and could be used as playing cards, they should be taxed as playing cards. This ruling, at the rate of two cents per pack, became law in 1894. Full decks of insert cards had to be packaged and sealed like ordinary playing cards, then broken down and placed one at a time into packages of tobacco.

THE FIRST TOBACCO TINS

The technical ability to mass-produce metal containers got its start in the 1870s and 1880s when a number of tin-making companies set up shop in large cities. A few became closely associated with the tobacco industry and produced tins exclusively for smoking and chewing products up to the turn of the century – Hasker & Marcuse in Richmond, and New York City's Somers Bros., Ilsley and Ginna firms.

By the 1880s, tin-makers, through the art of chromolithography, had achieved the luxury of two-color decoration. Ornamentation of tins was a new and exciting means of promotion and the tobacco men were quick to seize on the idea.

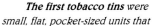

The first tobacco tins were small, flat, pocket-sized units that held a foil-wrapped chunk of chewing tobacco. Novelties included one of nickel-plated brass with a combination lock on the lid, plus another with a revolving celluloid disc portraying the presidential rivals of 1880. Others were adorned with color and finely detailed illustrations of the traditional Victorian style.

Trade journals, regional and national, began to appear in the 1870s and kept tobacco men abreast of the industry.

ROLLING STOCK:
THE KINNEY CIGARETTE CAR

In 1888, the Kinney Brothers of New York City, one of the country's largest cigarette manufacturers, put their advertising dollars to work in a flash of promotional brilliance. A special Pullman car, made to order by the Pennsylvania Railroad, hit the rails and made selling rounds from coast to coast. The exterior was painted bright green, gold and crimson, and the plush interior carried a display of Sweet Caporal and other cigarette brands, as well as a full line of cigars and smoking tobacco. The car was open to the trade (and curious visitors) at stops along the way, announced in advance by newspaper notices.

In 1882, the Lorillard company passed out a free booklet to customers entitled "Puffs of Wisdom" which contained odd bits of information such as Latin phrases, postal regulations, first-aid tips, and, of course, a few tobacco ads. It was the inauspicious start of a new trend in tobacco promotion–paper ephemera.

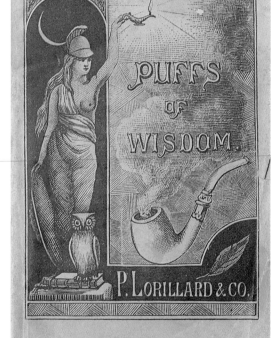

THE EMPIRE BUILDERS

The years that followed the Civil War spawned a new generation of entrepreneurs in American business. They created industrial machines that would survive unparalleled depressions, world wars and even the collapse of Wall Street. Among them were several tobacco magnates who, through innovative promotional tactics, guided their companies to the top of the heap during the hectic competition of the 1880s.

MARCH OF THE "BULL"

"STANDARD OF THE WORLD"

After the Civil War, John Green, whose tobacco warehouse in Durham Station, North Carolina, had been plundered by Union and Confederate troops, enjoyed new-found prosperity with his "Bull" Durham brand of smoking and rolling tobacco.

Green died in 1869 but prior to his death, he took in William T. Blackwell as a partner. Blackwell, in the smartest business move of his life, bought Green's share of the company for $2,000 from the estate and then hired two men, James R. Day and Julian Shakespeare Carr, to help him run the business operation, now renamed Blackwell's Durham Tobacco Company.

Blackwell sold out his interests in 1882 and Jule "General" Carr, the son of a Chapel Hill merchant and ex-Confederate army private, took over. Carr was the advertising genius of the group and continued to pioneer techniques of advertising deemed quite extravagant for the day.

But it paid off. Under Carr's leadership, the Blackwell company not only maintained the market momentum of "Bull" Durham but propelled the brand into national prominence, eventually making the firm the largest manufacturer of smoking tobacco in the world. The huge factory processed 20,000 pounds of tobacco daily.

Typical of the advertising excess engaged in by the Blackwell firm in the early years was the entertainment of a group of Royal Arch masons in Durham, North Carolina, in July of 1879. The festivities were described in effusive detail by the Raleigh News:

Blackwell's ambitious countrywide sign-painting promotion of the 1880s was made the humorous subject of a company trade card. Logo of the bull had been well established by this time.

PUTTING ON THE DOG

"On Thursday morning at 6 o'clock, a procession of thirteen four-horse spring wagons appeared in front of the hotel to convey the guests to Chapel Hill to witness the closing commencement exercises of the University and to partake of a barbecue, prepared by Blackwell & Co. on the grounds of the campus.

"The horses were richly caparisoned and all wore handsome covers and each had a flag attached to the head, on which was electrotyped on each side, the Bull, the trade-mark of the firm. In each wagon were two banners, white field, red borders; in the center a large painted bull with the words, 'Smoke Blackwell's Durham Smoking Tobacco.'

"These costly trappings were prepared in Philadelphia at considerable cost, expressly for the occasion, with the exception of the banners. These were painted by Mr. J.R. Lawrence (inventor of the packing machine) of Durham, an artist of no mean pretensions.

"Soon the delegates were comfortably seated and the procession proceeded to the University (12 miles distant). Near Chapel Hill, the procession was met by the Salem Cornet Band which accompanied the procession making music, each person smoking the 'Bull' brand of tobacco in long-stem pipes."

*The **Blackwell factory** as it looked in the 1880s. The sign of the bull can be seen on the front of the building. The town of Durham set their watches to the bellow of its come-to-work horn.*

In 1883, huge sums of money went into advertising space in newspapers – $100,000 in country weeklies and $50,000 in larger city dailies. In the same year, an additional $60,000 was expended for mantel clocks and razors used as premiums.

Small things counted, too. An enormous bull was painted on paneled sheet metal and hung up on the front of factory building. It was hooked up to a steam whistle that was made to imitate the sound of a roaring bull. When it blew, it was said that the sound could be heard 13 miles away.

The real marketing masterstroke came during the 1880s when four crews of sign-painters were hired and dispatched to all points in the country. They plastered the likeness of the "Bull" on anything that didn't move – barns, billboards, fences, large boulders, and sides of buildings. Some displays were enormous – one measured 80 by 100 feet.

The "Bull" went overseas and invaded the sanctity of foreign nations, his features reportedly left in indelible paint on a pyramid in Egypt, the Rock of Gibraltar and Mount Kilimanjaro.

By the 1890s, Carr and his "Bull" Durham brand had achieved worldwide recognition and had become the largest-selling brand of tobacco on the face of the earth. It was an incredible feat in days before mass media advertising methods were available, let alone envisioned.

Carr's commitment to promotion was aptly illustrated by his famous quote: "Yes, sir! As long as I have a dollar to spare, I will invest it in advertising!"

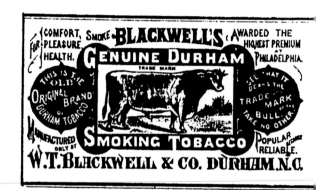

Advertising strategies of the 1880s and 1890s centered around premiums. Retailers were enticed with laundry soap, and smokers with cash, razors, baseballs, watches, and pipes.

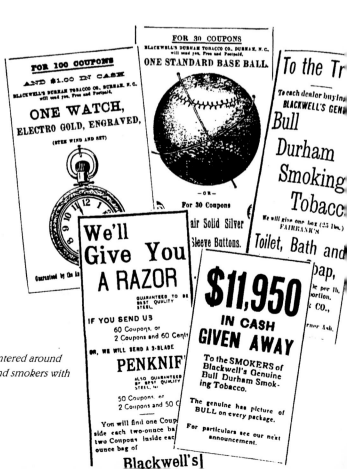

JAMES DUKE OF DURHAM
FATHER OF CONSUMER DEMAND

James Duke entered the tobacco world like a whirlwind in the 1880s. As head of his father's small smoking tobacco enterprise in Durham, North Carolina, W. Duke & Sons, the young Duke, within a decade, had driven it to the forefront of the market by employing unheard-of promotional schemes, some quite innovative, others rough and aggressive.

Stymied in his attempts to overtake the success of the crosstown rival brand, "Bull" Durham, Duke entered the cigarette business in 1881, determined to dominate the market. In 1884, he left Durham and set up headquarters in New York City.

There he waged a fierce and unrelenting promotional war on his competition.

Duke believed that advertising on a national scale could not only be made to pay off, but was one of the best investments a company could make. He essentially fathered consumer demand.

Duke's first order of business was to establish his cigarette brands. In October of 1881, he blanketed the nation for several months with newspaper ads boosting Duke of Durham tobacco and cigarettes. These early ads featured endorsements from tobacco dealers and consumers, a marketing device that he used with extreme effectiveness throughout his career.

He purchased 400,000 folding oak chairs in 1884, had them decorated with an advertisement for Duke's Cameo cigarettes and placed them free of charge in tobacco shops all over the country.

With such ploys, sales reached $600,000 in 1885. This was quite a change from the $70,000 estimated net worth of his father's business in 1880.

65

In 1888, Duke purchased the rights to a paper cigarette holder and used the device to add a glamorous touch to Cameo cigarettes, praising it in a little jingle:

*"I am wiser and I'm older,
And I've burned my upper lip
For I smoked without a holder,
(Duke could give this man a tip)."*

With Cameo cigarettes, Duke tried out a little invention of his own, a slide-and-shell cardboard box which he patented in 1886. Regarded by the press as "a perfect scream," it proved a vast improvement in packaging and immediately became standard in the industry.

Portland, Oregon, was the scene of a typical promotion in 1888. Large portraits of Madame Theo and Lily Langtry, 35 of them in ornate gilded frames, were placed in the windows of local tobacconists' shops and were awarded as prizes to those who turned in the most empty boxes of Cameo cigarettes.

Duke, in New York City, put into action personally devised and unique promotional stunts. He posted agents at the Immigration Station at Ellis Island who handed a sackful of cigarettes to every male passenger who stepped off a boat.

More unusual and aggressive were Duke's street tactics. Men, hired as shills, made the rounds of tobacco shops and loudly demanded Duke's brands of cigarettes. Street urchins were also employed to stand in front of these same shops and hand out free samples of Cameo and Cross Cut cigarettes.

The 1880s were closed out by Duke when he took one of his lesser brands, a cheap smoking and chewing tobacco called Honest Long Cut and, through extensive promotion, turned it into a national best seller.

This merchandising coup was accomplished with the help of G. Houtaling & Co., at the time the largest sign painter and bill poster in the country, who decorated the United States from Maine to California with advertisements for the brand.

Trade in Honest Long Cut was also spurred by distributing a plethora of free advertising, paper ephemera and such offbeat items as stereoscopic photographs and glass paperweights.

It worked. The cost of this large-scale advertising program, amounting to over $175,000 annually, was rewarded by phenomenal sales exceeding one-half million pounds of tobacco each month.

By this time, Duke was spending about $800,000 yearly on advertising out of sales of $4.5 million, almost a 20% re-investment. This was unheard of in his day.

THE ADVERTISING GENIUS OF EDWARD SMALL

One of James Duke's first traveling salesmen was Edward Featherston Small, a Southerner with a natural-born flair for promotion. Small was the handsome scion of a wealthy family and had served with the South's crack Washington Grays during the Civil War.

It all started one day in Atlanta in the 1880s. Strolling along Peachtree Street and looking idly in shop windows, Small came across a large portrait of Madame Rhea, a French actress currently on tour.

Later that day in his hotel, a brainstorm came to the salesman. He penned a note to the actress and had it delivered immediately. It read:

"Dear Madam Rhea:
"I write to ask if I may use one of your life-size lithographs to have the same duplicated in oil on canvas with the inscription below, 'Atlanta's Favorite'? Also extended in the right hand a package of Duke cigarettes?
"Yours truly, Edward F. Small, Salesman"

"Certainly," Rhea responded. Furthermore, she stated, she was "proud to be called 'Atlanta's Favorite.'"

A few mornings later, Atlantans awoke to find the beautiful and enticing Rhea offering them cigarettes, not only from an advertisement painted on the side of a building but also from a half-page ad in the local newspaper. The first celebrity endorsement had been landed in the tobacco business.

Soon orders for cigarettes flooded in, as Rhea's likeness continued to pop up on billboards and in store windows all over town. When the Atlanta campaign came to a close, Small had netted orders for a phenomenal 800,000 cigarettes.

"You made a happy hit with Rhea," an impressed Duke wrote his enterprising salesman.

This novel idea of Small's was adopted and continued. The Duke company soon began offering dealers colorful pictures of Madame Rhea with each order of a carton of 500 smokes.

When Small hit St. Louis, however, he found the dealers there unimpressed with his promotional antics. Despite heavy drumming, he took few orders. Undaunted, Small put his ingenious mind to work. He ran the following ad in the St. Louis Post-Dispatch:

"WANTED: Saleslady. Call at 103 North Fifth street between 10 and 11 A. M. tomorrow."

The next morning Small was surprised to find a dozen young women waiting for him. After interviewing the lot, he selected an attractive, red-headed widow, Mrs. Leonard, and instructed her in her new duties over a bottle of wine and lunch in a French restaurant.

Dispatched on her rounds, Mrs. Leonard landed 19 orders her very first day and was immediately written up in the papers as "the first and only lady in the world selling cigarettes." A female in the tobacco business at the time, needless to say, was unthinkable, but the effect was profound and magical.

Tobacconists in St. Louis soon looked forward to the pretty young woman who entered their shops. They showered her with orders.

Small, in grateful appreciation of Mrs. Leonard's accomplishments, bought her a new spring outfit. After the experience, in his letter sent to Duke, Small set down his personal recipe for sales success. Despite its mild racial slur, it was timeless in its application:

"The essential element in creating trade is a few grains of common sense, strategy and tact well sharpened, properly administered and rubbed in with a little nigger luck. Above all, judicious advertising, especially if the same is novel and astounding in magnitude."

Small's successful sales innovations were expanded by Duke who saw in them tremendous potential for brand promotion. They soon led to pictures of attractive young stage starlets and other female celebrities which were enclosed in Duke's cardboard cigarette boxes. These insert cards were the start of a huge marketing program. The idea was immediately copied by rival companies who recognized a good advertising thing when they saw one.

One of Small's last promotional coups was the organization of a uniformed team of roller skaters, dubbed the 'Cross Cuts of Durham" (the name of one of Duke's cigarette brands). Touring the Midwest, the team took on a succession of local challengers playing polo on roller skates.

As spectators left the arena, each gentleman was handed a package of Cross Cuts cigarettes and each lady was presented a pack of assorted photographs. The idea succeeded as sales of the cigarette brand skyrocketed.

By the 1880s, improvements in lithographic technique allowed the production of finer quality colored paper images. They graced packages and boxes of the weed, stood propped up on counters as posters and hung from the walls, light fixtures and ceiling fans of shops conducting business in tobacco. The purpose of advertising posters and labels was simply to attract the public's attention and to establish a brand name. Nothing was done, however, to promote the pleasures of using the product or claim superiority over rival brands. The packaged goods were not portrayed in ads either, and advertising slogans were nonexistent. Technical adjustments like these would come later.

THE GROCERS LEND A HAND

The distribution of tobacco goods in America was accelerated through allied trades, chiefly grocers. It was a natural marriage, tobacco and foodstuffs. Major wholesalers like Austin, Nichols & Co. of New York City offered merchants a complete line of brand name cigars and tobaccos.

You could order "Bull" Durham, Dausman's Horse Head chewing tobacco and Liggett & Myers' plug brands, Star and Clipper.

Cigarettes, not yet an important market item, were also available – Marburg's Lone Fisherman, Pilkinton's Fruits and Flowers, Goodwin's Old Judge, Kinney's Sweet Caporal, and Kimball's Vanity Fair - plus some expensive specialties like My Uncle Toby and Little Brown Jug all-tobacco cigarettes with cornhusk mouthpieces.

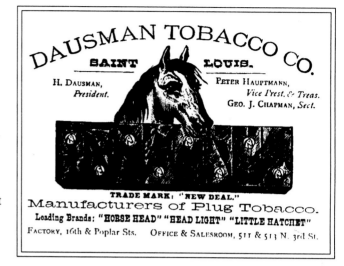

Tobacco ads as they appeared in an 1880 issue of Merchants' Review, *the retail grocers' weekly tabloid. Tiger Durham tobacco (below), made by a small firm in Durham, Roulhac & Co., was pushed by wholesalers as a more affordable, sound-alike option to the real (and more expensive) thing,* "Bull" Durham. *Enterprising companies like Roulhac became pesky business nuisances to powerful firms like Duke and Blackwell who often had to go to court to protect their trademarks from infringement.*

THE TOBACCONIST'S SHOP

The height of mercantile splendor in the vending of tobacco was achieved in the well-appointed tobacconist's shop that flourished in America between the 1870s and the 1930s.

This specialty emporium had evolved from its predecessor, the general or country store, where cigars, tobacco and smoking articles were relegated to dusty niches among canned and textile goods, into an elegant structure that occupied a prominent place in the busy social and business life of downtown America.

The old-time tobacconist's store was an institution of leisure. But, unlike the general store, it possessed special qualities – warmth, camaraderie and congeniality – that appealed strongly to male senses. It became a pleasantly informal neighborhood forum with back rooms for pinochle, stud poker or just plain conversation. Regular customers paid their tabs monthly – or when able.

This bastion of togetherness, a well-frequented social club, took on an atmosphere of exclusivity and privacy only surpassed by the local saloon. The price of admission was only a five-cent cigar.

Running a tobacco shop in the old days was a common profession. The Census Bureau reported in 1917 that there were an estimated 580,000 cigar and tobacco shops operating in the United States.

A DIFFERENT WORLD

The special flavor offered by the old-time tobacco shop started outside. Many businesses, up to the 1920s, possessed a carved wooden figure that stood faithful and silent sidewalk guard – usually a weatherbeaten old squaw in faded hues and chipped paint, holding aloft the traditional handful of cigars and standing proudly on a wooden pedestal.

Cigar stores were noted for their window displays. It was their stock in trade; they were designed to turn the heads of the most imperturbable passers-by.

Most displays were elaborate productions. Stacks of cigar boxes were placed snugly among large and colorful stand-up or hanging posters plugging cigar and cigarette brands. Every bit of space in the window area was utilized.

By the 1910s, the setting up of cigar store window exhibits had developed into a highly skilled art. Professional help was available from wholesale cigar houses, whose salesmen provided the service and the posters free (as long as their brands received front-row prominence). Tobacco shops not on the drummer's beat were supplied with detailed instructions mailed to the dealers.

Stepping across the threshold and into the tobacco store, the unmistakable aroma of fresh tobacco greeted the nose, a unique and agreeable olfactory experience for smoker and non-smoker alike. Once sampled, it was never forgotten.

The smell was even richer and stronger in those shops that catered to the pipe-smoking trade. A full line of smoking tobaccos was carried for making up house blends or personalized formulas for special clients. Each tobacco, stored in bins or jars, lent its distinctive fragrance to the air – Maryland and North Carolina leaf, Virginia cavendish, Louisiana perique, and imported Latakia and Turkish leaf.

Counters were filled to the brim with an enormous selection of cigars, both domestic brands and imported Havanas.

Boxes of twenty-fives, fifties and one-hundreds were packed side by side, their lids opened fully to reveal the enticingly pretty embossed labels inside. Open boxes rested on the countertop offering the customer the owner's private hand-rolled labels at bargain prices.

Stogies from Wheeling, the workingman's favorite, were also available for the hardier connoisseurs (light them up outside, please!).

For many years chewing tobacco was the staple commodity of all tobacco merchants. Long flat bricks of

bulk tobacco were sliced into small pieces with heavy cast-iron tobacco cutters and dispensed in small paper envelopes.

The lavish window dressing put on by Frankle Bros. of Youngstown, Ohio, seen here around 1915, was quite an eye-catching sight. Retailers had learned that a strategic location downtown, preferably a busy street corner, was critically important in ensuring good trade.

Cigar store windows were transformed from barren and dusty catch-all niches into colorfully extravagant displays. Cigar boxes, packages of cigarettes and smoking tobacco, pipes and other smoking paraphernalia were often set off by posters, ribbons, streamers, and fancy bunting. Freshened up weekly, the sight was guaranteed to drag a man inside from clear across the street.

ELEGANT INTERIORS

Cabinets made of the finest mahogany, oak and walnut, darkly stained and varnished to a high gloss, reached to the ceiling behind the counters and held rows upon rows of cigarette packs, wrapped plugs of chewing tobacco and small glass jars of Scotch and Maccaboy snuff.

A large gleaming and ornate brass cash register marked the place of business transaction at the counter.

Ample smoking accessories were on hand. Pipes, pipe tools, pipe cleaners, match holders, lighters, and cigar and cigarette cases were spread out on shelves or piled high in wooden crates on the floor and priced to sell quickly.

Quantity and a small mark-up in profit was the key to business success.

Every self-respecting tobacco emporium was fitted with a gas lighter, either mounted on the wall or on the counter. The flame, turned on during business hours, allowed smokers to light up their cigars and cigarettes without delay and join the proprietor and other patrons in conversation along the tobacco counter.

Care was absolutely necessary around the gas lighter – a gentleman might singe his mustache, a lady her expensive mink coat.

All sorts of mechanical devices for cutting and notching the ends of cigars were available. These, too, were dangerous instruments for the careless and unwary (and the foolish) who could lose a fingertip in a flash in one of these razor-sharp miniature guillotines.

Floors of the tobacconist's shop were either made of tile or marble. No one appreciated this choice of floor composition more than the unfortunate clerk whose job it was to clean it up at night after a day's accumulation of tobacco spittle that missed the brass or porcelain cuspidors lining the walls and counters.

Ceilings were typically high and covered with the decorative tin plate popular in Victorian days. Elaborate glass electric lights or gas models that threw out bizarre and frightening sheets of flame hung down from the ceiling and illuminated the interior.

Now step inside the Frankle Brothers' store and take note of the neat and orderly interior that served the needs of a fastidious tobacco-using clientele. Noteworthy accouterments included glass encased counters and cabinets filled to overflowing with boxes of cigars. Potted palms, recessed ceilings and fancy electric light chandeliers added a nice decorator touch. The cigar-making cage occupied the far end of the shop. Barely visible in the back room were stacked wooden buckets of fine cut chewing tobacco—Bagley's Fast Mail, Scotten's Hiawatha and Cotterill & Fenner's celebrated North Star brand from nearby Dayton.

HEADQUARTERS FOR ADVERTISING

To enter one of these establishments was also to step into a world of concentrated advertising. Every bit of marketing guile, persuasion and allure was poured into their environments to tantalize the senses – visual, olfactory and tactile.

The interior of the tobacco shop was filled with a wide choice of brand selections in every form of tobacco desired.

The very best of advertising was employed to attract the customer's attention. Vivid images of beautiful women on paper, promoting a cigar or cigarette brand, dotted the walls above or between the cabinets behind the counter. They were particularly effective when hung in a row. From their lofty stations, they looked down on patrons and sent out their subliminal message: "Buy me!"

Brightly colored packages of cigarettes and chewing and smoking tobaccos were stacked by the score behind glass cabinet doors or on open shelves, forming an enticing array of shape, size and color. Counter mats and change trays - even glass and metal cigar cutters and lighters – were emblazoned with brand names and attractive colorful imagery.

There was really no escape.

Tobacco and related smoking paraphernalia were not the only products sold in these establishments. Space permitting, magazine and newspaper racks were installed where customers could pick up the latest issue of Police Gazette or the evening edition of the daily journal.

The nattily dressed and courteous tobacco shop staff eagerly awaits a morning rush of business. Bargain-priced pipes fill the baskets on the floor and the row of cigar advertising posters form an impressive display on top of the cabinets. This was a small but first-class business establishment.

Every tobacco store attracted its own individual set of devotees. There was always a young-man-about-town crowd who frequented the stores more than they should have. Some called them idlers. The counter help had more polite terms for them in their shop lingo: showcase loungers.

Many men were just lonesome and came in to enjoy the company of others and chat a while, sometimes to the point of insufferable boredom to those around them. These experiences were especially painful to the clerks who had no means of escape.

Some of the customers were memorable characters, like the old man in Ft. Wayne who sat in a chair all day nursing his only purchase, a three-cent cigar, and recounted interesting stories about himself. He never returned when the proprietor, in total exasperation, simply removed the chair from the shop. The peace and quiet was well worth the daily three-cent loss.

Many tobacco shop owners and their families lived upstairs above the premises. When young ones came along, they eventually found their way downstairs. The floor of the shop served as an auxiliary playroom, sometimes to the annoyance of customers.

A professional appearance was important and staff dress codes were strictly observed. Male clerks wore starched, white shirts with ties. Jackets were added in the winter. It lent an air of decorum and taste befitting the clientele. In 1905, the average clerk in a cigar store earned $12 a week in wages.

Sundries were commonplace – so were gum and candy. A few shops boasted of their own soda fountains; some even served sandwiches on the side. At times the lunch end of the store became busier than the tobacco end and, during the Depression years of the 1930s, many a cigar store changed into a restaurant – and then sold cigars on the side.

THE CUSTOMERS (GOD BLESS 'EM)

Clientele, like the weather, varied.

Regulars from all walks of life passed through the portals of the downtown cigar store – the banker picking up his after-lunch panatela, the machinist stopping off for his favorite chewing plug and the college student selecting a fine smoking mixture or the latest brand of Turkish cigarette. Youngsters came in to cadge empty cigar boxes to hold their marble collections or fishing worms.

MAKING CIGARS AS A SIDE BUSINESS

Some business owners manufactured cigars on the premises for private retail and local wholesale markets. The factory area, usually located at the rear of the shop, was separated from the store proper by a metal mesh cage, as required by federal law.

Cigars were usually sold locally, regionally if the operation was a large one. Most cigar-making businesses were one-man enterprises, however, and the owner spent a good deal of time peddling his smoking wares around town. Saloons, hotels, sandwich shops, restaurants, and candy stores were his best markets. In tough times, proprietors used cigars and tobacco to barter for food from local farmers and grocers.

Tobacco shops slowly slipped into obscurity, done in by the economic ravages of two world wars, a major depression and the transformation of many downtown business districts into near ghost towns as human populations fled to the suburbs to escape urban blight.

Paramount in the demise of these venerable institutions was the overwhelming market preference of cigarettes which could be purchased in vending machines conveniently located all over town. Cigars had fallen out of favor, chewing tobacco and snuff were outmoded and, with their passing, so was the need for tobacco specialty shops. Most had closed their doors forever by the time World War II came to an end.

A nostalgic moment in time is frozen in this scene from a cozy Cincinnati tobacco shop around 1905. The boss poses stiffly while a clerk handles a phone order. A female employee, not an infrequent sight in such a male world, tidies up her paper work, and boxes of newly rolled cigars, stacked on a counter, await delivery. Tobacco could be stored for years, but once made into cigars, deteriorated rapidly. Wall posters advertising Ramleh and Mecca cigarettes form a colorful backdrop. The spittoon is curiously positioned to the right facing the cash register (did chewers favor this direction?). Working hours were long and grueling–sun-up to ten at night, seven days a week and 52 weeks a year (with maybe Christmas off) were typical.

Trade stimulators in
the form of slot
machines and other
ornate contrivances
were commonly found
around the turn of the century
and paid off in metal slugs which were
redeemable for cigars or cash. Considered games of
chance, they were eventually outlawed.

ADVERTISING LEGACIES OF THE OLD-TIME TOBACCONIST'S SHOP

Felt change mats

Cigar box tools

Tobacco cutters

Small figurals
– stern-looking Indians and
turbaned Turks – made of
plaster of paris and resting on
counter tops

Glass and metal change trays

Fancy cigar cutters, gas lighters
and match holders

Large, *framed posters* and
metal chargers, rendered in
dazzling colors

MAKING CIGARS

The making of cigars has historically been by hand. Even introduction of automated cigar-making machines in the early 1920s did not displace hand-rolling as quickly as might be expected. Cigar connoisseurs were a finicky bunch and many never gave up their taste for hand-made models. There was just something about the touch of the human hand that set them apart.

The art of hand-rolling cigars, from the 1870s to the present day, has changed very little. Seated in rows at tables, workers faced a slab of hard wood. An outer wrapper of Havana tobacco was selected from a pile of dampened leaves and smoothed free of creases and wrinkles. Then it was cut with a short peculiarly shaped knife (like ones used by shoemakers) into a rough semicircular piece.

The outer wrapper was the most important step in making a cigar. It gave the cigar its final form and hence its appeal. Many vain smokers were more drawn to the appearance of a cigar in their mouths than its smoking qualities.

Short leaves used as filler tobacco were squeezed into a loose bundle and placed inside the wrapper. With a dexterous twist, edges of the wrapper leaf were pulled up and over the filler.

The business end of the cigar was molded into the required conical shape and the point secured by a drop of paste; the other end was cut off straight and smooth. The cigar was then placed on the wood slab, rolled under the flat blade of the knife a few times, and it was ready to be smoked. By tradition, every cigar-maker was entitled to keep four or five "smokers" for himself each working day.

The finished articles were lastly tied into a bundle. A ribbon was stretched out flat on the table and the cigars heaped on it in quantities of 25 or more. The worker took the ends of the ribbon, brought them together and, with another deft move, tied the knot and dropped the bundle into an undersized box, forced into place by a screw press. The cover was nailed shut, the government tax stamp was applied and the box of bundled cigars was ready for shipment.

This was how clear, 100-percent Havana cigars were made. Stems and refuse of the tobacco were not used. Cheap cigars were filled with cuttings or fine shavings of

Under gas light illumination, this hardy and predominantly male work crew, a small, family-run business, fashions an endless stream of cigars (ca 1900).

domestic tobacco and wrapped with domestic leaf (so-called "clear seed" cigars). Tobacco was expensive and nothing was left to waste.

Cigar molds of various sizes and shapes came into use around 1870. They consisted of wooden trays roughly 18 inches long and 6 inches wide which held about 20 cigars. Freshly rolled smokes were placed into the hollowed-out depressions before application of the wrapper leaf and compressed into shape by clamps.

Molds saved time (and skill) and were capable of doubling output. Cheaper seed and Havana-wrapped cigars – nickel cigars and practically all – were made with molds.

Cigar-makers were regarded as craftsmen. Apprenticeships usually lasted three to five years and the individual skills learned in rolling cigars were guarded like military secrets. Workers were paid "by the piece" and received a stipulated sum for each 1,000 cigars rolled. An experienced journeyman could turn out 250 in a 10-hour day and averaged $15-20 a week in wages.

Thanks to a strong union forged by that grand old man of labor, Samuel Gompers, cigar-makers of last century were some of the best paid workers in America, true aristocrats of the labor world.

PEST HOLES

Not all cigar manufacturing of last century was carried out under clean and sanitary working conditions. A blight plaguing the unionized cigar industry was the tenement house system which first appeared in New York City around 1876.

Greedy manufacturers rented large apartment houses and forced workers ("turning men," they were called) to rent rooms as a condition of securing employment, usually $4 -5 more than the going rate.

There armies of cigar-makers became enslaved. In scenes reminiscent of pre-Dickensian England, two-room living spaces were converted into crowded, filthy miniature cigar factories, where entire families labored day and night rolling and packing cigars to eke out a meager existence. The finished products were then sold to jobbers and wholesalers at bargain prices and ultimately peddled on the retail market to unsuspecting consumers.

The principal victims were children. An estimated 24,000 of them, some as young as five years of age, stripped and rolled tobacco leaves alongside family members. New York Governor Theodore Roosevelt branded tenement houses as "pest holes." Although eventually prohibited by city law in 1882, the squalid tenement factories remained a social and business nuisance for decades. Sweat shops and luxury goods, it seemed, always went hand in hand.

A READY-MADE PROFESSION

Hard-working entrepreneurs, many of them immigrants seeking the American dream, found an attractive business opportunity in making cigars. With little capital, a skilled cigar-maker could register his factory with the Internal Revenue office and lay in a stock of tax stamps, tobacco leaves and cigar boxes.

Using only a knife and cutting board, he could turn out cigars in the corner of his room. Other necessities were not expensive; a well-made cigar box could be purchased for about 7 cents; a pretty colored lid label ran 3 cents.

Through hard work and a few sales, the cigar-maker could afford to rent a larger work space and perhaps hire an assistant or two. The average cigar manufactory in 1880 was composed of 2 to 3 people, a statistic that remained remarkably constant for decades.

SMOKING VICTORIAN CIGARS

The cheapest cigars sold in the 1870s were those made of domestic tobacco. These crudely made rolls of tobacco, saloon favorites, sold at two or three for a nickel ("two-fers" and "three-fers") and appealed not only to thrifty smokers but also to those who could not tell the difference between smoking a cigar and a piece of rope. Domestic brands were usually put up in imitation Havana boxes with imitation Havana labels, and brand names rendered in a plethora of Cuban or Spanish appellations.

The next best class were those with Havana fillers and Connecticut or Sumatran wrappers. They were often palmed off as real imported cigars. Upwards in grade were cigars made entirely of imported Cuban tobacco, the best in the world; they ran anywhere from 15 to 50 cents each.

True nabobs of society could afford the very best smoking articles: genuine imported Havanas, good for 50 minutes of smoking pleasure. They were scarce indeed and ranged in price from 20 cents to a dollar and over apiece.

The best-selling cigar in history, however, was the nickel cigar. No other cigar ever achieved the mass consumer appeal this variety did and, despite advertising claims, one brand was just as good as another. The original five-center was not a cheap cigar; to the contrary, it was a luxury smoking item. It contained more Havana leaf than more expensive cigars that came later.

The average cigar smoker in 1899, statistics claimed, went through six smokes daily and spent about a dollar a day on his habit. Some men didn't smoke cigars, they chewed them. These "dry smokers," as they were called, could gnaw their way through as many as 25 in a single day. Other men with artistic inclinations smoked according to their moods and often kept three or four different-sized cigars on hand.

Of presidents who smoked cigars, no one ever matched Grant's voracious chain-smoking appetite. Chester Arthur enjoyed one now and then and Harrison put away a half dozen a day and thought no man should exceed eight.

McKinley came into office a prolific cigar consumer, smoking 18 a day. His robust habit became so well publicized that any unpopular political decision he made was blamed by opponents on excessive smoking which they claimed was making the president "nervous." On the advice of his physician, McKinley reduced his cigar consumption, as much for health concerns as for political strategy.

Matchbooks and matchboxes (right) were personalized with business or brand names.

Pocket cigar holders
(above) made of stiff paper
or leather were supplied by
manufacturers to dealers
who in turn passed them
on to customers.
Advertising playing cards (below)
were also distributed.

Coin-operated cigar despensers like this fancy Doremus model of 1902 were forerunners of an invention that hastened the demise of the tobacconist's shop-the cigarette vending machine.

CHEAP CIGARS

Smokers who were not fussy about the looks of a cigar or impressed by gilded bands, labels and other glitzy foofaraw provided a number of cigar merchants with a thriving mail order business in the 1900-1920 period. These enterprising marketeers pawned off factory seconds or arranged orders "direct from the factory" at truly bargain prices and sealed the deal with gifts and a money-back guarantee. There was no going wrong with this kind of business proposition.

Cigars go to bat. This amateur baseball team of Cincinnati, enjoying the luxury of two substitutes and a bat boy, was sponsored by the hometown Ibold cigar company (ca 1910). Community participation was good for product publicity and employee morale.

Modern American cigar stores of the 1920s featured glass showcases, enclosed shelves, carefully humidified smoking stock and, most importantly, prompt and personalized customer service.

THE MAGIC OF STONE CHROMOLITHOGRAPHY

Cigar labels of the classic 1870-1920 period were printed by means of stone lithography, a laborious and time-consuming process, but it was through this medium that cigar label art reached its highest form of expression and beauty.

Improved printing techniques such as photolithography which became standard in the industry by the 1920s never matched the superb technical and artistic appearance of these old prints. Quality tends to be sacrificed with new processes saving time and money.

Stone chromolithography combined art with science. Original watercolor prints supplied by a vast pool of commercial artists, typically unsigned, were transferred with pen, pencil or greasy crayon onto the surface of polished slabs of natural Bavarian limestone of varying dimensions, usually about 24 inches square and 3.5-4 inches thick.

The sketched surface was then inked with a roller, a sheet of paper was placed over the stone and, under pressure of a steam press, the image was transferred onto the paper, the print being called a lithograph. In the production of colored images (chromolithography), a separate stone was prepared for each color needed; lavishly colored images required as many as 24 stones.

Quality of this old-fashioned printing process was improved in the 1880s when the use of two textured steel rollers gave the appearance of labels being printed on cloth.

But it was embossing with its three-dimensional effect, introduced in 1889, that gave life, definition and eye appeal to coins, medals, female curves, and other forms depicted on labels. Embossing was expensive but it added class and was worth it.

The embossing technique, however, only worked with high quality, unbleached, linen rag paper. This costly stock allowed stretching during the embossing process and, lacking wood fiber, it aged well, too, without yellowing. Labels today, a century later, look as fresh and new as the day they rolled off the presses.

Time, money and artistic talent, plentiful commodities in Victorian times, were not spared when it came to printing intricate cigar labels. The investment, as it turned out, was generally worthwhile. When cigar labels were created, they were created for a lifetime of business use. Many sold for years afterward.

Making cigar labels the old-fashioned way with engraved limestone slabs and 38-ton presses. Shown here is the busy printing department of the Calvert Lithographic Company of Detroit (ca 1920s), one of the nation's largest image-makers.

ELEGANCE WITH OSTENTATION

Manufacturers the country over sold the cigar's snob appeal to the masses. Brand names reaching into the tens of thousands flooded the land. So many cigar brands were on the market in the 1880s, for example, that it was possible to find 100-200 private labels for sale in a city of 20,000 inhabitants.

FROM WHENCE THEY CAME

The profusion of century-old cigar labels that reside in collectors' hands today emerged from various sources. Many were discovered in dusty basements and attics of long-defunct cigar factories, and ranged in quantities from a handful to wrapped bundles of thousands. Copyright files of large companies, cigar box factories and lithographic houses also yielded considerable numbers. Labels came in three basic formats–samples, proofs and those that were actually used. Salesmen's sample books, paperbound or leatherbound, were crammed full of labels, each one showing the name of the printer

.....and the price. Proof labels were typically lithographed on heavy stock, lacked embossing and carried color bars and registration marks used to align the paper during printing.

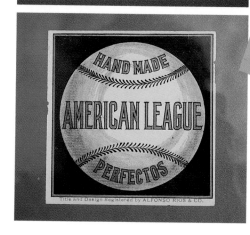

GILDED TREASURES

With rare exception, the prettiest and fanciest examples of Victorian advertising art were found on the inside lids of cigar boxes circulating between 1880 and 1900.

GREAT CHIEF

No. 6334 Ins.
No. 6335 Outs. | Price for Set: 2½ cts. net.
ALSO BLANK

CHAMPIONS

O. L. SCHWENCKE,
33-35-37 Bleecker Street.

No. 2239 ins. $3.00, No. 2240 outs. $1.50

BULLY

282

BULLY

COOL

F. HEPPENHEIMER'S SONS
19TH ST. AND 4TH AVE., NEW YORK,
108-110 RANDOLPH ST., CHICAGO,
723 BRYANT ST., SAN FRANCISCO.

No. 3358 Inside $2.00 per M. Net.
No. 3359 Outside $1.00 per M. Net.
ALSO BLANK.

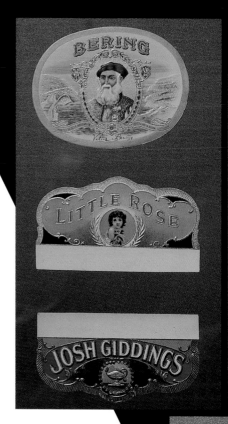

BY ANY OTHER NAME

Spelling the word "cigar" as "segar" is a throwback to original references made to the smoking article in the last century. In 1859, Webster's dictionary frowned on the latter word and referred readers to the more acceptable term, cigar. A larger encyclopedia of 1889, in defining a cigar, formally declared "segar" as grammatically incorrect. Nonetheless, many men in the trade continued to use the quaint but old-fashioned spelling (or variations of it) to spice up slogans, brand names and advertising copy.

By the 1920s, male responses to cigar advertising images had changed. Out went heavy and ornate Victorian ornamentation; in came clean and simple logos with snappy brand names such as Call Again, Yellow Cab and Hi-De-Ho. They were designed to catch the attention of connoisseurs of cheap cigars by sound, not quality. The golden age of label-making had come to an end.

Note the medals. They meant nothing, but manufacturers liked to think that their cigars could win medals.

INSINCERE FORMS OF FLATTERY

The custom of cigar makers naming brands after people in the news was not without problems. In their haste to cash in on the moment, cigar men hardly ever bothered with trifling details such as securing legal permission to do so. While most honorees were flattered by the act, others became angry and called their lawyers. A few cases ended up in court and made entertaining headlines. Bringing a $100,000 suit in 1925 against the Lorillard company was John Philip Sousa, the famous band master and composer. He was not so much upset that his name had been attached to a cigar, but that it was for such a cheap one, selling for three cents, and making him the butt of endless joking by his friends. Henry Ford also went to court over a brand of cigars named after his automobile. The auto maker lost and was informed by the judge that he, Ford, held no monopoly on his name.

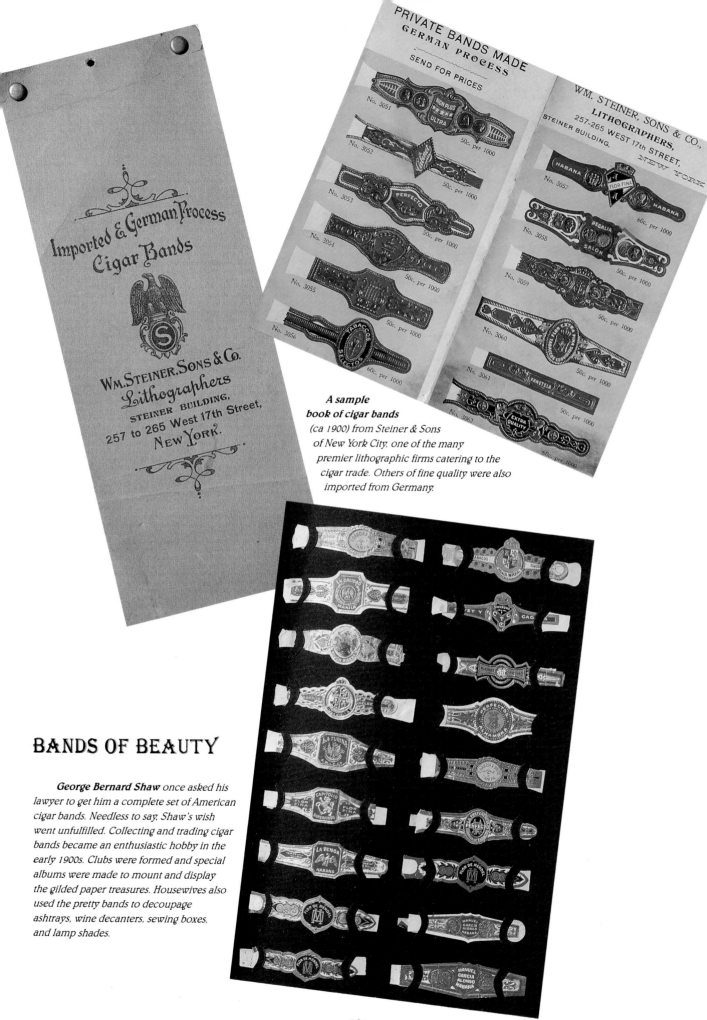

WM. STEINER, SONS & CO.,
LITHOGRAPHERS,
257-265 WEST 17th STREET,
STEINER BUILDING,
NEW YORK

No. 3051 NON PLUS ULTRA 50c. per 1000
No. 3052 50c. per 1000
No. 3053 PERFECTO 50c. per 1000
No. 3054 50c. per 1000
No. 3055 50c. per 1000
No. 3056 TABACOS S.P.ACTOS 60c. per 1000

No. 3057 HABANA FLOR FINA HABANA 60c. per 1000
No. 3058 REGALIA SALON 60c. per 1000
No. 3059 50c. per 1000
No. 3060 50c. per 1000
No. 3061 PANETELA 50c. per 1000
No. 3062 EXTRA QUALITY 60c. per 1900

Imported & German Process
Cigar Bands

WM. STEINER, SONS & CO.
Lithographers
STEINER BUILDING,
257 to 265 West 17th Street,
NEW YORK.

*A sample
book of cigar bands*
*(ca 1900) from Steiner & Sons
of New York City, one of the many
premier lithographic firms catering to the
cigar trade. Others of fine quality were also
imported from Germany.*

BANDS OF BEAUTY

George Bernard Shaw once asked his
lawyer to get him a complete set of American
cigar bands. Needless to say, Shaw's wish
went unfulfilled. Collecting and trading cigar
bands became an enthusiastic hobby in the
early 1900s. Clubs were formed and special
albums were made to mount and display
the gilded paper treasures. Housewives also
used the pretty bands to decoupage
ashtrays, wine decanters, sewing boxes,
and lamp shades.

THE GOLDEN AGE
(1890-1915)

Between 1890 and 1915, the so-called Gilded Age of America, was a period of unprecedented economic growth, rapid technological advancement and, vitally important to those in the tobacco business, remarkable innovations in advertising methods culminating in high quality, tantalizingly beautiful artwork.

The general population, well conditioned to traditional means of tobacco promotion, pretty labels, posters, trade cards, tin tags, and other examples of Victorian decorative excess, watched with eager fascination as new merchandising ploys hit the market.

Sales of cigarettes grew with each passing year, threatening to become the nation's favorite among users of the heathen weed. By 1912, the tobacco industry ranked eleventh in the nation based on value of its products and employed nearly 200,000 people. This was not the result of accident.

The development of tobacco manufacturing had created an industry not only of great commercial importance, but one that was surpassed only by the income tax in generating revenue for the federal government, a fact that figured prominently in all future political decisions affecting the tobacco industry, both nationally and locally.

The period also saw the birth in 1890 and cataclysmic rise of the American Tobacco Company, the so-called "Tobacco Trust," which played a significant role in spurring demand for tobacco. It grew into a corporate giant so large and so powerful that it virtually choked out all competition until its industrial stranglehold was broken by a U. S. Supreme Court decision in 1911.

The biggest event of the day, however, belonged to temperance, educational and religious groups. Years of hostility generated by these organizations toward tobacco and particularly cigarettes finally reached the breaking point and burst on the social and political scene with explosive force. Beginning around 1900, flames of reform, stoked by waves of anti-cigarette propaganda and paranoia, led to nationwide enactment of laws prohibiting the sale of cigarettes.

KICKING MACHINES, POETRY CONTESTS AND "BULL" IN THE OUTFIELD

Fueling the national call for tobacco was advertising which literally thundered across the land in scope and breadth. Attention was directed to newspapers and magazines. What had for years lain as vast, overlooked and underestimated avenues of communication had, by 1900, come to the front as a fresh, new way of merchandising a full range of goods to the nation's consumers. By the 1920s, tobacco companies would become one of the heaviest subscribers in this vital marketing sector.

In 1908, tobacco tycoon James Duke ran a limerick contest, offering cash prizes for the best rhymes extolling the smoking pleasures of Old English Curve Cut tobacco. Makers of chewing tobacco, oblivious to a spate of advertised tobacco cures and growing anti-tobacco sentiments, confidently assured the public that chewing "pure" tobacco preserved the teeth and pushed for more sales.

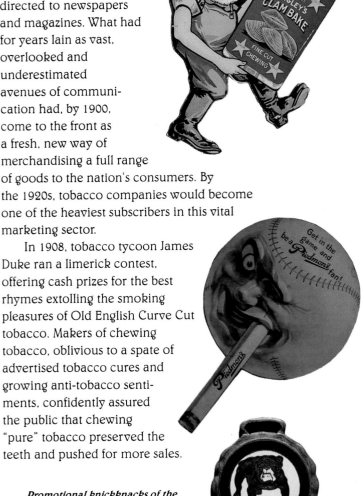

Promotional knickknacks of the period *included die-cut cardboard hangers, watch fobs and fans for spectators to whisk away annoying cigar, pipe and cigarette fumes at baseball parks.*

The Biggest "Hit" at the Ball Game

In 1896, a tobacco journal cursed the bicycle. An estimated one-half million males, formerly addicted to the long weed, had abandoned it in favor of the wheel craze sweeping the country. It was difficult, the article pointed out, to ride and smoke at the same time, resulting in a loss of sales of about 700 million cigars annually and a significant drop in overall tobacco consumption.

Tobacco, an important advertiser since the 1870s, turned to big-city firms for professional help. Admen, skilled at newspaper and magazine advertising, convinced tobacco companies that their services were essential if products were to be sold nationally. As a result, major advertising agencies, Ayer & Son, Lord & Thomas and J. Walter Thompson, aligned themselves with major tobacco corporations.

A few tobacco men, however, continued to invent promotional ideas the old-fashioned way – by instinct and the seat of their pants. Crafty and single-minded R.J. Reynolds, for instance, introduced the Schnapps kicking machine in 1897.

It was a hanging metal contraption with a pull cord. Chewers of plug stepped up to the machine and, pulling the cord, gave themselves a well deserved kick in the pants for not chewing Schnapps. Crude and outrageous, but remarkably effective, the kicking machine remained popular for well over a decade with plug-chewing plowmen the country over.

An enterprising New York City barbershop owner sold advertising space on his ceiling to merchants. His first customer was a tobacco store proprietor.

The American Tobacco Company, always on the cutting edge of promotional novelties, bankrolled the "Hit the Bull" campaign in 1912 and 1913. In promoting

"Bull" Durham tobacco, the company took advantage of the established popularity of baseball by erecting large cut-out wooden signs of the bull on the outfield grass of major and minor league parks. Hometown players scoring a direct hit on the sign with a fly ball were mailed a check for $50.

It was a smash hit with fans and players alike; a total of $10,500 was paid out in 1912. The campaign was finally halted when too many outfielders ran into the sign, injuring themselves.

Duke's company elevated celebrity endorsements to record levels in newspaper and magazine advertising. In 1912, the American Tobacco Company recruited opera star Enrico Caruso and a number of well-known sports figures, especially baseball stars such as Ty Cobb, John McGraw and Christy Mathewson who eagerly signed their names to ringing endorsements of Tuxedo smoking tobacco (for a fee, of course).

Duke also pioneered the use of comic strips in national advertising. Bud Fisher, creator of the popular Mutt and Jeff series, lent his artistic talents for the Tuxedo brand.

PRIMING THE PUMP

Cigar and tobacco salesmen, now indispensable adjuncts to merchandising, were dispatched far and wide to pay regular calls to all stores selling tobacco. There they established good will, solicited orders and distributed circulars announcing new brands, special sales and ordering information.

Praises were sung over Reynolds' advertising calendars of the early 1890s featuring ravishingly beautiful Victorian beauties. Railroad cars leaving factories filled with manufactured tobacco were decorated with huge banners bearing the names of the manufacturer and brands being shipped. The advertising messages were carried along miles of track throughout America.

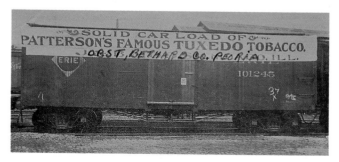

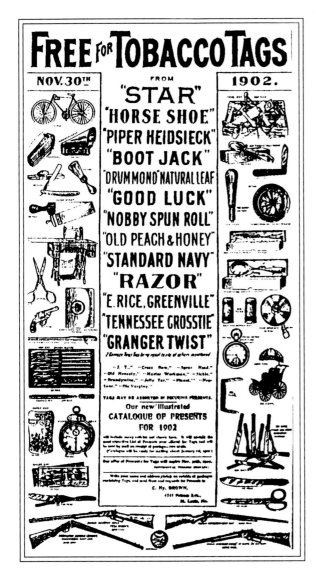

THE CONSUMERS' ACHILLES HEEL

The tobacco industry's first national premium system, tin tags, continued to enjoy uncommon success. To chewers living off the beaten path in rural America, the opportunity to obtain big city goods in exchange for the little tags of tin was a strong incentive to chew more and to chew often. "Save the Tags!" tobacco companies exhorted consumers in ads and on the tags themselves. In 1893, the Sorg firm turned the redemption of Spear Head tags into a contest and offered $170,000 worth of gifts, including gold-plated toothpicks, French opera glasses and Elgin watches.

In 1902, the American Tobacco Company published a list of chewing brands whose tags qualified for redemption. This was necessary to keep quid chewers up to date with the Trust's voracious habit of acquiring new companies and new brands. Whether it was a shotgun or a bicycle in exchange for tin tags, or something as simple and crass as cash, the public's appetite for receiving something "free" created an unprecedented demand for products. The premium system became an essential feature of many future tobacco promotions and remains popular today.

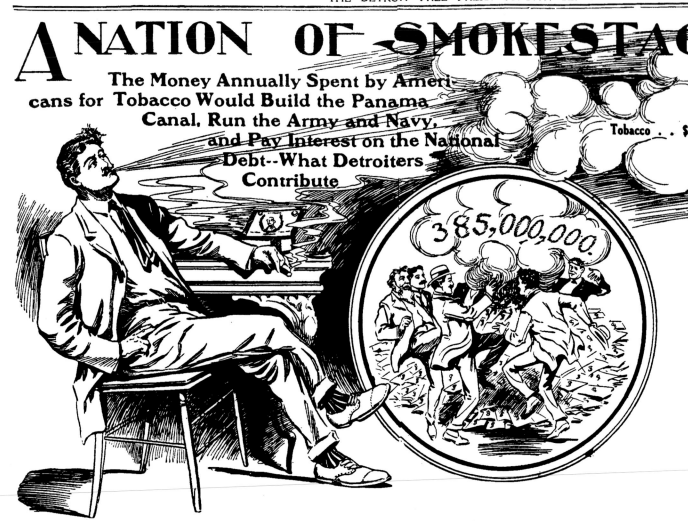

A NATION OF SMOKESTAC

The Money Annually Spent by Americans for Tobacco Would Build the Panama Canal, Run the Army and Navy, and Pay Interest on the National Debt--What Detroiters Contribute

Tobacco companies continued to be faithful and enthusiastic exhibitors at state and national shows. The World's Fair in 1893 in Chicago, the Columbian Exposition, generated unparalleled cultural and business excitement. Advertising displays introduced at the show ran a full range: posters, catalogs, calendars, cards, and circulars of all sorts.

Some idea of the effort and extravagance expended by tobacco companies in forming displays was found at the Atlanta Exposition in 1895. There the Reynolds Tobacco Company, in a room lavishly papered in imitation of chewing tobacco, erected an immense pyramid of tobacco boxes representing various brands of plug on top of which sat a figure of "Liberty Enlightening the World," illuminated by strong lights.

Trial samples of smoking and chewing tobacco were mailed out from factories for the price of a few pennies, a postage stamp or cut-out ads from newspapers. Others were supplied to dealers free of charge.

By this point in time, many tobacco manufacturers were discovering that advertising not only paid, but it paid well. A good example was Richard Joshua Reynolds. The North Carolinian, in the 1880s and 1890s, cautiously reinvested 2-3 percent of gross annual income in advertising; he was rewarded by significant increases in sales.

These figures were to pale later when, by 1915 and after Reynolds' death, as much as 80 percent of his company's net earnings were plowed back into promotion, chiefly with Camel cigarettes.

Another major means of marketing came to life in the 1890s and grew with blinding speed: outdoor advertising. It first took the form of glittering electrical displays on downtown buildings and then spread to wooden billboard signs which soon blighted urban and suburban neighborhoods.

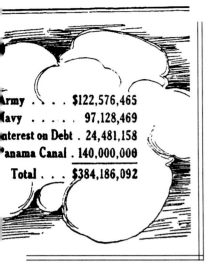

Army	$122,576,465
Navy	97,128,469
Interest on Debt .	24,481,158
Panama Canal .	140,000,000
Total . . .	$384,186,092

SECRET OF THE FIFTY-CENT JACKKNIFE

In 1897, Duke's American Tobacco Company introduced Dragoon chewing tobacco, first in Indiana, then in Ohio. Each purchaser was handed a card to hold Dragoon tin tags which, when filled, was redeemable for a pocket knife. It was an expensive but highly successful promotion.

A company salesman, interviewing customers, made a startling discovery: 60 percent of those chewing Dragoon did it simply for the knife, 20 percent did it because they liked the tobacco and the rest did it for no reason at all. The last group, when asked what brand they chewed, responded: "Any kind."

Similarly, in 1911, a Holton, Kansas, man saved enough tobacco tags to send away for a rocking chair. His wife calculated that the money he had spent on chewing tobacco would have bought a bedroom suite, kitchen stove, parlor table, and a living room rug.

Tobacco companies had inadvertently stumbled onto the greatest selling secret of all time -- the American public's vulnerability to premiums. People could be induced to buy a product if they received something "free" in exchange.

This marketing phenomenon was exploited to the hilt by every business in the United States with something to sell, but the pioneers and masters of the art were the tobacco men.

TOBACCO CLOUDS OVER AMERICA

Between 1890 and 1915, tax records of the Internal Revenue Bureau revealed that the consumption of cigarettes in the United States had increased nearly eightfold, from 2.2 billion in 1890 to over 16 billion in 1915. In this same period, cigars, although tapering off in popularity, were also going up in smoke at a steady rate of 6-7 billion a year. Likewise, ever increasing amounts of smoking tobacco were being incinerated in pipes and hand-rolled cigarettes. The use of tobacco had grown with exponential force.

Few people, aside from those interested in statistics, realized the hold tobacco had taken on the population. So common was the sight of a man with a cigar or cigarette between his lips that he scarcely attracted passing notice. Rather it was the man who refrained from the weed who seemed to spark comment. America had truly become a nation of smokers.

In 1908, a Detroit newspaper editor made interesting observations on the subject of tobacco consumption. The person, the newsman said, who considered construction of the Panama Canal a foolish waste of money was the same one who plunged his hand deep into his pocket several times a day to pull out coins in exchange for cigars or cigarettes.

He joined the rest of the country in paying out a sum of money conservatively estimated at $385 million a year for smoking pleasures. This was enough to build the Canal, run the Army and Navy, and pay off interest on the national debt – and still have a few dollars left over to spend elsewhere.

IS SMOKING AN ILLUSION?

A popular parlor trick of the 1890s went like this: Select a smoker to wet the ends of two cigarettes. Blindfold him and light one of the cigarettes. Allow him to randomly inhale from both. After a few draws, the smoker cannot distinguish the lighted from the unlighted cigarette.

REIGN OF THE TRUST

DYNASTY OF THE AMERICAN TOBACCO COMPANY (1890-1911)

In its two decades of dominating the tobacco industry, the American Tobacco Company relied heavily on advertising aimed at building brand loyalty and persuading more people to smoke cigarettes. Between 1893 and 1910, approximately 10 percent of the company's sales were reinvested in promotional schemes, chiefly newspaper and magazine advertising, and premium programs of one sort or another.

In February of 1890, newspapers carried a small item that a new company, the American Tobacco Company, had been formed in New York City. It was the inauspicious start of a business giant that would soon rock the foundations of the tobacco industry.

The company brought together the five leading cigarette manufacturers in the nation: W. Duke & Sons of Durham, Allen & Ginter of Richmond, Goodwin and Kinney of New York City, and Kimball of Rochester. The merger was orchestrated by James Buchanan Duke. For the lanky, red-haired North Carolinian, it was a matter of great personal triumph and satisfaction as one of his new partners, Lewis Ginter, had rudely snubbed him six years earlier when Duke approached him with the same plan.

Duke's aggressive and innovative promotions had catapulted his tobacco and cigarette brands into leading market positions, destined for even greater success. It had not taken long for Ginter and the others to understand their vulnerability in this wild, free-for-all war Duke was waging on them. They were far better off to join Duke than to fight him.

The formation of the American Tobacco Company caused great fear among competitors and for good reason; simple arithmetic spelled it out. Five manufacturers, accounting for 85 percent of national cigarette production, resulted in the same monopoly concentrated in a single company. The prospects looked ominous for the outsiders.

Referred to as the "Tobacco Trust," the "Tobacco Combination," or simply, "The Trust," the American Tobacco Company went quickly about their business and became the object of bitter hatred by others in the trade.

STRONG-ARMED TACTICS

Duke embarked on a course of rapid business expansion, utilizing ruthless methods. One of his first moves was to neutralize the role of the wholesalers and jobbers. These middle men soon learned Duke's new rules of the tobacco game. By handling the Trust's brands exclusively, they earned higher commissions and, more importantly, they were assured of a continuous supply of American's tobacco goods. Since many of Duke's brands were market leaders, the net effect was to stifle competition. In this manner, Duke established absolute control over distribution of goods and the setting of wholesale and retail prices.

The Trust's manner of doing business ran like this:

American "sold" no tobacco, they "consigned" it. But then, ten days after delivery, dealers had to pay full retail value. Three months later, Duke's agents balanced their books and paid long overdue commissions to the dealers. During this time, tobacco merchants made no profit on sales for a full three months while the Trust enjoyed their money, in full and up front.

Those who dared to fight the Trust flirted with fate. By handling brands other than American's, or discounting the Trust's pre-set prices, they suffered the ultimate penalty; they were not allowed to purchase American Tobacco's products.

Since 90 percent of all cigarette brands sold around 1896 belonged to the Trust, this hasty action was tantamount to business disaster. Forgiveness was granted if the dealer promised to sell American's products exclusively in the future. Penitence (and economic survival) came at a high price.

Overseeing and enforcing these iron-fisted activities was the Trust's Gestapo-like detective force which policed the trade and "handled" any infractions of the rules. Dealers had no choice but to play ball or find some other line of work. Such were the harsh business realities facing tobacco retailers as they dealt with the Trust at the turn of the century.

BUTTING HEADS

And so the undaunted Trust, disliked by many doing business with it and despised by all who weren't, marched on. With the lucrative cigarette market cornered, it turned its attention to manufactured tobacco (chewing and smoking tobacco). Having already purchased several large producers in this field in 1891, Duke wanted more. He saw

his competition, namely Lorillard, Liggett & Myers and Reynolds, as ripe plums ready to be picked. When they refused to join him, Duke turned loose a vicious marketing attack.

In what has been termed the "plug wars," the marketplace between 1894 and 1898 was the scene of a bitterly fought battle over chewing tobacco. The independents' brands, Lorillard's Climax and Liggett & Myers' Star and Clipper, contested strongly with Duke's fighting brand inadvertently but so appropriately named Battle Ax.

Wholesale prices plummeted. Quid chewers everywhere rejoiced at the rare opportunity of buying their favorite brands at bargain prices. At one point in 1895, "Battle Ax" sold at thirteen cents a pound wholesale when, a short time previously, consumers were paying fifty cents a pound retail.

The financial losses sustained by all parties was staggering. The Trust, due to extravagant advertising and price-cutting, lost well over $4 million. It was, however,

offset by huge profits made on cigarettes. The others were not so fortunate.

In the process, Duke's marketing assault forced traditional plug makers into the cigarette business. Drummond in St. Louis distributed coupons in chewing tobacco redeemable for cigarettes; Liggett & Myers released a flood of new cigarette brands.

The steady war of economic attrition finally came to an end in 1898 when, brought to their knees, most of the battle-weary independents, including Lorillard, reluctantly came to terms and joined the Trust's newly formed company for the occasion, the Continental Tobacco Company.

There still remained two major hold-outs: Reynolds and Liggett & Myers. A little later, in 1899, Reynolds, short of cash, signed up with Duke but Liggett & Myers found a new ally in its desperate attempt to remain free of the Trust.

The "savior" was a wealthy group of Wall Street financiers, the so-called "traction crowd," headed by Thomas Fortune Ryan. These enterprising interlopers championed the cause of the independents by forming a new firm in 1896 aimed at competing with the Trust, the Union Tobacco Company.

Fully intending to do tobacco business, at least on paper, they acquired the National Cigarette Company in 1896 and, two years later, purchased the stock of Blackwell's Durham Tobacco Company. The Liggett & Myers firm eventually joined forces with the Union Tobacco Company.

Suddenly, though, Union sold out to the American Tobacco Company in March, 1899, for nearly $7 million in cash and over $12 million in stock. The principals of both parties profited handsomely in the deal.

Ryan and his associates pocketed a quick 200% profit on their investment in three years; Duke bought peace. There was little doubt in Duke's mind that Union, with its financial backing, could have caused him trouble and the high price for the company was well worth it in the end.

And, in the process, Duke ended up with a trade bauble that he had coveted for many years, ownership of "Bull" Durham tobacco.

CROWDING THE FIELD

During the 1890s, the American Tobacco Company eliminated competition by gobbling up one company after another. Their advertising and promotional devices completely dominated the marketplace.

Those who defied Duke's juggernaut faced intense competition; many small companies were forced out of business as a result. The independents' feeble but proud battlecry, "Not Made by a Trust," was prominent in advertising copy as they desperately took their case to the public and played on sympathy for support.

The Trust's routine in acquiring new businesses became a familiar one: The Trust dispatched the previous owners into early retirement with fistfuls of money in return for a signed promise not to re-enter the tobacco business, usually for a period of 10 to 15 years.

Employees with exceptional leadership or sales qualities were stripped from the old company and integrated into the Trust's personnel corps. Prominent brands, previously major competitors, now appeared on American's wholesale and retail price lists and were given big promotional pushes; the rest were abandoned.

If the old company did not fit the Trust's long-range plans, or was of marginal value, the factory was simply closed down. A good example was the Drummond Tobacco Company of St. Louis, a long-established manufacturer. Drummond cost the Trust nearly $3.5 million and then was shut down shortly after acquisition.

Acquisition tactics soon changed. The Trust, instead of buying rivals outright for cash, bought up controlling stock in the company. This was cheaper and allowed the newly acquired firm to carry on business as usual but with new ownership, a fact not always publicly disclosed.

This arrangement of secret ownership was taken to the epitome of subterfuge and dishonesty when the newly controlled company was falsely advertised as being independent of the Trust. A new low in business ethics was reached, all in the name of profits.

THE TIDE TURNS

As complete and ruthless as the Trust's ways were in establishing and maintaining a monopoly of the industry, they proved, in the end, to be their undoing.

During the 1890s, a constant stream of formal complaints and lawsuits were filed by defiant tobacco men still standing up to the Trust. They complained

TOBACCO TRUST

Decoration Day.
(Plaschke in the Louisville Evening Post).

bitterly of American's harsh and unfair business practices and claimed restraint of trade.

The storm of protest accelerated in the early 1900s and the mounting cries finally reached receptive ears of justice officials in Washington. But it would take President Theodore Roosevelt's trust-busting terms in office before federal officials stepped in to make serious trouble for the American Tobacco Company.

Finally, in 1909, the government, led by U. S. Attorney General George Wickersham, filed suit against the Combination, claiming violation of the Sherman Anti-Trust Act. After two years of legal wrangling and maneuvering, the U. S. Supreme Court, on May 29, 1911, upheld the judgment made against the American Tobacco Company and ordered dissolution of the giant, $240 million-a-year corporation.

By 1912, Lorillard, Reynolds and Liggett & Myers were re-established as independently operating corporations and each awarded a proportional share of the Trust's cigarette and tobacco brands. Thus, a fairer balance of trade and power was created in the tobacco industry.

The stripped-down American Tobacco Company now faced the market on equal footing with its competition, as it had when it first started business 21 years previously. Then the battle for market supremacy started all over again.

Advertising, as expected, became the chief weapon in the hands of the competitors.

THE RISE AND FALL OF ADMIRAL CIGARETTES

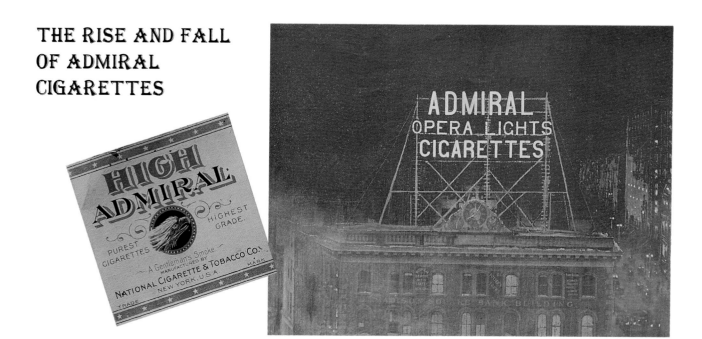

The story of the National Cigarette and Tobacco Company in the 1890s was a brief but sad account of a company's attempt to buck the Trust. Small but ambitious, the New York City firm started an elaborate and extensive preliminary cigarette marketing campaign in 1892.

In many cities the company erected large signs with the cryptic message, "Wait the Arrival of the Admiral." They attracted considerable attention. More curiosity was aroused the next year when, during the Columbian Exposition, residents of New York witnessed elegant carriages driven around the city carrying a woman in the uniform of an admiral.

Attractive young ladies were hired to ride around Central Park in carriages driven by liveried coachmen and on bicycles covered with gaily colored signs. They drew large crowds and caused so much commotion over a two-week period that police threw them out.

Following this, the company constructed a model of the battleship New York on a carriage bed and toured the country with it, spending three months in Chicago as an exhibit at the Exposition. A midget, "Admiral Dot," stood within the display. Signboards nationwide were decorated with the likeness of Admiral Farragut standing in the rigging of his flagship, damning the torpedoes as he watched the progress of the Battle of Mobile Bay.

The mystery was finally revealed in New York City in February, 1894. High atop the Madison Square Bank Building at the corner of Twenty-third Street and Broadway, a huge sign in gilded letters announced the company's two cigarette brands. Admiral and Opera Lights. Every night, from 6 p.m. until midnight, it was lit up with banks of electric lights which could be seen far up and down Broadway.

A coupon was inserted in each box of cigarettes. Fifty could be redeemed for a copy of one of 40 books covering a wide range of authors such as Dickens, Scott and Jules Verne. It was the Admiral Cigarette Coupon Library.

The merchandising campaign generated tremendous consumer interest and demand for the two brands ran rampant. The idea paid off...for a while. Then, in a bullying move that had come to mark the Trust's cut-throat business ways, the American Tobacco Company clearly informed all jobbers that henceforth American would no longer supply their brands to those dealers who also handled Admiral and Opera Lights cigarettes.

While some wholesalers, notably those in Indiana and Missouri, defied the Trust, it was only a matter of time before they, too, buckled under, forcing the National Cigarette Company to bypass jobbers and supply retail dealers directly.

The competition was too fierce for the young company. In 1896, failing in business, it was taken over in a power move by the Union Tobacco Company, a New York-based rival to the Trust, as its cigarette-making arm.

The American Tobacco Company eventually gained control of National in 1899 but, by this time, the firm was practically worthless and no attempt was made to continue the manufacture of its cigarette brands.

Admiral and Opera Lights cigarettes, born in a blaze of advertising hoopla, came to an inglorious end, victims of murderous business competition.

WINNERS AND LOSERS

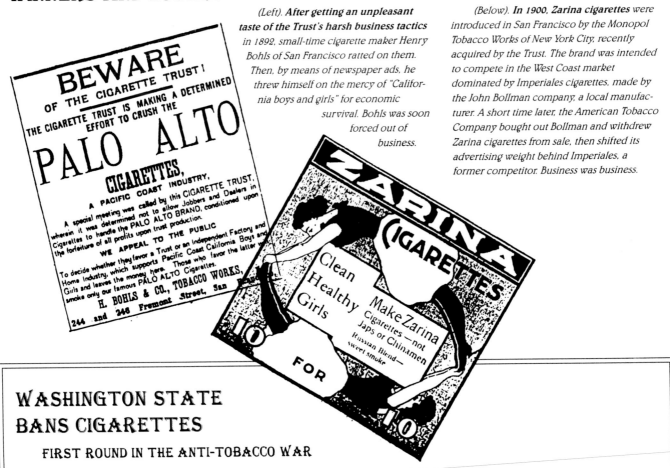

(Left). **After getting an unpleasant taste of the Trust's harsh business tactics** in 1892, small-time cigarette maker Henry Bohls of San Francisco ratted on them. Then, by means of newspaper ads, he threw himself on the mercy of "California boys and girls" for economic survival. Bohls was soon forced out of business.

(Below). **In 1900, Zarina cigarettes** were introduced in San Francisco by the Monopol Tobacco Works of New York City, recently acquired by the Trust. The brand was intended to compete in the West Coast market dominated by Imperiales cigarettes, made by the John Bollman company, a local manufacturer. A short time later, the American Tobacco Company bought out Bollman and withdrew Zarina cigarettes from sale, then shifted its advertising weight behind Imperiales, a former competitor. Business was business.

WASHINGTON STATE BANS CIGARETTES

FIRST ROUND IN THE ANTI-TOBACCO WAR

In March of 1893, the State of Washington passed a bill making the sale of cigarettes illegal, the first such statewide ban in the country's history. The legislative move ushered in the three-decades-long anti-cigarette era in America.

But the reason for the no-cigarette law was not for reform. Ninety percent of the legislators who voted for the bill admitted that they had done so to strike a blow at the American Tobacco Company which monopolized the cigarette industry.

Dealers were glad to see the Tobacco Trust get a taste of their own medicine. As one said, "I am glad the bill has passed. I am tired of getting off my stool 250 times a day to sell a five-cent package of cigarettes and then making only ten cents on the whole lot." (A good cigar, or a piece of cut plug, bore a nominal mark-up.)

The bill went through the legislature so swiftly that it caught the American Tobacco Company flat-footed. Hastening their lobbyists to Olympia with $20,000 in funds to compass defeat of the measure, the Trust was too late – or so they thought.

The tobacco firm went to court. The Trust's lawyers contested the new law on the grounds that the sale of cigarettes was a matter of inter-state commerce, which, being a business regulated by federal law, was therefore beyond the jurisdiction of state authorities. The judge agreed.

The new statute, barely three months on the books, was struck down in June when it was declared unconstitutional by a federal court in Seattle.

"Ridiculous," a New York Times editor commented in the aftermath of the fiasco. He leveled a timeless warning of the dangers of trying to outlaw cigarettes:

"The smoking of cigarettes may be objectionable and may be more injurious than other modes of smoking tobacco, but it is an evil which cannot be remedied by law, and it is not the kind of evil to the community at large that is a legitimate subject for legislative action. That kind of law is pretty sure to be evaded, and it begets a contempt for law in general and for public authority that is more pernicious than selling cigarettes or even smoking them."

THE GIANT KILLERS OF DUBUQUE

Not all tobacco concerns fell before the Trust. A good example was the Myers, Cox Company of Dubuque, Iowa. Since 1866, the year of its founding, this maker of cigars and smoking tobacco had established itself as the largest independent jobber and manufacturer west of the Mississippi.

The Myers, Cox firm had long marketed a brand of smoking tobacco, Fragrant, when the Trust came to town in the early 1900s, determined to steamroll its way over local competition. The Trust's agents sent samples of Fragrant back to their factories. There it was analyzed and a similar product was formulated, one called Dot, and over six tons of it was shipped to Dubuque to do battle with Fragrant.

And then the trouble started. The Trust's best salesmen ran headlong into a defiantly loyal corps of dealers who, having handled Fragrant for over 40 years, simply refused to stock Dot. The Trust, well accustomed to such temporary acts of impertinence and false bravado, next played their trump card; it cut the wholesale price of Dot in half.

The ploy didn't work. The dealers in Dubuque steadfastly held their ground. Finally, in a rare act of desperation, the Trust's salesmen left free packages of Dot with each dealer and threw in free pipes as well. This move failed, too.

After sitting unsold on shelves for months, the packages of Dot were thrown out by the store owners. The Trust conceded defeat and left town, never to bother the dealers again.

BIG CITY SCHOOLS TAKE THE LEAD
CIGARETTES COME UNDER ATTACK

The first organized attack on cigarettes in America was mounted in the public schools of Chicago and New York City in 1894. Both cities faced the same problem: local shop owners were selling smokes to school children. Boys given money and sent out into the neighborhood came back with cigarettes, as many as they could buy.

It was an outrage but education officials were unable to stop the practice. Eventually, upon the urging of local women's auxiliaries, schools set up anti-smoking clubs in an attempt to discourage the habit among students. They failed.

It took several years before the City of Chicago was persuaded by health officials, educators, and civic leaders to take action. In May, 1897, the mayor finally signed an ordinance placing a license fee of $100 on any merchant selling cigarettes.

It was an innovative move, one made extremely effective due to dictatorial wholesaling practices of the Tobacco Trust. The average package, containing 10 or 12 smokes, sold for a nickel which allowed the seller a minuscule profit of nearly 1.2 cents per pack. At this rate, a dealer had to sell over 8,300 packages of cigarettes a year just to meet the cost of the license.

To the average shopkeeper, this was an excessive amount of money, and he had little choice but to abandon a once tidy little business of selling cigarettes.

In a statement of profound prophesy, the mayor of Chicago said: "I think more can be accomplished by this plan of licensing than by a prohibitory statute."

School teachers rejoiced. As one remarked with no less candor and insight: "At least the principals can get at the small storekeepers who

sell cigarettes to the boys. It was in vain to talk to boys about the evils of smoking when it was possible for them to slip around the corner and buy all the cigarettes they pleased."

Chicago's answer to the cigarette problem did not go unnoticed. Other cities, like Kokomo, Indiana, copied the idea and passed similar licensing laws.

It was too good to be true. The bubble burst when dealers' attorneys challenged the constitutionality of the city ordinances and won. As the license laws were rescinded, police forces exhaled a collective sigh of relief.

Of the thousands of shopkeepers, only a handful obeyed the law and purchased licenses, sparing police departments the tiresome chore of hunting down and arresting noncompliant merchants.

WANTED

1000 GIRLS AND 500 BOYS

BETWEEN THE AGES OF 14 AND 21 YEARS.

TO LEARN TO MAKE LITTLE CIGARS

Boys and Girls can make from $6.00 to $9.00 per week after they learn, and are paid while learning.

Our factory is perfectly clean, no dust and no bad air; perfectly ventilated, and with every modern convenience, such as dressing rooms, toilets and dining rooms.

THE WORK IS CLEAN, EASY and LIGHT

You can get good board here very cheap, and if any families desire to move here, they can rent good, comfortable houses at a reasonable rate.

For further information apply or write to the

DANVILLE BRANCH,
The American Tobacco Co.
601 BRIDGE ST., DANVILLE, VA.

Advertising flyer (ca 1905)

THE WAR WITH SPAIN

The country's patriotic rush to colors during the Spanish-American War of 1898-99 provided tobacco companies with fresh themes to work into poster copy, brand names and advertising text. The American Tobacco Company, for instance, thanked the nation's home front for "patriotically" chewing its way through tons of Battle Ax plug, indirectly helping to finance the war effort through payment of tobacco taxes.

The makers of "Bull" Durham scored favorable publicity when they provided free postcards for the exclusive use of "soldier boys" in army camps. The men, many of whom had run away to enlist, were encouraged to write home by Red Cross personnel.

The war had drawbacks. A blockade of Cuba for several months in 1898 reduced importation of Havana-made cigars, causing temporary anxiety among cigar devotees in the States.

Surgeon General Rixey of the U.S. Navy expressed alarm at the increased cigarette smoking by shipboard sailors during the war. He threatened to ban cigarettes aboard ships but backed down in the face of a possible mutiny.

Courtesy of Gene Semel

"Hurrah! Battle Ax has come."

Everybody who reads the newspapers knows what privation and suffering were caused in Cuba—by the failure of the supply of tobacco provided by the Government to reach the camps of the U. S. Soldiers.

BattleAx

Uncle Sam.—"You're a credit to the nation!"

Every man who chews Battle Ax has the satisfaction of having helped the U. S. Government pay the expenses of the war with Spain.

BattleAx PLUG

pays four million dollars' tax into the U. S. Treasury !!! More than all the money paid by any five other brands of chewing tobacco. It is QUALITY that does this — real excellence :— actual superiority.

Remember the name when you buy again.

"At the Front"

RECRUIT

5c. Cigar

It has taken the lead, and keeps it.

AT ALL DEALERS.

SMOKE BLACKWELL'S GENUINE BULL DURHAM TOBACCO.

PUT TWO CENT STAMP HERE

SMOKE BLACKWELL'S GENUINE BULL DURHAM TOBACCO

AWAITING CAMP INSPECTION

SMOKE BLACKWELL'S GENUINE BULL DURHAM TOBACCO.

PUT TWO CENT STAMP HERE

SMOKE BLACKWELL'S GENUINE BULL DURHAM TOBACCO

ON THE MARCH

DRUMMING THE TRADE
THE MEN WHO SOLD TOBACCO

George Washington Duke, *struggling to establish his tobacco business after the Civil War, often hit the road to peddle his goods. Some years after the Duke name had become famous in tobacco, a Missouri retailer recalled his first meeting with "Wash" Duke: It was a cold morning in the early 1870s when a mature and neatly dressed gentleman in a broad-rimmed hat opened the door of the tobacco shop, sauntered halfway toward the office, then walked back to shut the door. Then, speaking in a deep drawl, he announced, "Good morning. I did shut the door and I'm from North Carolina." Setting his well-worn carpetbag on the floor, he continued, "I've got some mighty good smoking tobacco in here and believe you could sell a heap of it if you had it in your store."*

THE CIGAR SALESMAN

From beginnings like this was born the tobacco salesman.

Those men who worked the road last century were called "drummers," a curious human link that joined the two extremes of commerce, the maker of goods and the buyer of goods. The cosmopolitan wanderers became the lifeblood of the tobacco business as they scoured cities, towns and rural hamlets all over America in search of sales.

Selling tobacco was like selling any other product, but the trade possessed one distinct advantage. Through advertising and the power of suggestion, customers could often be induced to buy something they didn't know they wanted.

Ever since Dr. Paul Wesley Ivey wrote his first book on merchandising, many sales techniques used with tobacco wares came and went. The ones that stayed were the ones that worked, and the ones that worked relied heavily on advertising.

With proper promotion, the way was paved for the salesmen. If the sales force was properly trained, the rest was easy. Key to improving sales was to make drummers enthusiastic about their products. Hard work was rewarded by greater sales and, with it, the pride that came with being part of a successful business operation.

The men who peddled tobacco in Nineteenth Century America were generally colorful characters who have long faded into history. Many were recalled later with special fondness and, as time so often does, embellished in romantic terms.

Best remembered were those men who sold cigars, an industry that relied almost solely on salesmen, not advertisements. Cigar drummers, on the whole, were great showmen who had learned the art of the pitch from the likes of carnival barkers and vaudeville stage performers.

These roving knights of the gripsack were a sight to behold. They knew how to wear good clothes: tailcoats, high silk hats, striped lavender pants, and medals and other decorative emblems dangling from heavy gold chains stretched across their double-breasted vests.

They were not only good dressers, they were good talkers, too; it came by them naturally. They could hold a conversation with anyone on any subject ranging from the attributes of corn juice to making vinegar pies. On

Newspaper ad (1891)

116

trains they could quiet a weary mother's bawling baby and keep it spellbound, or draw a pretty girl's attention from the passing landscape to themselves with tales of dubious authenticity.

Sly, smooth-tongued devils they were; they could sell iceboxes to Arctic Esquimaux. They knew everybody and everything worth knowing. They were gentlemen - polite, gallant and chivalrous to a fault – but, above all, the drummers knew their products and they knew their territory.

The jolly, irrepressible souls travelled the country-side with their leather sample cases and their visits to a tobacconist's shop were orchestrated with the precision of a battlefield commander. After a hearty handshake, slap on the back and brief interlude of story telling, out came the sample case and the rolling of fragrant cigar selections under the dealer's nose.

Inducements – premium coupons, cigar cutters, lighters, matches, or dazzling cards featuring stage actresses or prize fighters – were used to help cinch the deal. Orders were taken and then the drummer was off to the next town and another round of shops.

TOBACCO TRADE JOURNALS

FINGERS ON THE BUSINESS PULSE

Trade journals, by the 1890s, had expanded in numbers and had improved in quality. They played a vital role in keeping tobacco men abreast of current events in the industry; their service ran well into the 1950s.

ADVERTISING SLOGANS
THOSE LITTLE WORDS OF IMPORTANCE

By the 1900s, professional admen had taken a critical look at tobacco advertising slogans and refined them to better fit the tantalizing imagery being rendered on posters, labels and other promotional material. It was a change long overdue.

The new advertising look favored the ethereal approach. Slogans were designed to enhance product desirability by using the consumer's imagination. What the brand name, logo and accompanying graphics lacked in suggestion, the rest was made up by slogans. They were the finishing touch administered to tobacco products, like frosting on a cake.

Short, catchy phrases took their place in advertising copy and the words were chosen with care, light and purely subjective. Gently and subtly, the words seemed to transport tobacco users into a higher state of contentment and pleasure.

Confidence in brand selection – cheap or expensive, it made no difference – was projected by means of well-dressed gentlemen in top hats or refined young ladies with ingratiating smiles portrayed in advertisements or on labels complimenting the consumer on his (or her) taste.

New areas of promotional potential were entered. Slogans accompanying cigarette brands began to dwell on tobacco's "taste," an advertising trend that started in the 1920s. The subject, however, has always been the center of controversy.

Do cigarettes have taste? In 1923, Dr. John B. Watson, then employed by the J. Walter Thompson advertising agency, determined that smokers were unable to distinguish one cigarette brand from another based on taste. His results were later confirmed using blindfolded subjects.

Similar findings were obtained in a study at Reed College in Oregon in 1928, leading cynical observers to comment that the only sure way to tell cigarette brands apart was to look at the labels. Cigarette makers paid no attention; Nebo cigarettes were advertised by the American Tobacco Company as tasting "delicious," just like candy.

References to aroma and strength of tobacco also crept into advertising lingo. Smokers were led to believe, through repetitive advertising statements, that these qualities could be detected and differentiated as well. Experts disputed these notions, too, and also claimed that there was no connection between the aroma of a cigar or cigarette and its nicotine content.

By the same token, the designation of tobacco as "mild" or "strong" probably depended in large part on physiological effects caused by the nicotine content, or simply differences in individual perception. The bottom line was that cigars and cigarettes were not always what they seemed, or what they were touted to be.

Common consumer misconceptions about cigars arose along the way, namely that dark-colored cigars, especially black ones, were "strong" and light-toned ones "mild," and smoking the latter was considered much better for your health.

When it came to promoting cigars, many manufacturers practiced advertising license on an unprecedented scale, dispensing immodest slogans with free and reckless abandon. There were few brands sold in America, for instance, which were not claimed "best in the world," the most overworked cliche in cigar advertising history. It made Vice President Thomas Marshall's famous whispered remark on the Senate floor, "What this country really needs is a good five cent cigar," seem tongue-in-cheek.

Starting in the 1930s, the terms "flavor," "taste" and "aroma" became vital catch words in cigarette advertising. Inserted in just the right place, they looked, read and sounded good, but they really said little. Being difficult to define, let alone quantify, the abstract words were aesthetically pleasing and legally unassailable. It was really a safe, smart and effective thing to do.

CAVALCADE OF SUPERLATIVES

"Cigarette of Quality" – Piedmont cigarettes (1912)

"The Original Egyptian Cigarette" – Schinasi Natural cigarettes (1915)

"A Distinctive Cigarette in a Distinctive Case" – Bud cigarettes (1912)

"The Charm of Egypt" – Arabs cigarettes (1915)

"You Can't Help But Like Them" – Beech-Nut cigarettes (1919)

"Think of the Name When You Buy Again" – Battle Ax chewing tobacco (1896)

"The Old Reliable" – Sweet Caporal cigarettes (1894)

"Ask Dad, He Knows" – Sweet Caporal cigarettes (1918)

"The Old Time Turkish Cigarette" – Condax cigarettes (1919)

"Each One Recommends One More" – Nebo cigarettes (1914)

"One Man Tells Another" – Blue Boar cigarettes (1923)

"A Breath of Oriental Luxury" – Haidee cigarettes (1915)

"Mild as May" – Marlboro cigarettes (1929)

"There's Something About Them You'll Like" – Herbert Tareyton cigarettes (1916)

"The One Cigarette Sold the World Over" – Melachrino cigarettes (1923)

"A Taste for Grays Is a Taste That Stays" – Grays' cigarettes (1915)

"Treat Yourself to the Best" – Mail Pouch chewing tobacco (1915)

"Quality Superb" – Helmar cigarettes (1917)

"The National Joy Smoke" – Prince Albert smoking tobacco (1910)

"Fragrant & Delicious" – Lucky Strike pipe tobacco (1904)

"The Height of Good Taste" – Piper Heidsieck chewing tobacco (1907)

"Sweet as a Nut-Clean as a Whistle" – Beech-Nut Chewing Tobacco (1915)

"The Utmost in Cigarettes" – Egyptian Deities Cigarettes (1913)

"Generously Good" – Geo. W. Childs Cigars (1899)

"Metropolitan Standard" – Murad Cigarettes (1907)

"Everywhere-Why" – Murad Cigarettes (1914)

"Generously Good"
(Geo. W. Childs cigars, 1899)

"Everywhere–Why?"
(Murad cigarettes, 1914)

"The Utmost in Cigarettes"
(Egyptian Deities cigarettes, 1913)

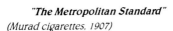

"Sweet as a Nut–Clean as a Whistle"
(Beech-Nut chewing tobacco, 1915)

"The Metropolitan Standard"
(Murad cigarettes, 1907)

THIS IS SMOKERS WEEK IN NEW YORK

The makers of a billion cigars a year will open their exhibition at the garden tomorrow. A miniature Virginia tobacco plantation one of the features

Group of Turkish Girls to Roll Cigarettes at Tobacco Exposition

-From New York Herald, 1906

The Onondaga Indian Band — Wards of N.Y. State, — Which Will Play at the Exhibition.

THE NEW YORK TOBACCO SHOWS

In an attempt to gain public support for their cause against the American Tobacco Company, a group of independent tobacco manufacturers sponsored annual tobacco shows in New York City in 1905 and 1906.

The first show in 1905, a weeklong event, was overrun by so many curious visitors that it was repeated on a much more lavish scale the following year. The tobacco men rented the spacious accommodations of Madison Square Garden and threw a two-week bash that had all the makings of a Hollywood spectacle.

Posters pasted on the building's exterior displayed "beautiful girls in startling costumes handing trays of costly souvenirs to splendid gentlemen in evening clothes and monocles," the New York Times reported. Inside a circus-like atmosphere prevailed. A small-scale cigar-rolling factory was set up and boxes of the newly-made articles were auctioned off by local celebrities. A 40-year collection of cigar butts smoked by some of the world's greatest personalities was also proudly exhibited.

A display of Irish tobacco included an automatic cigar-smoking machine that was used to test the burning qualities of the tobacco. Real peasants from the "auld counthry" enlightened the public on its operation.

Another feature included a package of the world's smallest cigars (25 of them fitted into a walnut shell). male visitors were draw to six costumed cancan dancers from Paris who worked the French cigarette booth and Hundreds of veiled Turkish beauties rolling cigarettes. Field workers tilled the soil of a miniature tobacco plantation and background music was provided by a band of Onondaga Indians dressed up in native costume.

It was truly a smoker's paradise.

UNITED CIGAR STORES
MODERN MEANS OF MERCHANDISING

accessories, as well as sundry items like candy, gum and ice cream.

Carefully composed ads appeared frequently in newspapers, announcing promotions such as new shipments of cigars or cigarettes, special sales, double-coupon days, and even guessing contests. At Christmas women were cordially invited to drop in and purchase cigars for the men in their lives.

The business philosophy of United Cigar Stores was based on small profit margins derived from large volumes of sales. This approach allowed the company to undersell competition which brought a surge of business. The shops with their distinctive red, white and blue shield logos became familiar sights in urban, suburban and even rural neighborhoods all over the nation. In October, 1905, over 300 stores in 36 cities were in full operation and, by 1907, the number of outlets had swelled to over 1,000.

The rapid success of the United Cigar Stores chain and others like it signaled the end of the sole-proprietor tobacconist's shop which, since colonial days, had been the primary place of business in America.

Another offshoot of the Trust, organized around 1906, was the National Cigar Stands Company. It was designed to control retail cigar trade conducted in drug stores. This subsidiary supplied druggists with showcases, window displays and all necessary advertising on the condition that they agree to carry the Trust's goods exclusively, in addition to paying a nominal rental fee.

A new look in the mass marketing of tobacco products was introduced in 1901 when the United Cigar Stores Company in New York City was formed. Organized and financed secretly by the American Tobacco Company, as it came to light years later, the stores served as outlets for the Trust's goods.

The first shop opened in October at 84 Nassau Street and, with a grand total of two employees, rang up $3.70 in sales on its first business day. It was an unpromising start for what would become the largest retail chain of tobacco stores in the world.

In communities far across America came the smoke shop extraordinaire: the United Cigar Stores smoking emporium. It was an all-purpose convenience store, modern in appearance, well appointed and strategically located at well-travelled intersections. It was a place where smokers (non-smokers, too) could stop in and make selections from a full line of smoking goods and

PRETTY PACKAGES

STRENGTH OF THE VISUAL SELL

One of the most compelling reasons people have been tempted to try tobacco over the years has been the attractiveness and appeal of product packaging.

Up to the Civil War, tobacco was retailed in bulk. Packages provided by shop owners, other than simple paper wrapping, were a rare indulgence. Manufacturers were eventually forced to pre-package tobacco at the factory when, in 1868, passage of federal law required the affixing of prepaid tax revenue stamps to all tobacco products.

Packaging ultimately proved a boon to merchandising, and pretty containers, as instruments of competition and consumer seduction, quickly became a tradition in the tobacco industry. They emerged as an art form in the 1870s when chromolithography first allowed manufacturers the luxury of dressing up packages of tobacco with colorful labels, giving life and allure to brand names and trademarks.

Smoking tobacco, granulated or otherwise shredded to fit the pipe bowl, was supplied in bags, pouches and sacks. These were the original tobacco packages and were usually made of woven fabric, cloth, leather, sometimes burlap, and, for the frugal shop owner, paper. The attaching of paper labels followed shortly; many were painstakingly lettered and glued on by hand, one at a time.

It was more expensive but some manufacturers, in the 1870s, marketed smoking tobacco in small, pocket-sized cardboard boxes fitted with lids, prototypes of metal containers which followed shortly and became the preferred means of packaging with large companies.

By the 1890s, the range of packaging options for smoking tobacco had expanded considerably. Standard forms, leather and cloth bags fitted with drawstrings, and square-cornered paper pocket models lined with tinfoil, now came into regular use. Some manufacturers, however, preferred individual, custom-designed units which imparted brand distinctiveness.

Chunks of chewing tobacco formerly found snug but messy storage in waistcoat pockets of casual chewers of the weed until packaging came along, initially paper bags and envelopes. It progressed to tinfoil wrappers and small pouches made of leather, cloth or paper with fold-over flaps, and, lastly, tins.

Prior to the Civil War, cigars were commonly sold in "wheels" or "bundles" – 25 or 50 bound up in colorful ribbons. Sold singly or by the bunch and typically unbranded, smokers paid their money and took their chances.

Wooden cigar boxes, initially made of imported Spanish red cedar, did not achieve widespread use until well after the Civil War. By 1907, worldwide supply of this elegant wood dwindled considerably, forcing manufacturers to substitute other woods and reluctantly for the really cheap brands, cardboard.

In the 1880s, small paper sacks and envelopes with personalized advertising logos made cheap means of dispensing tobacco that did not come pre-packaged.

Beginning in the 1870s, plug chewing tobacco in sizes ranging from one-half to four ounces was factory-wrapped in protective tinfoil and commercially distributed. Trademark logos (plus the obligatory tax stamp) were typographed in blue or gold to enhance eye appeal. This style of packaging extended well into the new century.

CIGARETTE PACK ART

Cigarettes of the 1870s were offered to the public in soft, foil-wrapped bundles with wrap-around paper labels, ten for a nickel. The Kimball firm of Rochester, New York, also utilized an oval cardboard box with a fold-over lid to carry its Excelsior brand.

Invention of the small cardboard slide-and-shell box by tobacco magnate James Duke in 1886 provided a better means of packaging and protecting the dainty articles. It also lent itself well for advertising purposes.

Cute and compact, the box slipped in and out of pockets with ease (a few purses, too). Colorful and eye-catching labels were applied to the lid; insert cards and other promotional material fit neatly inside.

Manufacturers of Turkish cigarettes found this format extremely well suited for their needs and the boxes faithfully served that specialty smoking market for many years.

In 1913, soft cigarette packs (called "cups" in the trade) were introduced and became the standard format of cigarette packaging. A heavy layer of tinfoil was glued to the paper liner which preserved moisture.

Cardboard cartons holding ten soft packs of cigarettes were also introduced in the early 1910s. In 1930, outer cellophane wrappers were added to all soft packs.

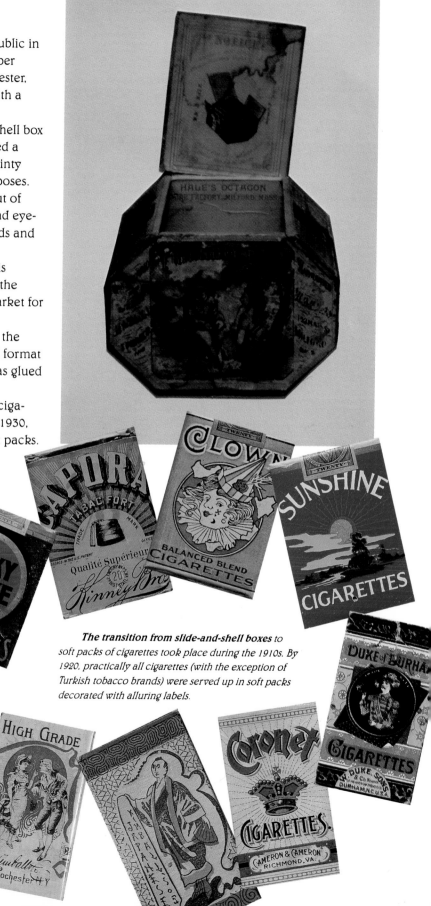

The transition from slide-and-shell boxes to soft packs of cigarettes took place during the 1910s. By 1920, practically all cigarettes (with the exception of Turkish tobacco brands) were served up in soft packs decorated with alluring labels.

TOBACCO BAGS

Introduced in the 1870s, pouches, sacks, and bags made of cloth, burlap, leather, and other fabrics were the original commercial tobacco containers. Many were branded with pasted-on paper labels; drawstrings were added later in the decade.

PAPER PACKAGES

Improvements in packaging by the 1890s led to foil-wrapped paper packs of smoking and chewing products. Later, outer cellophane coverings were added. More room for brand advertising was available with this form of packaging.

TOBACCO TINS

Brilliantly conceived and artfully implemented, the use of metal containers for tobacco was an extraordinarily successful marketing idea and contributed greatly to the weed's appeal to the masses. Tins were utilized primarily for brands of smoking and cigarette-rolling tobacco, cigars and, much less often, chewing tobacco and cigarettes.

First developed on a commercial basis in the 1880s, the industrial life of tobacco tins spanned the decades, experiencing ups and downs in use with changing tobacco preferences, wartime metal shortages and the Depression. By the 1950s, the market dominance of cigarettes and ever-increasing manufacturing costs brought a virtual halt to this novel and once popular form of packaging.

The pretty metal units became instantly popular with the consuming public and, by 1910, people were buying them as much for the containers as for the tobacco inside. Many tins, as a result, enjoyed second lives on kitchen shelves, desktops and fireplace mantels as decorations or storage bins long after their contents had been used up.

Capitalizing on compulsive consumer habits, the design of tins was modified to fully exploit their newfound appeal. Between 1900 and 1915, the market was inundated with tobacco tins in all sizes and shapes, the more unusual or outlandish, it seemed, the better.

Imaginations ran wild. There were triangular and octagonal tins, egg-shaped tins and kidney-shaped tins, humidor tins, tins to hold kitchen staples (including the labels) and even tins in the shape of a football, gold nugget, beer stein, pail, lunchbox, barrel, and creamer. One company unabashedly issued a container in the form of a casket; others marketed tin purses, complete with a carrying handle.

The new age of metal containers for tobacco caused a minor shift in advertising strategy. Tins were now incorporated in magazine, newspaper and poster advertisements and, by 1910, the practice had become widespread. Not only did this cement brand recognition, but depiction of tins maintained consumer consciousness.

***Squarecorner
boxes.*** *Flat and upright
units with hinged lids were
darlings of the trade
during the 1890s.
Hundreds decorated
handsomely in two- and
three-color artwork were
issued. Round-cornered
boxes came a bit later.*

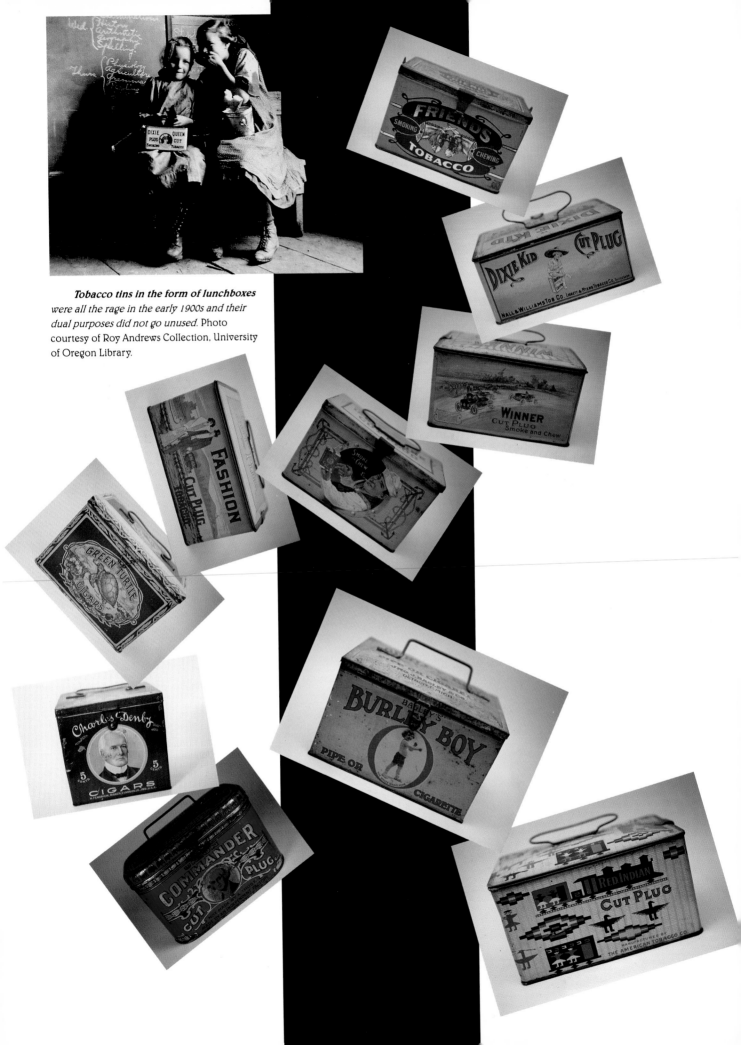

Tobacco tins in the form of lunchboxes were all the rage in the early 1900s and their dual purposes did not go unused. Photo courtesy of Roy Andrews Collection, University of Oregon Library.

"Pieshapes." Round, flat commercial tins punctured with ventilation holes served up chewing tobacco to zealous masticators of the weed.

Large tins with prominent graphic decoration were designed to rest on tobacco shop counters. They held small, paper-wrapped packages of smoking and chewing tobacco.

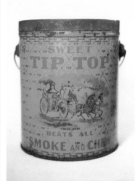

Round tins with slip-off or
humidor tops *and pails fitted with*
wire handles were also in demand.
Paper labels were commonly seen
with this style.

Some of the most dazzling lithography rendered on tobacco tins was reserved for small, flat, round-cornered units that circulated in the 1890-1910 era.

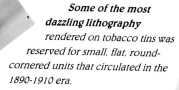

Cigar tins. While a few were marketed as early as the 1880s, their use did not peak until the 1910-1930 period. They came in round, oval and square-based formats: most held 25 or 50 cigars. Pocket-sized models carrying five or ten smokes were also popular.

TAKING ADVERTISING OUTDOORS

Wheeling, West Virginia (ca 1900)

It was the custom long ago for merchants to crudely apply various statements in whitewash upon rocks along roads and railways to announce their products or services. Then farmers were persuaded to let the sides and roofs of their barns, for the sake of having them painted, to be illustrated with advertisements. Outdoor displays were thus born.

Following this, placards were nailed to wooden posts in fields, intersections and along rural roadways. The idea was carried to town where broadsides and posters were pasted up on walls of buildings or on fences, or large notices painted on the bricked sides of office buildings.

Outdoor displays, no matter the form, did not appear to have suffered from the growth of literacy and reading habits in the United States. Before the days of the great newspaper and magazine circulations, the motive in using outdoor advertising was to reach the masses of people who were not regular readers or subscribers of periodicals, perhaps seldom opening them at all.

Aberdeen, South Dakota (1911)

ELECTRIC SIGNS

A branch of advertising that was strictly American in origin was the night display. Ever since Barnum's huge gaslit sign plugging his museum in the 1840s, said to have "illuminated Broadway for several blocks," drug stores, tobacco shops, theaters, and saloons made effective use of this form of street advertising.

The first fixed electric sign roared to life in 1891 on New York's Broadway, later to reach such an intense concentration of bright, glaring lights that they gave the famous thoroughfare its popular nickname, "The Great White Way."

Since that time, a seemingly endless stream of electric signs made their appearance in every large and medium-sized city in America until, by the 1910s, they utterly glutted urban areas.

Some were immense in size and, either mounted on rooftops or on the sides of buildings, were ingenious mechanical marvels fitted with moving lighted figures and other special effects.

PAINTED BARNS

Barns adorned with advertising signs for Mail Pouch and Red Man chewing tobacco dotted rural landscapes many years ago. The custom, begun in the last century, hit its promotional peak in the early 1900s and ran up to 1964 when it was officially outlawed by the federal Highway Beautification Act.

Appalachian coal and steel communities, home to some of the nation's heaviest chewers of tobacco, were specifically targeted for barn ads. Farmers were approached with the deal of a lifetime. They got their barns painted (just the prominent side, though) for which they were paid a nominal leasing fee, usually ten or twenty dollars a year. Painting crews returned every several years to touch up their handiwork.

Now regarded as examples of early American folk art, a small group of painted barns are maintained today in the State of West Virginia.

TROLLEY SIGNS

Streetcar advertising has been around since the 1870s when enterprising merchants began posting signs around the car's coal-burning stove, or suspended them in bunches from the ceiling by a string along with the notice, "Take One."

Sketches made during the Philadelphia Exposition in 1876 show streetcars with advertising panels covering the windows. In the 1880s, the interior of horsedrawn stages in New York City had a glass-covered frame over the door where retail stores placed announcements, paid for on a contract basis.

Selling advertising on city trolleys and street trams was turned into a nationwide business by the late 1880s and made formal when the advertising rack, an 11 x 21-inch space, became a standard trolley car appurtenance around 1890.

Major tobacco manufacturers made ample use of trolley ads beginning in the 1910s.

THE WEED ON PARADE

It was the custom long ago for trades to march as a unit in parades. Tobacco manufacturers, almost exclusively local or home state firms, were eager participants. Witness the Spear Head chewing tobacco sign draped over a water wagon in Vermontville, New York. Makeshift floats were used to publicize cigar brands, such as the giant stogie weighing down a flatbed truck in Joplin, Missouri, in 1911, while another, drawn by a pair of caparisoned steeds and accompanied by two midget circus clowns, pulls a wagon load of female cigar rollers somewhere in Ohio.

Youngstown, Ohio

Louisville, Kentucky

TOBACCO SHOPS ON WHEELS

Loaded down with cartons of cigarettes and boxes of cigars, plus reams of advertising material, the salesman's vehicle literally became a rolling tobacco store.

Peoria, Illinois

PAPER GIVEAWAYS
A NEW FORM OF ADVERTISING

Tobacco manufacturers, between the Civil War and World War I, generated a tremendous amount of free advertising paper items. Typically handed out at the point-of-purchase and intended to be nothing more than something pretty to look at or interesting to read, they were meant to be thrown away. Surprisingly, however, they turned into an effective means of promotion despite their short life and cheap cost of production.

This form of advertising grew out of the development of chromolithography, die-cutting and embossing techniques that had their beginnings in the 1870s. They produced an avalanche of colored and printed scraps of paper that found their way all over the country. To the general public accustomed to only seeing printed images in black and white, the response was overwhelming; they couldn't get enough of them.

Paper giveaways were collected and much of it was pasted up in family scrapbooks. The abundance of this material in collectors' hands today attests to its once vast popularity as a Victorian parlor pastime.

Tobacco advertising ephemera took on many forms. The early prototypes, trade cards, business cards, and cigarette insert cards, gave way to counter display cards, stickers, premium coupons, illustrated booklets, and company magazines, offering the reader advice, general information, jokes, cartoons, and other odd bits of entertaining copy and graphics.

PREMIUM COUPONS
SOMETHING FOR NOTHING

Offering gifts for tin tags proved a surprisingly effective means of promotion, but the program had one serious drawback: its use was limited to chewing tobacco.

By the 1890s, manufacturers were facing major changes in consumer tastes. Chewing tobacco, long the staple of the American worker, was on the decline. Smoking tobacco and particularly cigarettes were now in heavy demand.

Tobacco men, chiefly those at the American Tobacco Company, were not about to allow a golden moment of opportunity pass by, as they applied the format of the tin tag redemption system to these fast-selling items as well. After all, it was important to foster the consumer's notion of seeming to get something for nothing.

The result was the introduction of the premium coupon, a merchandising tool that revolutionized the field of advertising and which was quickly copied by other major industries in America.

Early examples were seen in the 1880s. The Butler Tobacco Company of St. Louis, for instance, inserted paper "profit sharing" coupons inside each foil-wrapped plug of chewing tobacco. They were redeemable for gifts.

A wide range of prizes – pocket knives to fireproof safes, catchers' mitts to upright pianos, watch fobs to double-barreled shotguns – were offered in exchange for various devices. In the early days, between 1895 and 1900, these usually amounted to cut-out labels or fronts of boxes of cigarettes, little cigars or packs and sacks of smoking tobacco; even cigar bands counted.

But as convenient and economical as this marketing gimmick was, it lacked the

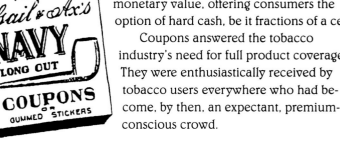

organization and sophistication that had come to mark the tobacco industry's scrupulous attention to detail. Eventually gift giveaway programs were replaced by the paper coupon system which became the standard of the industry.

Tobacco premium certificates were strictly utilitarian articles. Visually unappealing, small pieces of paper were imprinted with filigreed backgrounds to discourage counterfeiting, labelled, and occasionally decorated with a simple graphic sketch. They were released in prodigious numbers beginning in 1900 and were inserted in containers holding tobacco.

The coupons went by various names: vouchers, bonds, vouchments, or just plain "certificates." The term "coupon," though, was most commonly used.

Redeemable gifts were either displayed on the back of the paper scrip or, more commonly, were listed in premium catalogs issued free to the public. Some coupons were accorded token monetary value, offering consumers the option of hard cash, be it fractions of a cent.

Coupons answered the tobacco industry's need for full product coverage. They were enthusiastically received by tobacco users everywhere who had become, by then, an expectant, premium-conscious crowd.

Tobacco giveaways of the late 1890s, redeemed for box fronts, coupons and stickers.

PAPER NUISANCES

Problems of a annoying nature soon plagued the redemption system during the period of transition from tin tags and other devices to paper coupons.

Due to the variety of premium-giving programs, it was not unusual for smokers or chewers to have accumulated an odd assortment of certificates, tin tags, cigar bands, labels, and box fronts of different brands, many of them issued by the same company. Tobacco companies had no choice but to make them all redeemable and interchangeable in value, but not necessarily at the same rate. In 1910, for example, a tin tag from Horse Shoe or American Navy chewing tobacco carried twice the value as one from the Newsboy or Black Bear brands.

Consumers remitting large collections of redeemable articles presented monumental headaches. One can imagine the tedious task that faced office clerks at, say, the Floradora Tag Company in St. Louis, one of the American Tobacco Company's national redemption centers. Here a constant stream of shipments arrived every day that had to opened, sorted and counted. Ignorance or carelessness on the part of the remitting public was legion with packages lacking return addresses, forms incompletely filled out or errors made in counting.

Angrily worded letters were received from remitters demanding action on parcels that had been missent through the mail. Senders were cautioned again and again not to send accompanying letters with their packages. This constituted a first class rate and double postage but, most importantly, the sender incurred a $10 fine. Nothing was easy in the old days.

The use of tobacco coupons continued well into the 1910s but fell off drastically after World War I, reflecting paper shortages and a thinning out of companies and brands caused by the war.

RETAILERS' COUPONS
FOR THE MAN BEHIND THE COUNTER

In the early days when selling a single popular brand of cigarettes such as Camel or Lucky Strike brought in enough income to carry a company, tobacco manufacturers traditionally relied on sales of a long line of products to maintain profit margins. The list covered everything from a nickel plug of chew to $4.50-a-pound latakia pipe tobacco.

Marketing such a broad range of products required a great deal of cooperation from middle men in the trade: jobbers, wholesalers and dealers. To ensure compliance, manufacturers extended them inducements in the form of secret discounts, free goods, bonuses, and other "deals" which became a standard business practice.

Part of the currying of favor was the issuance of special retailers' premium certificates which were inserted in bulk shipments of tobacco products. These coupons circulated profusely for a decade or so before the war.

Big companies even went to the trouble of helping dealers maintain profitability against undercutting chain outlets like Riker and Liggett drugstores in the past. This protective solicitude, however, vanished quickly when huge profits from cigarettes materialized, necessitating larger increases in advertising appropriations and drastic reductions in product lines. The dealers were now on their own.

**Few advertising pieces surpassed the dazzling
colors** of this premium flyer of 1904, issued by the American
Tobacco Company. It featured the Dixie Queen logo, one of
tobaccodom's prettiest. The brand originally belonged to the A. H.
Motley firm of Reidsville, North Carolina. Motley was bought out by the
Trust around 1900, and a few of its brands, like Dixie Queen, were
rushed to the front of the market through aggressive promotions.

PREMIUM CATALOGS

This catalog of the Pinkerton Tobacco Company of Zanesville, Ohio, acquired by the American Tobacco Company in 1903, contained 48 pages of redeemable gifts. The exchange medium was a departure from the ordinary, cut-out logos from paper packages–a deer's head from the Buckshoe brand, or a plow from Tiger Stripe tobacco. Customers were warned not to send in cut-outs from free samples; they didn't count. The catalog dates to around 1905 and represents another example of the Trust's habit of buying out competitors and turning up the advertising heat on their most popular brands.

Premium catalogs circulated freely in the 1910s following the break-up of the Trust. It was important for major companies to continually update catalogs and change the menu of presents offered to the public.

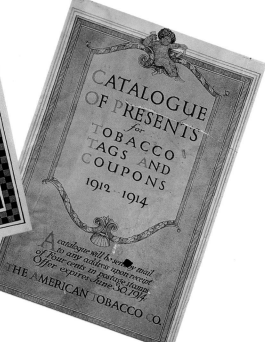

CIGAR STORE COUPONS
FUN FOR THE ENTIRE FAMILY

Cigar store coupons were introduced in 1902 by the United Cigar Stands Company. This firm conducted business on a hard cash basis, a far cry from the informal ways of the old-time tobacco store, and the premium-yielding certificates were designed to embellish the company's reputation and bid for patronage.

Popular from the outset, the first premiums clearly catered to a male clientele. But it was not long before management recognized that feminine members of the smokers' families were fast becoming aware of the coupons' worth and significance. The list of redeemable gifts were thus expanded to include silverware, cut glass, gravy boats, and other household articles of interest to women.

And so it was that housewives, long opposed to smoking in the household, now had reason to urge their husbands to light up more often. Before father's suits were sent to the cleaners, the pockets were searched for vagrant coupons. In business offices, stenographers and telephone operators cadged the valuable slips of paper from male co-workers. Even children enlisted in the army of coupon gatherers, bold ones standing outside cigar stores and greeting departing customers with: "Coupon, mister, please."

During the heyday of the cigar store coupon, the United Cigar Stands company distributed over $4 million worth of merchandise in one year alone, embracing an assortment of some 500 gifts ranging from a cigar cutter for five coupons to a silver-plated tea set for 1,000.

Specialty shops soon appeared in the vicinity of redemption centers and trafficked solely in cigar store coupons. There certificate collectors, too impatient to accumulate the required number of coupons, exchanged theirs for cash. These establishments saw brisk business just before Christmas.

Eventually business competition among the chain stores, marked by drastic price-cutting, plus waning public interest, brought an end to cigar store coupons. By 1930, their use had been abandoned completely.

ADVERTISING BOOKLETS
LIGHT READING FARE

Fatima
A DREAM OF PASSION

Sweet FATIMA sat in her boudoir one day
to conflicting emotions and passions a prey,
She had health, she had beauty and treasure galore,
But to-day she was restless, and for something more,
Something dearer and sweeter than riches she sighed.
"Alphonso, my darling, my loved one!" she cried,
(And her white bosom heaved like a tempest tossed sea)
"Alphonso, my darling, Oh, hasten to me,-
Oh hasten to fold me in loving embrace,-
Oh haste on my lips thy warm kisses to place.
Oh hasten to- But what she would have said more
Is uncertain,- just then came a ring at the door.

"SWEET FATIMA SAT IN HER BOUDOIR ONE DAY."

ANOTHER Fatima

A DREAM OF PASSION

GENUINE DURHAM
Smoking Tobacco
W.T. BLACKWELL & CO
Durham N.C.

"SMOKING - IS WHAT?"

OLD
VIRGINIA CHEROOTS
LIBRARY

THE
TELL TALE
BRACELET

Throwaway paper advertising literature, delivered to dealers from the factory or supplied by drummers on the beat, ended up in the hands of the public. Designed purely to entertain, humor and lots of colored pictures were essential ingredients. Customers, for instance, enjoyed booklets like Bull Durham's "Tales of Sweet Fatima" relating a young lady's exasperating experiences with her likeable but bumbling oaf of a suitor, Alphonso La Grande, who never seemed to grasp the importance of smoking the right tobacco–or reading Old Virginia Cheroot's miniaturized library of thrillers–or Honest Scrap's sad tale of a bobtailed terrier that made the fatal mistake of tangling with a mean cat–or reading about the life of General Hood. There were hundreds more like them.

HONEST Scrap

A SHORT HISTORY OF
GEN. D.C. BUELL

A SHORT HISTORY OF
GEN. HOWARD

A SHORT HISTORY OF
GEN. JOHN B. HOOD

HONEST Scrap

The man he cussed and he ripped and he swore
And he gathered a big brickbat
And he swore he'd be darned eternally
If he didn't kill that cat.

The dog he howled and the hair it flew,
As the claws went into his hide,
The man he cussed and he ripped and he swore
As the dog kerflummuxed and died.

CIGARETTE INSERT CARDS
SECOND TIME AROUND

Those attractive pieces of colored cardboard slipped into tobacco packages enjoyed a second surge of popularity beginning in 1912 when cards promoting vying brands of Turkish and domestic blend cigarettes hit the market. The renaissance lasted until paper shortages of World War I brought the fad to a final close.

Variations in themes abounded:

There were toasts (some with biting sarcasm) and birth month information...

Cards that told fortunes...

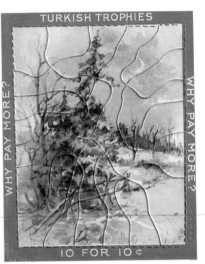

Cards cut up into miniature puzzles...

Battlefield scenes from the Great War...

Animals...

154

College sports (it took 15 of the smaller to get one of the larger)...

Medals...

Cartoons...

Baseball players...

And, the venerable favorites, faces of pretty women.

155

COMPANY MAGAZINES
PENROD FOR A NICKEL

Some well-capitalized tobacco manufacturers went to the trouble and expense of publishing company magazines. They were aimed at consumers and distributed free or sold at nominal cost in tobacco shops; a few were published in-house exclusively for factory employees or for chain retail outlets.

The few publications of last century, such as the one printed by the Blackwell firm in the 1880s, were single or short-run series with pedestrian contents. After 1900, however, company magazines took on a refined look and mimicked high-quality commercial publications; money took care of that. Then customers had to pay for them, a nickel a copy.

Duke's Magazine (later renamed Duke's Mixture Magazine after the Trust dissolved), was a serialized periodical that ran from 1902 through 1911. It contained a healthy diet of cartoons. The Lorillard company issued a classier version in 1915 (Above) which featured short stories written by contemporary authors such as Booth Tarkington, Irwin S. Cobb and O. Henry. It is said that Penrod first saw the literary light of day in this magazine. There was plenty more. Accompanying the usual assortment of jokes, cartoons and extraneous bits of information was a special "Home and Woman's Page–Edited by a Real Woman." Ads were not done up cheaply, either. Striking, full-page plugs in color appeared for Lorillard's chief brands of tobacco–Climax, Stag and Union Leader.

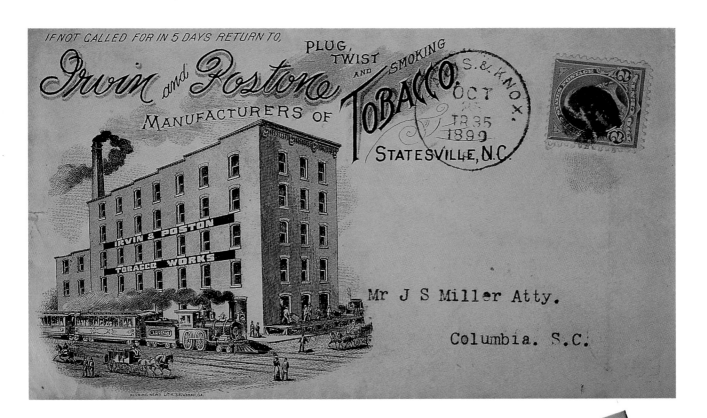

DRESSING UP THE STATIONERY

Following the Civil War, printed matter underwent dramatic change, hand in hand with new and exciting advances in lithographic and printing techniques. Artistic embellishment became the order of the day.

The new look was far-reaching and filtered down to such everyday items as business correspondence: letters, envelopes, billheads, and the like. These items were turned into added avenues of advertising by tobacco companies and dealers who splashed their company names, products, logos, and brand names in great flourishes of ornately engraved artwork.

The spectrum of decoration ran a full range – from simple inked handstamps modestly applied to a corner of an envelope to large, steel-engraved sketches covering the faces of all business missives leaving the office. Typical of the times, the size of buildings was exaggerated far out of proportion to street traffic. Images of factories in particular were rendered with chimneys belching out huge volumes of dark smoke, the Victorian symbol of industrial size and might and a nightmare to modern-day environmentalists.

The Goodwin company made more promotional use of the reverse of the envelope than the front. It dates to 1887.

Fine examples of the steel engraving art were found on advertising envelopes used by Southern plug manufacturers and cigar houses in the 1890s and early 1900s.

LETTERHEADS

Major manufacturers, dealers in leaf tobacco, wholesale jobbers, small-time retailers–it really made no difference. Few things lent such a touch of class to something as ordinary as office stationery than decoration with a finely engraved illustration. It fit most budgets.

—OFFICE OF—

ROBINSON & CO.,
MANUFACTURERS OF
FINE CIGARS,
And DEALERS IN LEAF TOBACCO,
BROADWAY AND FIFTH AVE.,
Troy, N.Y.,

LOUIS F. WENTZ.
WM. W. STEWART.
ANCHOR
STOGIE FACTORY
12, 13, 14 & 15 CHURCH AVENUE.
Wentz, Stewart & P
Manufacture Cigars and Sto

The Winston Manufacturing Co
WHOLESALE MANUFACTURERS OF CIGARS.
Individual Responsibility
Over $100,000.00.
N. . N.C. U.S.A. NOV 1 1893

The Largest firm in this line any where in the Southern

DEAR SIRS:
About
Filled ELGIN Wa
package. We adv
owing to the e
Watches we had
surplus quanti

ROBERT. WILSON President
B. McCALLAY, V. President
CHAS. H. BARKELEW, Secretary
E. L. McCALLAY, Treasurer
WILSON & McCALLAY COMPANY
FOR A CHEW TAKE ONLY HALF AS MUCH AS OF OTHER TOBACCO NO HEARTBURN FROM GOLD ROPE
GOLD ROPE
SPUN ROLL
The WILSON & McCALLAY
TOBACCO COMPANY,
Manufacturers.
Middletown, O. ber 31st, 1901.
I.W. BECKER

WALTER J. FRIEDLANDER.
The Day & Night Tobacco Co.
TRADE MARK
MANUFACTURERS OF
Chewing & Smoking
TOBACCO.
REGISTERED
Red Light Mixture
Cor. PLUM, CANAL AND GENESEE STS.
Cincinnati, July 3rd, 1901.
this day sold
anufactured
ture and
the

POSTCARDS

Postcards were the standard form of mail promotion utilized by American businesses between 1900 and 1920. Referred to as "advertising post-cards" today, they represent a relatively short-lived but quite prolific means of product promotion before their use was curtailed by World War I.

The first postcard models, called government postal cards, were issued between 1893 and 1898 and bore an imprinted stamp. Messages could only be written on the front side. Americans discovered the picture postcard at the Columbian Exposition in Chicago in 1893 where "souvenir cards," bearing images on the backs of government postal cards, were mailed for two cents.

The postcard, as we know it today, came legally into existence by an Act of Congress on May 19, 1898. They were named "private mailing cards" and private printers were allowed to issue and sell them. Postage was one cent and the back side was undivided. In 1907, the mailing side was changed. It was divided with a vertical line and the left half could be used for written messages.

Germany supplied most postcards printed before World War I and shipped about 35,000 tons of them yearly to our shores. Postcard albums were manufactured to fill the demands of a new collecting craze in America that took place between 1905 and 1910.

Tobacco manufacturers, as well as other industries, were quick to recognize the pass-along value of this new mass media device and the golden age of postcard advertising began. Free cards were distributed at all levels of commercial trade including point of purchase. Others were offered as premium incentives to consumers who probably mailed a few, but hoarded millions in scrapbooks that never saw the light of day.

THE TALKING POSTCARD

A remarkable sales gimmick was a postcard fitted with a detachable miniature phonograph record that could be played on home gramophones. It dates to 1913 when Lorillard, makers of Stag smoking tobacco, issued it to boost sales. Such postcards were originally an English novelty item.

POSTCARD PANORAMA
(1907-1919)

Cigarettes and smoking tobacco were advertised on postcards. Some, like the Mecca cigarette series, were handed out free at United Cigar Stands outlets in 1912; the Murad cards were folded and inserted in boxes of cigarettes. The patriotic themes of World War I were the work of J.C. Leyendecker, a renowned artist and illustrator.

A SALESMAN WILL CALL

Drumming the tobacco trade long ago was governed by strict Victorian standards of politeness and decorum. A salesman's visit in the field was announced in advanced by postcards, a practice that began in the 1880s and lasted well into the new century.

Cards were considered personal extensions of the companies and, as such, were generally stiff, formal and filled with language that today would be judged as overly patronizing. Later, humor was interjected.

Postcards were important to business.

They were used to advertise brands, confirm orders, announce price changes, and make special offers to retailers and to customers.

POSTER STAMPS

Poster stamps were employed from the 1890s through the 1930s to advertise a variety of products. Die-cut and gummed, they were affixed to anything requiring a little splash of color and pizzazz. Most stickers were perforated like postage stamps and represented a miniaturized version of poster art, a fad left over from the 1890s.

THEATER PROGRAMS

Theater programs have been around as long as plays have been staged, primarily in cities with large theater communities such as New York City, Chicago and Philadelphia. The playbill's marketing value was realized as early as the 1860s when advertisements run by local businessmen first appeared on their pages.

In the beginning, programs were provided by printing companies specializing in the field who kept advertising revenues as payment. In New York City, Frank V. Straus developed a theater program business into a vast operation in the 1880s and merged in 1900 with a competitor, Leo Van Raven, forming the New York Theater Program Company. By 1928, this firm was supplying well over 1.5 million programs per month to theater houses nationwide.

Playbills presented a unique opportunity for advertisers to reach a sizable and affluent audience. In 1908, for example, the combined seating capacity of New York City theaters alone exceeded 120,000, largest in the world. This advantageous situation was not overlooked by the ever-vigilant tobacco companies with money to spend for advertising.

Manufacturers like the American Tobacco Company and Lorillard were frequent advertisers in theater playbills. In the early years they tantalized the carriage trade with spot or full-page advertisements, many in striking colors, for high-priced Turkish cigarettes and aptly named Between The Acts little cigars which found special favor with male theater-goers.

THE LITTLE THINGS
SILKS, RUGS, AND LEATHERS

An enormously popular and successful promotional device was the use of small fabric novelties made of satin, leather and flannel. Chiefly employed as insert giveaways with Turkish brands, they were important weapons used in the cigarette wars being fought by major producers. The fad, which had strong feminine appeal, came to life in 1912 and ran up to the outbreak of World War I.

SILKS

Attractive and colorful images, many rendered in striking detail, were either directly lithographed onto or woven into patches of satin ("silks" were really made of satin).

The use of chromolithography on textiles was an extension of the art form developed by Louis Prang, father of the Christmas card and one of the world's pioneers in color printing. He was the first to transfer colored pictures onto satin, mostly in the form of greeting cards.

This breakthrough found its way into the cigar industry in the 1880s as gaily colored ribbons and streamers which were used to tie up freshly wrapped bundles of cigars. It allowed the identification of brands at a quick glance.

Sizes of silks varied. Most were uniformly small, averaging two by three inches; others ran larger (five by seven inches, in some cases). The largest, measuring one square foot, was offered by Liggett & Myers as a premium for Fatima cigarettes.

Silks were meant to be sewn into decorative household items by women. Manufacturers offered a long list of possibilities: doilies, sewing bags, belts, parasols, hair bands, belts, lamp shades, pin cushions, dolls' dresses, and door curtains. They could also be sewn into the designs of "crazy quilts," table linens and cushion covers.

As an added touch of practicality, tobacco companies conveniently placed the brand name and factory information near the edge of the silks so they could be trimmed before they were sewn into place. The tobacco men thought of everything.

The subject matter depicted on silks duplicated themes already beaten to death on insert cards. Sets portrayed animals, coats-of-arms, colleges, flags, flowers, Indians, famous sports and stage personalities, and much, much more.

Silk inserts were expensive premiums; in one year alone they ran the American Tobacco Company over $300,000 in costs. Consequently, silks were never placed in cheaper brands of cigarettes, but as competition stiffened, that policy changed.

Old Glory arrives in the mail, a four-by-six-inch patch of colored silk, straight from a premium distribution center in Jersey City. Also included were illustrated suggestions for silk-sewing projects.

GEORGETOWN

ZIRA
THE NEW
CIGARETTE
5 CENTS
A SATIN WONDER
IN EACH PACKAGE
RECOMMENDS ONE MORE

Adding to the pleasure of cracking open a new pack of cigarettes was finding a pretty silken treasure inside.

RUGS

Multicolored miniature rugs made of fringed or plain-cut flannel or silk were other fabric giveaways. They were the bulkiest of all cigarette inserts and were either contained in cellophane envelopes or wrapped around packages of tobacco, held by a strip of paper. Larger rugs were folded into quarters; outsized ones were mailed from distribution centers as premiums. The latter rugs were utilized to promote cigarettes, not cigars, a common collector misconception today.

Sizes of rugs ranged from small two-by-four inch models to larger eight-by-eleven inch carpets. Standard themes were employed: conventional and Indian rug patterns, flags, college pennants and official seals, baseball players, and the like. Brand names were sometimes stamped on the back but most came unmarked.

As with silks, rugs were intended as gifts for the womenfolk, to be sewn together in ambitious sewing projects: pillow cases, bedspreads and table mats. Many ended up as carpets in doll houses.

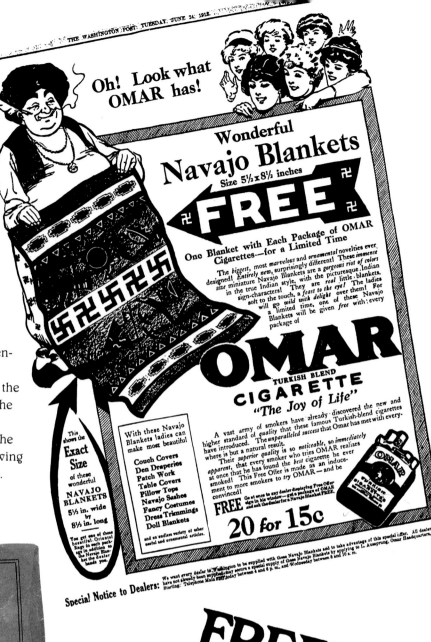

The ads' influence was subtle. Women were nudged into wondering what other pleasures awaited them in that pack of cigarettes besides a free rug.

167

Other flannel novelties included kewpie dolls, Indian rugs, college pennants, and major league ball players.

FREE LEATHERS

Manufacturers also offered lithographed leather patches as premiums for a short time in 1912. Most were produced in two or more colors, with or without frame designs. Mammoth soft leather creations existed, measuring a whopping 30 inches square and obtainable only with Helmar or Turkish Trophies premium certificates. They were intended to be sewn into pillow or cushion covers.

168

ROLLING YOUR OWN

Not all consumers smoked convenient packaged cigarettes; many preferred to manufacture their own with cigarette paper and their favorite brand of smoking tobacco.

"Rollers," they were called. They firmly believed that a self-made cigarette possessed a number of smoking advantages, a notion fostered by tobacco companies.

Rolling cigarettes proved an adroit art and a certain mystique evolved around the ritual and the man who mastered it. Being able to roll a cigarette with a single hand, a minimum of saliva and in a strong wind seemed to confer an air of manliness, independence and self-assurance.

The delicate and socially elegant art of fashioning a self-made cigarette.

Cheap smokes, 40 for a nickel, was the advantage of buying a sack of "Bull" Durham in 1914.

It must be remembered that in the early days, smoking cigarettes was looked upon as an effeminate and sissified pastime, one reserved for limp-wristed dudes and dandies. Rolling helped dispel that attitude.

"Rollin'" with the "makins'" got its start in the 1880s, soon after the introduction of the handmade commercial cigarette. It became a style of smoking that found particular favor in rural areas but could be found almost anywhere whenever times got hard.

This was, of course, the most compelling reason for "rolling your own" – it was a cheap smoke. This indisputable fact formed the central theme of advertising by those who made rolling tobacco.

Some manufacturers, the American Tobacco Company being a prime example, ran full-page ads to show the public how easy it was to roll cigarettes.

CIGARETTE PAPERS AID PROMOTION

A half-century (1900-1950) of handsomely decorated cigarette paper packets, each an advertisement in itself.

Cigarette paper was originally imported from France. While domestic production existed, it was not until the 1930s that American manufacturers matched the superior quality of French-made brands like Riz La Croix, Tam Tam and OCB.

Rolling paper was made from linen rags but it was not unusual to see it referred to as "rice paper" or "wheat paper," falsely implying that these were the sources of the paper. These misnomers lingered for years, probably for aesthetic reasons; "rice paper" sounded more elegant than "rag paper."

Packages of imported French cigarette paper were initially sold in this country as separate smoking articles, usually costing a nickel. This was expensive fare. A good hand-rolled Havana or a two-ounce tin of first-rate smoking tobacco could be bought for that kind of money.

In the 1890s, a few tobacco companies, recognizing the promotional value of little things, began providing American-made rolling paper in packets tucked under the outer labels on bags and sacks of smoking tobacco.

Some firms with fatter wallets, like Reynolds and the American Tobacco Company, sprang for the good stuff by importing genuine French paper and providing it to consumers free of charge.

Rollers liked that. They also liked the brightly colored packs of domestic papers, that eventually dominated the scene and helped advertise the many brands of rolling tobacco on the market.

PINBACK BUTTONS

Celluloid pinback buttons made their debut in 1896. They were an immediate success and found widespread use in the political, religious, souvenir, and advertising fields. The makers of bakery goods, breakfast cereals, candy, and chewing gum inserted pinbacks in their products as the buttons' strong commercial promotional value was recognized.

Celluloid, a synthetic plastic material, was first introduced in 1856. Its commercial application blossomed in the late 1860s when it was used to make everyday articles such as combs, hair brushes, men's shirt cuffs, and collars–and billiard balls. In addition to celluloid's natural properties of strength, luster, durability, and low cost, it was the material's ability to take up colors well that led to another important use, the making of pins and badges, book covers and other similar devices.

Pinback buttons were the invention of George B. Adams of Irvington, New Jersey. Interestingly, the prototype was a trousers strap made of celluloid patented by Adams in 1894. In July, 1896, Adams patented the classic "badge pin." The inventor assigned the patent rights to a manufacturer of novelty items in Newark, New Jersey, the Whitehead & Hoag Company which became the nation's premier maker of pinback buttons.

Newspaper ads in 1896 *announced the availability of Sweet Caporal pinback buttons. The celluloid novelties were handed out to customers by tobacco dealers.*

Tobacco companies put the buttons to enthusiastic use. Most were used to advertise cigarette brands, but some also saw service with cigar, smoking and chewing labels. To maximize eye appeal of the colorful buttons and to eliminate clutter, many carried the brand name on a small piece of stiff paper inserted on the reverse side under the metal pin assembly.

The best known tobacco celluloid buttons were those issued in 1896 by the American Tobacco Company which handed out hundreds of thousands to promote Sweet Caporal cigarettes. A wide variety of subject matter was portrayed: actresses, baseball players and comic pictures and sayings, first in sepia tones, later in full color. All were manufactured by Whitehead & Hoag. In the 1910s, following the breakup of the Trust, the American Tobacco Company issued a profusion of pinbacks with the advertising of Hassan, Tokio and Perfection cigarettes.

High Admiral cigarettes
were advertised on celluloid buttons in 1896 and featured Henry Outcault's famous cartoon character, the "Yellow Kid." Celluloid scarf and lapel pins in the form of flags were also used to advertise Sweet Caporal cigarettes.

172

ADVERTISING MIRRORS

Advertising mirrors – oval, round or rectangular with a mirror
on one side and eye-catching graphics rendered on celluloid on the
other – inundated America in the early 1900s. They were an outgrowth
of the pinback button craze and were used to push everything from
manure spreaders to mortuaries. All were given out free and were more
in vogue with women than with men.

TOBACCO POSTER ART
(1890-1915)

This was an era of tumultuous technological advancement in color printing. Progress in the manufacture of new inks and coated paper made constant headlines in trade journals. By 1890, the novelty of chromolithography had faded in favor of collotype, photolithography and photo-engraving techniques which were used to enhance printed images.

A result of the blending of art and American business was the great poster period of 1890-1915. Big, bright, bold, and beautiful, images in eight colors or more were printed on paper, tin, linen, glass, cardboard, or any hard surface, and hung on walls, propped up on counter tops and placed in windows.

Posters were advertising necessities of the tobacco trade. They attracted attention and helped etch brand names of cigarettes, cigars and smoking tobacco in the viewer's mind forever.

"It is only shallow people who do not judge by appearances."

- Oscar Wilde

"The average man can be counted on to see better than he can think."

- Anonymous

COUNTERTOP POSTERS

Stand-up tri-fold counter displays made of cardboard or tin were tabletop versions of wall-mounted posters and signs. Their use dates to the 1880s when colored images were first transferred onto three-piece die-cut sections. When unfolded, their visual impact was stunning. Used through the 1950s, triptychs advertised everything there was to smoke and chew. Few tri-fold posters exist today; dealers were required to buy them, unlike wall posters which were provided free of charge.

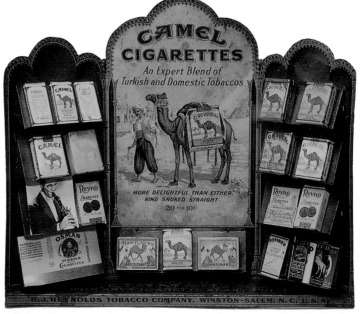

THE TURKISH CIGARETTE FAD

Years ago, smokers in America had a love affair with Turkish cigarettes. Also called Egyptian cigarettes, these specialty smokes were the smoking rage between 1890 and 1920. The cigarettes were made from a small-leafed variety of tobacco grown only in the hilly regions of Asia Minor and particularly the Balkans which, prior to World War I, belonged to Turkey.

The fad of Turkish cigarettes first started in the 1870s in New York City and Boston. They were smoked by small colonies of immigrant Syrians and Armenians who opened quaint little coffee houses and served coffee and the special cigarettes to customers.

Making Turkish cigarettes as an industry was established late in the 1880s. Foreign exporters with depots in eastern Mediterranean ports came to the United States via London and set up manufacturing facilities on the East Coast, primarily in New York City.

The light-colored Turkish leaf tobacco, said to have an agreeable, mild and subdued flavor, also possessed another advantage: once lit, it never went out. It was an improvement in taste and aroma over domestic Virginia and burley tobaccos.

Turkish cigarettes, hand-rolled and expensive, became big-city items with snob appeal and attracted a small but loyal carriage trade clientele. But, surprisingly, the trendy smokes caught the fancy of many connoisseurs of the weed and their demand surged in the 1890s.

The new type of cigarettes were made differently from factory-made American brands. With the latter, tobacco was rolled inside paper and then sealed. With Turkish smokes, the cigarette paper was wrapped around an oval form and the seam sealed with a starch paste; then the empty paper tube was allowed to dry. A mixture of Turkish tobacco, the leaves carefully selected and shredded by knife, was rolled into a long cylinder with a piece of stiff cardboard, then inserted into the paper tube.

Domestic blend cigarettes sold for five to ten cents a package. Turkish models ranged from ten cents to as much as 75 cents for choice brands; the average package cost 25 cents.

Companies making Turkish cigarettes were traditionally small business operations (some were family-run) and relied on word-of-mouth advertising. While the tobacco itself claimed many converts, demand was created and sustained through simple, cheap but remarkably effective merchandising techniques.

Selection of brand names and packaging details were turned into a highly refined art. Logos in full color with "Oriental" motifs greeted the eye: pyramids, swaying palm trees, Egyptian symbols and hieroglyphics, turbaned pashas, and veiled harem women. They covered the lids of the characteristic flat, hinged, cardboard boxes that became instantly recognizable as holding ten oval-shaped Turkish "bombers."

Creative minds conjured up a long list of intriguing brand names, putting a final touch to the suggestive imagery. Many brands were prefixed with the magical word "Turkish" or "Egyptian." As a result, labels such as Egyptian Prettiest, Egyptian Mysteries, Egyptian Emblems, Turkish Guards, Turkish Trophies, and Turkey Red were created. Others had a similar ring – Arabs, Fez, Minaret, Sultan, Delhi, Durbar, Soudan and Otez.

The numbers of those making Turkish smokes rose as rapidly as their popularity. The original pioneers, Schinasi, Stephano, Nestor Gianaclis, Melachrino, and Anargyros, were soon joined at century's end by a host of operators wishing to get in on the action.

Turkish cigarettes made significant inroads in the marketplace. By 1902, they had taken the country by storm, accounting for a whopping 20 percent of national cigarette sales. Naturally, this sort of business action did not escape the watchful eye of the cigarette king, James Duke, who purchased two major manufacturers of high-grade Turkish cigarettes, the Monopol Tobacco Works in 1899 and S. Anargyros in 1900.

Taking two brand acquisitions, Murad and Ramleh, Duke pumped hundreds of thousands of dollars into advertising and, by 1911, made them market leaders (Ramleh was renamed Helmar in 1907 by reversing the letters).

MAGAZINE WARS

Between 1912 and 1920, a marketing war was fought over Turkish cigarettes on the pages of national magazines. Some of the most striking imagery seen in tobacco advertising appeared as a continuous parade of classy, full-page illustrations in color that enticed readers (including many women) into buying Murad, Helmar, Fatima, Egyptian Deities, and other brands.

NEWSPAPER ADVERTISING
(1890-1915)

Newspaper advertising of tobacco products slowly grew in strength between 1890 and 1910. After the break-up of the American Tobacco Company, it became prolific.

CIGARETTES GO TO WAR
WORLD WAR I AND THE COST OF VICTORY

During its course, from 1914 to 1919, the Great War thrust the domestic blend cigarette into national prominence, killed the Turkish cigarette market virtually overnight, drove scores of tobacco dealers out of business, and dealt a lethal hammerblow to the anti-tobacco movement.

In a macabre twist of fate, veterans of the war who took up the cigarette habit overseas formed an unwitting test pool of human guinea pigs. Two and three decades later, their sudden and alarming development of lung cancer, previously a rare disease, provided medical scientists with the first strong hint of the causal relationship between cigarette smoking and lung cancer.

CASUALTIES OF A DIFFERENT KIND

A nurse hands out free smokes to U. S. soldiers at an aid station in France. Many of these boys came home addicted to cigarettes and paid the price later by dying of lung cancer.

TOBACCO AT THE FRONT LINES

15 CENTS

HELMAR

TURKISH CIGARETTES

'If you love me, can you fail
To send Helmar every mail?"

Anargyros Makers of the Highest Grade Turkish and Egyptian Cigarettes in the World

⊕Quality-Superb

Tobacco ads like this preyed on the public's conscience. Who could possibly resist the appeal to send cigarettes to boys risking their lives for the cause of freedom?

"Tobacco is as indispensable as the daily ration; we must have thousands of tons without delay." So cabled General John J. Pershing, commander of the Allied Expeditionary Force in France, to officials in Washington, D.C., in 1918. His message was clear and urgent.

"Send us cigarettes and more cigarettes!" was the same plea echoed in many letters sent home by soldiers at the front.

Historically, tobacco and wartime have always maintained an inseparable alliance; military commanders long ago had discovered that tobacco was indispensable at the battle front. General George Washington was one of the first military leaders to observe that soldiers well supplied with tobacco fought better. He uttered the same appeal as did Pershing 150 years later: "I say, if you can't send money, send tobacco."

The influence of tobacco on troops was well illustrated during the Franco-Prussian War. It was stated by military authorities that the crushing defeat of the French was to a large extent due to their lack of personal comforts on the battlefield, chiefly tobacco.

German hussars charged into battle with huge cigars in their mouths; the infantry stood shoulder to shoulder while pulling at their pipes. Bismarck himself was seldom seen without a cigar. The Iron Chancellor used to walk among the wounded and, taking cigars from his pocket, light them and hand them out to soldiers. General Count Moltke took tobacco in the form of snuff and kept it in a handsome gold casket which stood at his elbow while he pored over war charts in his field tent.

The First World War did great things for cigarettes, and for smoking in general. American Army doctors sent home glowing reports of the cigarette's uplifting properties, how it acted as an incomparable builder of morale, reliever of tedium and solace to pain and suffering, better than any medicine could provide.

Cigarettes became the doughboy's best friend. They spurred him "over the top" and comforted him as he lay wounded. Soldiers were allowed to smoke while being operated on. "Wonderful," one army surgeon described the cigarette's calming effect at a frontline hospital, "as soon as the lads take their first whiff, they seem eased and relieved of their agony."

Tobacco for the boys. Boxes upon boxes of "Bull" Durham reach to the rafters and beyond in this army warehouse somewhere in France. This was the brand of choice for many soldiers who preferred to roll their own or stoke their pipes during respites from battle. -Courtesy Library of Congress, Prints and Photographs Division.

UNUSUAL DELIVERY SYSTEM

After the war, interesting stories came to light. Martin Merle of San Francisco, a playwright, originated the plan of supplying cigarettes to men by means of airplanes. While attached to the 27th Pursuit Squadron of the 1st American Air Group at St. Mihiel, he conceived the idea of having aviators drop cigarettes to the doughboys at the front.

"It was while the fight was commencing at St. Mihiel that I persuaded Major Hartley, commander of the first pursuit group, to allow the cigarettes to go by way of the airplanes," said Merle. "Eddie Rickenbacker of the 9th Squadron was one of the aviators who flew across the front lines with the smokes. Personal messages were written on the cigarette packages in pencil by the aviators. At first the doughboys were a bit bashful about picking up the hundreds of small packages which came fluttering down. But when they spotted the K-C mark they lost all fear. Thereafter the idea became a general one."

185

DOING THEIR PART

It was shortly after the doughboys landed in France in the fall of 1917 that the Army reported huge shortages of tobacco in training camps. The call went out. The U.S. Government responded by mustering the army of civilians at home into service of a different kind by convincing them that it was just as important to place a cigarette in a soldier's mouth as a rifle in his hands. The population answered enthusiastically.

"Buy tobacco as well as war bonds!" officials urged as money was raised to buy cigarettes, cigars and tobacco for the boys in France. Large-city newspapers lent their support and sponsored "tobacco funds," as well as celebrities who volunteered their time to solicit contributions.

High school girls formed "sister clubs," made contact with fighting units in Europe and mailed them tobacco supplies. The government established the National Service Committee in New York City to coordinate tobacco shipments overseas and asked civilians for names of boys in the service who had no friends or family back home and sent them cigarettes.

Civilian tobacco and pipe funds were established, encouraged in part by tobacco companies who had a good thing going and, in so doing, received a windfall of unscheduled publicity, all favorable.

A dime could buy a pipe for a doughboy through the "Soldiers Pipe Fund," sponsored by prominent public citizens.

Civilians sending tobacco were often surprised to receive a hearty "thank-you" in the mail from grateful soldiers. The messages were written on special postcards provided by the army.

Handy order forms made it easy for the folks at home to do their part by sending 25-cent tobacco kits to "our boys over there."

186

A colonel's daughter started the "Army Girls' Transport Tobacco Fund" in 1918 and issued an appeal for funds. "Every dollar received has been expended for smokes," she proudly proclaimed. Soon the group was packing and shipping 5-8,000 tobacco kits daily and for its unstinting effort received a grateful thank-you note from General Pershing.

Tons of "tobacco for the boys" – cigarettes, smoking and chewing tobacco – were purchased by the government and shipped to France where it was stockpiled in warehouses and then distributed to troops. Some idea of the government's enormous appetite for cigarettes was demonstrated in November, 1918, when the War Department placed orders for three billion cigarettes to meet military demands for the next two months.

Overseas in France, the smoking comforts of soldiers were tended to by the Y.M.C.A., Salvation Army and Knights of Columbus. Canteens were set up close to the front. Here cigarettes, fruit and chocolate were sold to the troops at scalping prices that raised bitter complaint until the problem was rectified. From dugouts located just behind the lines the Y.M.C.A. handed out free smokes to doughboys in, or just leaving, the trenches.

The tobacco drive reached Hometown, U.S.A. Theaters set up boxes where patrons dropped pennies – cigarettes were welcome, too. School children were sent out into neighborhoods to collect donations. The call even reached prisons where inmates not only gave up their tobacco rations but took up collections for the cause of defending democracy.

Finally, in May, 1918, shouts of joy rang out from America's fighting men as the War Department announced that daily tobacco rations would be issued to every soldier, sailor and marine in uniform.

To many people in this nation, it was utterly unthinkable, totally incomprehensible, that the day had arrived that the much maligned cigarette had shed its disreputable image and emerged as the shining symbol of civic duty, patriotism and the American way. Tobacco reformers shuddered in horror.

HOW ST. LOUIS FOUGHT THE WAR

The many tobacco funds that sprang up in public-spirited cities during the year of 1918 were similar to the one in St. Louis; it was sponsored by a local newspaper, the Republic.

Money was raised by sponsoring a variety of social activities, bowling contests, dances and theater shows, and by accepting contributions. The Helmar Club, named in honor of a Lorillard brand of Turkish cigarettes, hosted dances featuring the "pickle toe," the latest dancing rage from New York City.

"KICK IN, AMERICANS AT HOME!", the press trumpeted, "YOU must do YOUR duty along with all the rest!"

The funds were used to buy tobacco for the "thousands and thousands of American boys overseas," made easy by the convenient presence of the hometown firm of Liggett & Myers, makers of Fatima, Piedmont and Chesterfield cigarettes, which offered their products at wholesale prices.

Publicity like this could not be bought by tobacco men.

THE "BULL" GOES TO WAR

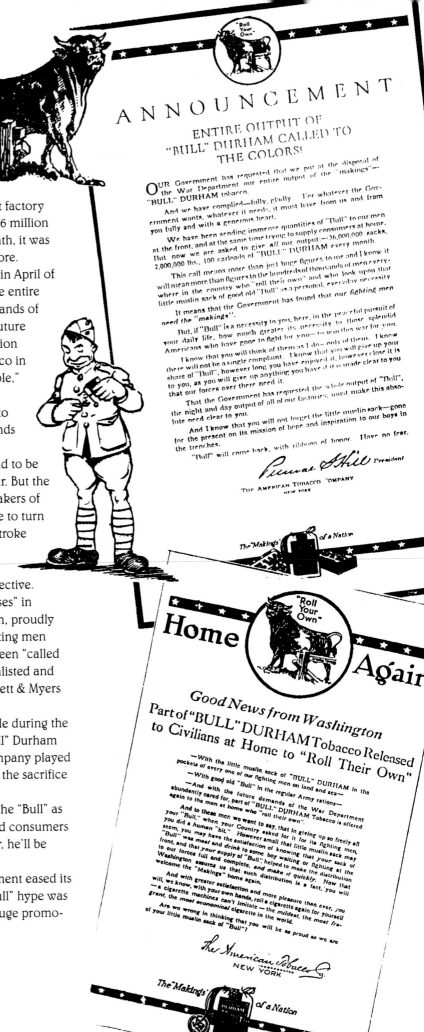

The funnelling of tobacco into military channels caused significant shortages in the civilian sector. Despite running day-and-night factory shifts and shipping 100 boxcars loaded with 36 million sacks of "Bull" Durham to the front each month, it was still not enough – the government wanted more.

So, without warning, federal authorities, in April of 1918, swooped down and commandeered the entire factory stores of "Bull" Durham and staple brands of other manufacturers, then requisitioned all future production. Reasons for the high-handed action were vague. "We need cigarette rolling tobacco in areas where cigarettes are not readily available," was the official explanation. Orders were simultaneously issued to the manufacturers to temporarily halt advertising of the same brands in order to reduce domestic demand.

Under the circumstances, such lumps had to be taken in stride by tobacco men in time of war. But the resourceful American Tobacco Company, makers of the popular "Bull" Durham tobacco, was able to turn a calamity into a windfall through a masterstroke of marketing genius.

They didn't advertise "Bull" Durham per se, in compliance with the government's directive. Instead they published periodic "news releases" in newspapers and magazines across the nation, proudly informing the smoking public that "our fighting men need the makings" and that the "Bull" had been "called to the colors." And indeed, the "Bull" had enlisted and gone to war. So had Duke's Mixture but Liggett & Myers chose not to make a big deal out of it.

Considerable promotional hay was made during the seven-month period that production of "Bull" Durham was taken over. The American Tobacco Company played up the mistaken notion that they had made the sacrifice willingly, and with patriotic intent.

Nonetheless the public took a shine to the "Bull" as he snorted, "So long, but not good-bye," and consumers found comfort in the assurance, "Never fear, he'll be back covered with medals of honor."

Finally, in November, 1918, the government eased its control but not before one last round of "Bull" hype was fired off. The entire operation had been a huge promotional success.

BOOM AND BUST

While it was argued that tobacco played a small role in winning the war, there was little doubt that the war greatly benefitted some segments of the tobacco industry.

The number of factory-made cigarettes produced during the fiscal year ending June, 1918, was 37 billion, six billion more than had ever been made before. Also, there was a large increase in the cultivation of the weed itself. North Carolina, in 1918, harvested over 242 million pounds of tobacco which was 38 million pounds more than that grown the previous year.

But it was not a bed of roses for everyone in the tobacco business during the war. Many dealers felt a severe economic pinch brought on by the conflict, namely, shortages of material, manpower and tobacco. Some were forced to close their shops.

Business in Turkish cigarettes, in full bloom before the war, suffered a mighty blow. The hostilities in Asia Minor, site of cultivation of the tobacco, cut sharply into production. Importation of Turkish leaf in the United States, four million pounds in 1914, fell drastically to 40,000 pounds a year later. The supply shrunk even smaller.

Manufacturers smart enough to anticipate supply problems stockpiled Turkish tobacco in neutral European depots to sustain manufacturing operations. Others with shorter foresight ran out of tobacco.

The final blow was administered by the U. S. government. To ensure fairness, purchase contracts for cigarettes were based on pre-war shares of the domestic market. Camel cigarettes, enjoying 30-40 percent of national sales, was the nation's number one seller. Consequently, billions of them, more than any other brand, were shipped to France and many a doughboy came home a dedicated Camel smoker.

Tobacco manufacturers were proud of their contributions of cigarettes to the war effort. Despite the ballyhooed millions of Liggett & Myers' Fatimas, a pure Turkish tobacco cigarette at the time, shipped to France to help fight the war, the numbers paled in comparison to those of the new domestic blend cigarettes, Camels and Lucky Strikes, which really "won the war." They also hooked countless American fighting men on the cigarette habit.

THE LAST HURRAH

A vigorous ad campaign was run in 1918 by the Lorillard company to save their Turkish cigarette brands hit hard by the war. In spite of stirring martial themes and catchy slogans, the bottom dropped out of this specialty market, done in by the rapidly rising popularity of domestic cigarettes. It didn't help either when Lorillard was forced to increase prices on these already costly smokes during the war.

THE SMOKE CONSUMER

DON'T SMOKE

IT'S WICKED

OUR WOMEN
DON'T LIKE IT

PART III
A NATION STANDS UP
TO TOBACCO

St. Louis Globe Democrat (1911)

WAR IS DECLARED ON CIGARETTES

THE GREAT ANTI-TOBACCO MOVEMENT (1893-1927)

It was a curious twist of fate. A nation that for decades tolerated the spittoon in business offices and the corridors of Congress, and the same nation that presented 11,000 cigars to General Grant after one of his Civil War victories, suddenly turned against the cigarette.

For the first time in history, businessmen, clergymen, temperance leaders, and legislators joined hands in a crusade to drive the slender rolls of tobacco from America. Beginning in the 1880s, banks and railroads prohibited cigarettes – but permitted cigars. For the next three decades, reformers, evangelists and churches denounced cigarette smoking as a form of moral turpitude.

Puffing their long Captain Marryats and Lillian Russells, men of importance solemnly declared the soul- and mustache-destroying cigarette a thing of evil. Rumors spread. Cigarettes were doped with opium, people whispered, the better to hook young folks with, and the paper wrappers were not safe, either; they contained arsenic.

The use of cigarettes, unlike a stylish pipe or a majestic cigar, was looked upon as a debasement of manhood, a pastime indulged in by sissies. Between the lips of a woman, a cigarette was regarded as a badge of the stage adventuress, or certainly one inclined to "the Bohemian persuasion."

A youth seen smoking was most assuredly heading for a life of crime, that is, unless "cigarette insanity" did not seize him first. An encyclopedia of medical horrors due to smoking awaited the unwary and the unwise.

How a nation so fond of tobacco, people wondered, allowed the cigarette to gain a respectable foothold in society remained a mystery.

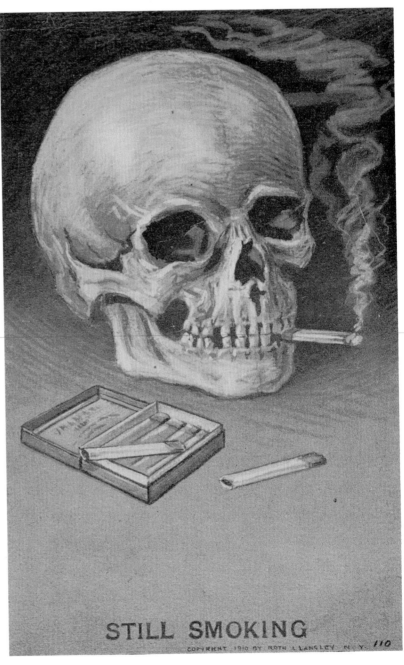

STILL SMOKING

COPYRIGHT 1910 BY ROTH & LANGLEY N. Y.   110

By the 1890s, general public opinion held that cigarettes, because the smoke was inhaled, were more harmful than other forms of tobacco. They also posed a serious threat to certain young people, described once by a Chicago judge as being of "weak and immature mind," who were irresistibly drawn to them.

192

TARGETING CIGARETTES

Voices of reform, by the turn of the century, had turned on tobacco and cigarettes were singled out for special attack. States passed laws prohibiting the barter, sale or giving away of cigarettes and cigarette papers, and, in some cases, storage of the articles in places of business. These restrictive ordinances found widespread support as the longstanding flow of anti-tobacco propaganda, running hot and heavy, finally permeated the mind of a nation.

The great anti-tobacco movement that arose in America in the 1890s and for the next three decades waged a fierce war on cigarettes was truly a freak of history. While scoring an impressive list of legislative triumphs, there was, in the end, little to show for the hard work done by the campaigners.

Tobacco fighters in the early days were an unorganized ragtag lot and most could be found in the ranks of temperance and suffrage groups. Organizations like the Anti-Saloon League, founded in 1894, and the Women's Christian Temperance Union which opened lobbying offices in Washington, D.C., in 1895, grew to exercise great political power. The groups stirred the national conscience and made demands of lawmakers for drastic social change. Alcohol and suffrage stood highest on their agendas, but the issue of tobacco rode closely behind.

By 1900, anti-tobacco agitators had grown into a large but loose-knit force composed of church and civic organizations, Sunday school groups, educators, the Y.M.C.A., and women's clubs. Largest of all was the National Anti-Cigarette League, a financed branch of the W.C.T.U. formed in 1899. It boasted of hundreds of thousands of members nationwide but its influence basically boiled down to a single person, the founder and outspoken banner carrier, Lucy Page Gaston of Chicago.

Small but well organized and wielding a surprisingly loud voice was the Methodist Episcopal church. This group, acting through its Board of Temperance, Prohibition and Public Morals, remained faithful fighters for decades and constantly lobbied for laws prohibiting cigarettes.

The marriage of social causes – suffrage, temperance and tobacco – proved highly effective and mutually beneficial. Early anti-cigarette statutes often followed on the heels of those prohibiting liquor.

Shock troops. *An advance guard of the W. C. T. U.'s "White Ribboners," in full battle array, pose for a quick curbside photo. These no-nonsense crusaders made the lives of lawmakers miserable as they crowded legislative offices and demanded sweeping anti-cigarette statutes.*

But it was an uphill battle all the way. When it came to tobacco, many legislators were reluctant to enact anti-cigarette decrees, knowing full well that such action cut into much needed tax revenue. These fence-riding politicians, however, proved relatively easy targets for hordes of feminine activists who crowded their offices and pressed for laws against the cigarette. On the heels of "this-or-nothing" reformers came men of the cloth, school teachers and leaders of civic, youth and women's clubs, making the same demands. The impact (and political pressure) was overpowering.

TOBACCO REFORM SWEEPS THE NATION

Next to election bills and tax initiatives, measures directed at outlawing the manufacture and sale of cigarettes occupied most state legislatures during the winter of 1900. The Chicago Tribune reported the next year that only two states, Wyoming and Louisiana, had not given any attention to enacting such a law. Eleven states had already done so, and the list was growing rapidly.

Massachusetts, on May 8, 1901, passed a law forbidding the sale or gift of cigarettes to any person under 18 years of age. Another act passed later that year covered snuff and other forms of tobacco. More than 30 states had now adopted similar laws, some making the age as low as 16.

THE WAR ON THE CIGARETTE

TOBACCO BANNED BY PRESBYTERIANS

Southern Assembly Opposes Use by Ministers and ch Officials — North Assembly for Grape ce at Communion.

Kansas City, May 27.—The general ssembly of the Presbyterian church in he United States (southern) went on record late today as opposed to the use of tobacco among clergymen, candidates for the ministry and church officials.

Rev. J. S. Lyons, Louisville, Ky., retiring moderator, recommended on behalf of the committee on bills and overtures, that the assembly reply in the negative to an overture that it should discourage tobacco.

ANTI-CIGARETTE LAW FOR GEORGIA

House Yesterday Passed the Bill by Large Majority.

ATLANTA, Ga., July 27.—(Special.) The anti-cigarette bill by Mr. Porter of Floyd, passed the house of representatives Thursday afternoon by the overwhelming majority of 107 to 9. The bill prohibits the manufacture, sale or distribution of cigarettes or cigarette material in Georgia. Violations of the anti-cigarette bill shall punishable as a misdemeanor

A Scene in a Tobacco Field.

law, which prohibits not along the selling of cigarettes to children less than sixteen years old, but makes it a misdemeanor to sell any kind of tobacco to youngsters. The law also makes it a misdemeanor for children to smoke in public places.

Violation of the law on the part of a merchant is made punishable by a fine not exceeding $300, and by imprisonment for not more than 100 days, though if the fine be unpaid, the offender may be imprisoned for as many days as he owes dollars. Children may be fined for smoking, though they cannot be imprisoned, even though they do not pay the fine.

As a matter of fact, the law is not well enforced. The big dealers obey it, but the smaller ones don't. In the poorer districts of the city are thousands of places where children can go and buy two cigarettes for a cent or as many more as they are able to pay for. If the dealer is caught, he

BAN

TOBAC CAN

DEA

W

bad money, Good ad most other to take it. to it

500,000,000 Cigarettes a Year Is the Problem tes Are Now Fighting

THE CIGARETTE FIEND.

OH! SEE THE SALLOW LOOKING WRECK,
OBSERVE HIS ONLY DIET;
AND THIS IS WHAT YOU'RE COMING TO,
WHY DON'T YOU PROFIT BY IT.

F. L. 373

make for effi competition became fierce e South found this out. That Drinking didn't pay. Sobri y. Hurrah for sobriety! ems like a pretty pulseless rality and high-mindedness. is. But it works where the didn't work. And the effect individual who is prevented

isconsin meant business and led the ssion. Wisconsin and the whole usually mean business, whether cigarettes or tariff that is before ouse. Cl were put in the class—e few m simil a with a and N whole an i aw r no r. ax um y se tual. iness wa ring. Business was d in its discrimination se who smoked the things ed with business. Men with ngers and thus became ore conscious of th hunting they c

business was h lislature. Some ho rohibiting the ma ure of cigarettes in Nobody smiled. Such legislatio passed the joke stage. The wisd the few had dribbled down into m rity. Therefore, a majority was easily counted in both houses. The Governor approved, and on July 1 the law became effective. Iowa had crushed out the cigarette, precisely as she had crushed out the legal sale of liquor— not because she listened to the plea of reformers, but because she heeded the commands of business.

Oklahoma Has Anti-Cigarette Bill.

OKLAHOMA CITY, Feb. 13.—A bill was introduced in the Oklahoma House yesterday making the use of tobacco in any form by minors a misdemeanor and the sale, advertisement or distribution of cigarettes w the State limits a felony.

NEW ANTI-CIGARETTE LAW.

Gov. Johnson Signs a Sweeping Measure Passed in Minnesota.

ST. PAUL, Minn., April 14.—Gov. Johnson today signed the Anti-Cigarette bill, which makes it a misdemeanor to manufacture, sell, or give ettes or cigarett lobber

Eight States, Through Their Legislatures, Have Taken Action to Prevent Its Sale

ANTI-CIGARETTE LAW SIGNED BY GOVERNOR

New Measure Makes It gal to Sell or Give T bacco to Minors.

CIGARET MEA

MAYOR SWIFT SIGNS FOR $100 IAC

Executive's Name Is A

THE SMOKER

Fitznoodle smoked a cigarette
Bigger than a cane;
All the fire went to his nose,
The ashes to his brain.

How would you like to be sausage or fish?
Smoked to a finish to make a good dish?
You smoked human being, you'll die in your tracks
If you don't give up smoking those old coffin tacks.

NEW REGULATION

as Students Must of Pipes, Cigars Speculation as to ty Members Who

MILWAUKEE P BAN ON CI

(BY ASSOCIATED PRESS
MILWAUKEE, Wis

ERY time I smoke a cigarette I say— er, my God, to Thee

Kansas Bans Cigarette Advertising.
Special to The New York Times.
TOPEKA, Kan., Feb. 8.—The House

BARS CIGARETTES

Chief Moore Issues an Order Prohibiting Employes to Indulge in the Habit.

HOUSE BARS CIGARETTES

CROSS BILL TO OUTLAW "COFFIN-NAILS" PASSES, 98 TO 22.

Measure Prohibits Men Carrying "Pills" or Having "Makings" and Papers, as Well as Manufacture or Sale in

POLICE TO ENFORCE THE TOBACCO

Cigarettes Must Not Be Sold to Children of Brooklyn.

ANTI-CIGARETTE MEASURE GIVEN HEARTY APPROVAL

DRASTIC CIGARETTE LAW.

Wisconsin Would Bar the Sale, Gift, or Importation.

MADISON, Wis., March 17.—A drastic anti-cigarette bill previously passed by the Assembly was passed by the Senate to-day

VIGOROUS ATTACK ON THE CIGARETTE

Aggressive Campaign Planned by Fighters Against "Coffin Nail"—Many Clubs Organized in Sunday Schools

ANTI-SMOKING LAW IN EFFECT MONDAY

THE ENEMY OF MANKIND

Legislative hammering of cigarettes also took place in Wisconsin and Indiana in 1904. These two states, however, did not need anti-cigarette laws as much as others. More white rolls, for instance, were going up in smoke each year on New York City's east side than in these two states combined.

By 1907, Wisconsin, Oklahoma, Nebraska, and Arkansas enacted no-cigarette laws. Washington state instituted a regulation prohibiting the sale of cigarettes, but just before it became law, two enterprising dealers in Tacoma sold off $200 worth of tobacco goods to the highest bidders in a street auction.

A monster petition, yards long and signed by thousands of Southern California voters, was carried to the state capitol in Sacramento in March, 1913, by members of the W. C. T. U. It urged legislators to immediately pass an anti-cigarette bill. Endorsements of the petition were hearty. Said the State Superintendent of Public Instruction: "Stamp the cigaret out of existence and give the boy a chance. It is the curse of the boy's body, mind and soul, the bane of society and the enemy of mankind."

On July 7, 1907, Illinois made it a misdemeanor to smoke cigarettes in public places. Retailers scurried about and divested themselves of their smoking stock, offering bargain prices and giving away fistfuls of premiums.

The activities led an editor of the New York Times to remark that it was unimaginable to think of Chicago without cigarette smokers. He also wondered how the city treasury was going to make up the $75,000 lost each year in business licenses sold to tobacco dealers. Six months later, the Illinois law was repealed.

The states of Iowa, Michigan, Minnesota, Missouri, Nebraska, Wisconsin, Indiana, and Illinois, by August, 1909, had passed laws prohibiting the sale or manufacture of cigarettes.

In the midst of this wild wave of reform, it was interesting to note that anti-cigarette bills secured the support of many legislators who were not only veteran users of the weed, but who were generally opposed to restrictive legislation of any kind.

Cigarettes were attracting as much national attention as liquor and the long string of legislative successes did much to buoy the hopes of the anti-tobacco forces.

YOUR CIGARETTE OR YOUR JOB: A NEW WEAPON

The best reformer was not necessarily a reformer. A vital boost to the anti-tobacco movement came from an unexpected quarter, American business, which stepped into the public picture around 1900 and for the next decade or so discriminated against the worker who smoked cigarettes.

Many railroads in the West and meat packing plants like Swift in Chicago demanded total abstinence from tobacco of their employees. Men under the age of 21 who smoked cigarettes could not find employment either at Wanamaker's department stores, Montgomery & Ward, or Sears, Roebuck & Co.

Company presidents were convinced that young men in their employment who were addicted to cigarettes were inefficient, that their nervous energies prevented concentration on work. It became customary for these same companies to not hire persons bearing yellow-stained fingers, the official badge of servitude to Lady Nicotine.

Businessmen simply gave the tobacco users a choice between cigarettes or their jobs; the call of the latter was usually the louder. Business didn't preach, it was said, it practiced.

ANTI - CIGARET POSTER GETS PRIZE
PRAISE LOS ANGELES BOY'S CARTOON

THE PRIZE-WINNING W. C. T. U. CARTOON AND ITS MAKER, MONT LOGAN

Sample of Youth's Work Will Be Exhibited at the
National W. C. T. U. Convention in Portland.
Evils of Smoking Habit are Depicted

THE ANTI-CIGARETTERS
GO TO WORK

In 1901, at the first meeting of the Anti-Cigarette League in Washington, D.C., President Willis Brown addressed an audience of 200 youngsters and informed them of the great strides the League had made. In the Midwest large merchant houses and offices were issuing orders forbidding their employees to smoke cigarettes and businessmen there were refusing to hire young men who smoked.

Brown asked the young ladies in attendance to urge their boy friends to abstain from the use of tobacco. Boys were encouraged to stand up and recite the "Clean Life Pledge" in unison; young ladies followed suit. The pledge read: "I do hereby pledge myself, upon honor, to abstain from smoking cigarettes or using tobacco in any form, at least until I reach the age of 21 years, and to use my influence to induce others to do the same." Initiates were then issued a special pin to wear.

After the yell of the League was shouted by the entire congregation and a hymn sung, the meeting adjourned. The yell went:

> "We have signed the pledge of freedom,
> On our honor bright;
> We are anti-cigaretters,
> We're the boys, all right!"

Within a week, the League had signed up over 1,000 new members.

Commander-in-Chief Brown also stressed that young ladies were not immune from the cigarette habit, either. His statement struck a familiar chord with teachers in the audience. One testified that 30 girls in her school were so addicted. It was difficult to detect smoking among females, the teachers admitted, because students removed telltale nicotine stains from their fingers with chemicals or smoked with cigarette holders – or wore gloves.

The director's work was not done yet. While anti-smoking regulations at school only applied to pupils during school hours and on school grounds, danger lurked just beyond the school yard. There the selling of cigarettes to minors by tobacco and candy store dealers, in direct violation of local ordinances, was widespread and contributed heavily to the smoking problem.

Lax law enforcement made it possible for a boy aged eight or ten to enter shops and purchase cigarettes without difficulty. It was a serious matter, Brown stated, which he intended to correct by reminding the police of their duties and prosecuting offending shop owners.

Brown's series of speeches galvanized the citizenry into action. More League branches sprang up in the metropolitan area. Local church groups and pastors promised full cooperation, as did many public school teachers, principals and superintendents. Expulsion of students who smoked was promised by the educators to prevent "contamination of others."

Parents caught their share of blame for the juvenile smoking problem. Brown admonished those adults who smoked, spared discipline or did not control the after-school whereabouts of their children.

True to his word, leader Brown, within a week of making his promise, had warrants for arrest served to 18 tobacco dealers, all of whom were charged with selling cigarettes and tobacco to minors. Principal witnesses were four youths under the age of 16 who visited the stores and made the tobacco buys without challenge.

The campaign was over. The nation's capital, as of 1901, was safely in the hands of the anti-cigarette army.

BAD AND BAD ONLY

Anti-tobacco crusaders received much-needed support from courts where judgments were made against lawsuits aimed at overthrowing or emasculating anti-cigarette laws.

A landmark decision was reached by the Tennessee Supreme Court in 1899. A tobacco dealer purchased cigarettes from a dealer in another state and sold a package to a customer in his shop in Tennessee. He was arrested, convicted and fined.

The dealer sued the state, contending that packs of cigarettes were articles of interstate commerce and beyond the state's jurisdiction, a legal loophole used with success in the past.

But not this time. The state high court upheld the statute in sharply pointed language:

> "Are cigarettes legitimate articles of commerce? We think they are not because they are wholly noxious and deleterious to health. Their use is always harmful, never beneficial. They possess no virtue but are inherently bad and bad only."

On appeal, a bitterly divided U. S. Supreme Court sided with the state's decision by a narrow margin. The federal justices ruled:

> "Without undertaking to affirm or deny their (cigarettes') evil effects, we think it within the province of the legislature...to prohibit their sale entirely."

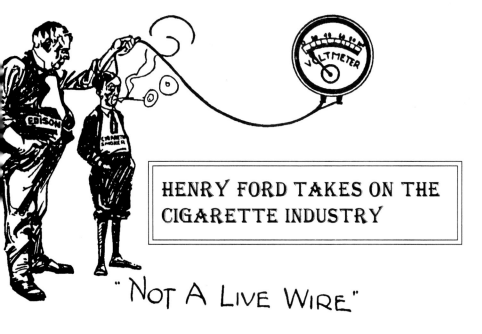

HENRY FORD TAKES ON THE CIGARETTE INDUSTRY

"Not A Live Wire"

In 1914, automobile tycoon Henry Ford, assisted by Thomas Edison, aimed a personal attack on cigarettes by publishing a book entitled "The Case Against the Little White Slaver." It was an extensive compilation of data condemning the physical and moral harm caused by the smoking of cigarettes, and was distributed free all over America in hopes of preventing spread of the habit among children.

The term "white slaver" was a contemporary one, used to define any young white woman unwantonly seduced into prostitution. The analogy to cigarettes was suitable as a title for Ford's four-volume encyclopedia.

The work also expostulated Edison's personal belief that the injurious agent in cigarettes did not arise from tobacco, but from the burning papers in which they were wrapped. Edison defined the toxic agent as acrolein and stated that the chemical had "a violent action on the nerve centers, producing degeneration of the cells of the brain, which is quite rapid among boys."

Based on Edison's experiments and conducting interviews of his own, Ford went on record by listing a litany of harms inflicted on the body by smoking cigarettes.

Ford's book caught the attention of Percival Hill, president of the American Tobacco Company. Hill moved to counteract the adverse publicity Ford was casting on the cigarette and issued Ford a challenge, asking for proof of his assertions. In a private letter dated May 16, 1914, Hill labeled Ford's statements erroneous and misleading and felt compelled to rebut them "in justice to the millions of intelligent men who use cigarettes."

"Scientific facts are all in favor of the cigarette," the tobacco man asserted. He cited numerous scientific studies conducted on the cigarette and its wrapper, alleging their safety and concluding that "the cigarette is absolutely pure...contains less nicotine than any other form of tobacco products...and its temperate use is in no way injurious to normal users."

According the Hill, proof rested with those with superior intelligence who chose to smoke cigarettes, "doctors, preachers, lawyers, bankers, business men, laboring men and men of all classes have deliberately turned from cigar and pipe to the cigarette," he claimed.

The clincher came at the end of Hill's letter: "the increase of cigarette smoking... which is growing all the time, is possible only because millions of American men have convinced themselves that cigarettes are good for them."

Ford's response to Hill's letter came from his quick-thinking secretary who, in Ford's absence, blunted Hill's wordy lance thrust in a brief, pithy note that ended with the question: "What beneficial result has ever been experienced by anyone through indulgence in this (cigarette) habit?"

The letter war between Hill and Ford ended at this point.

In 1900, cigarette smoking was banned among workers *at the National Weather Service in Washington, D.C. Those who chose to ignore the order, according to the bureau chief, would have their confidential personnel files so noted. The action grew from concerns that smoking was causing carelessness and laxity on the job. Likewise, in 1905, the sale of cigarettes at Ellis Island was halted, much to the disappointment of immigrants many of whom were devoted smokers. The Immigration Commissioner also discouraged cigarette use among employees.*

WHY ANTI-CIGARETTE LAWS DON'T WORK

LEGAL LOOPHOLES, POOR ENFORCEMENT AND MORALIZING LAWMAKERS

Anti-cigarette laws of the early 1900s looked good on paper, but didn't work out well and were doomed to failure, almost from the start.

Legal snags popped up right away. Legislators, in their zeal to put teeth into the measures, made the language so restrictive of the rights of tobacco dealers and manufacturers that when the statutes were appealed to courts of law, they were declared unconstitutional. Many anti-cigarette laws in the early years bit the dust in this manner.

Graft, back-room conniving and political chicanery were ever-present dangers to the tobacco reform forces. An anti-cigarette bill was made into law in Tennessee in 1897. The next year, a state representative testified that he had been approached by a lawyer representing the American Tobacco Company and offered $500 to sponsor a new bill repealing the old. The tobacco company flatly denied the charge but the lawyer could not be found; he had left the country.

Sometimes no-cigarette bills contained "jokers," an antiquated term for amendments deliberately added to emasculate or dilute the weight of the law, either by design, accident or glaring oversight.

In 1907, six months after an anti-cigarette law went into effect, the Illinois Supreme Court declared it unconstitutional. The bill prohibited the sale of cigarettes but contained provisions not spelled out in its original title. As a result, the sale of "all-tobacco" cigarettes was not affected. Red-faced tobacco reformers promised immediate remedial action.

Legitimate objections were raised by many newspaper and magazine editors who rankled at the idea of politicians legislating morals. They branded lawmakers as "undemocratic" when the politicians attempted to regulate the habits of individuals by passing laws, and to exercise a political right to prohibit adults from harming themselves by smoking. The press predicted ineffective results and they proved right. They were also correct when they foresaw a public backlash to such ordinances.

Following the passage of an anti-cigarette law in Indiana in 1905, the editor of Outlook Magazine brought up the issue of citizens' rights:

"It is entirely legitimate for a democratic community to exercise whatever authority may be necessary over great organizations, whether of labor or capital, to prevent them from violating the rights of the individual. This is something different from exercising control over the rights of the individual which do not violate the rights of others, and from the injurious effects of which he is the chief if not the only sufferer. Such an act as this...does much more harm than it can possibly do good, for it tends to arouse the American spirit of independence against law, and so to promote the spirit of lawlessness."

The strongest alternative to prohibition of cigarettes was requiring dealers to post bonds which were forfeited and their licenses revoked if they were found guilty of selling smokes to minors. The idea, oddly, was opposed by most tobacco vendors who preferred to take their chances bootlegging cigarettes at exorbitant prices. It was worth the risk.

A few governments tried it, anyway. West Virginia imposed a bond of $500 on all cigarette vendors in 1893; the city of Denver levied one likewise, to the tune of $1,000. Both fees were found unconstitutional, however, and were removed from the books.

FUNNY BUSINESS IN INDIANA

Political meddling by the American Tobacco Company became a full-time business in the early 1900s, as the Trust attempted to extinguish the brushfires of anti-cigarette legislation flaring up around the country, by weight of largess, if not by legal argument.

A former Trust executive once reminisced: "A bill would be introduced to legislature to prohibit the manufacture or sale of cigarettes; it would be referred to a committee, and our people would have to get busy and pay somebody to see that it died."

This devious practice backfired occasionally with embarrassing results. In 1905, a clumsy attempt at bribery was uncovered in Indiana which left the Legislature no choice but to enact an anti-cigarette bill. During a house discussion prior to a vote on the measure, a member stood up on the floor and waved an envelope given to him by a tobacco trust lobbyist. As he opened the letter, out fluttered five $20 bills.

Responsible was a shadowy figure, Oscar A. Baker, who achieved immediate notoriety and a suitable nickname in the press, "Cigarette" Baker. A warrant was issued for his arrest on attempted bribery, but Baker fled the country. Four years later, apparently missing the U.S., he returned and surrendered to authorities.

Enacting anti-cigarette laws was one thing, enforcing them was another. The statutes were frequently ignored by the two most important parties concerned, the police and shop owners who sold cigarettes. Without their cooperation, the laws were meaningless words on paper. Business and laziness kept getting in the way.

One of the earliest anti-tobacco laws in the nation was passed by the Pennsylvania State Legislature in 1889. It forbade the selling of cigarette papers, tobacco and cigars to boys. Violators were guilty of a misdemeanor, to be punished by a fine not exceeding $300. It was never enforced.

Rhode Island and Ohio also enacted anti-cigarette laws in 1901 but police never enforced the statutes until a public outcry was raised.

A good example of official lethargy and roadblocking took place in Oakland, California, in 1898. The city council took a hard swipe at cigarettes by prohibiting their sale by dealers, and smoking by minors. Strangely, the law only applied to factory-made smokes; those rolled by hand were exempt.

Both the mayor and the council were aware that the unpopular statute would create chaos. Nicotine fiends would find devious ways to obtain their slender rolls of pleasure, one way or another. Bootlegging, the officials agreed, was a foregone conclusion.

Sure enough. Law-bending tobacco dealers erected false walls in their shops like New York City gin mills and clandestinely served their cigarette-smoking clientele.

Mark Twain was seldom seen without a calabash pipe or an expensive cigar in his mouth. He remarked wryly: "It has been my rule never to smoke when asleep and never to refrain when awake. It is a good rule."

Although smokes were not sold openly, many drug stores and pool halls had them available under the counters. Cigarettes, in the end, remained easy to find as laws were winked at.

Worse yet was instructing the police in their new duties. The Oakland police chief summoned his bluecoats and, after admonishing those who smoked, asked those who preferred ready-made cigarettes to roll their own henceforth, and then go out and arrest those smokers in public who didn't.

A law in 1893 made it a misdemeanor in New York City for any boy under 16 to smoke cigarettes in public, or to purchase them in shops. Tobacco dealers in the vicinity of schools continually flaunted the law by selling their goods to patrons of legal age who then re-sold them to smoking juveniles at school. The Brooklyn school board prodded police into upholding the law and arresting offending tobacco shop owners.

It was a scene repeated in just about every state and city in the nation with an anti-cigarette law in effect. Little or no cooperation could be expected from those who made a living selling the rolls of tobacco.

While most big dealers obeyed the laws, small operators thrived on finding ways to circumvent them. In the poorest districts of a city there were hundreds of places where children could buy cigarettes, two for a penny. More creative retailers sold a book of matches for twenty cents...and threw in a package of cigarettes for free.

LOST CAUSE

PORTRAIT OF LUCY PAGE GASTON

The archenemy of the cigarette and driving force of tobacco reform in the early 1900s was a frail, hollow-cheeked spinster of Chicago, Lucy Page Gaston. Devoting her life to banishing the "coffin nail" from the land, no reformer in America labored as tirelessly or as valiantly as she, yet had so little to show for it. Gaston's story capsulizes the early anti-tobacco movement in the U.S.

Born in Delaware, Ohio, in 1860, Lucy Page Gaston was the daughter of staunch abolitionist and prohibitionist parents. She grew up in a state already astir with iron petticoats and sharp feminine elbows. At the age of thirteen, she was not eyeing little boys over the top of her slate, she was teaching them Sunday school. At sixteen, Lucy, now a full-fledged schoolmarm, was busting their knuckles with a ruler.

Her career as a reformer began while a student at the Illinois State Normal School where she led raids on local saloons, gambling halls and tobacco shops. After ten years of teaching school, the war cries of Frances E.

Willard appealed to Lucy's senses. She laid aside her school duties and entered public life as a bonneted member of the Women's Christian Temperance Union.

In the late 1890s, Gaston took her act of reform on the road and visited neighboring states where she addressed school audiences and church groups, preaching the word of clean living and abstinence from intoxicating beverages and all forms of tobacco.

During this time, Lucy watched with increasing concern and disgust as the physical health and moral fiber of the nation's youth was being threatened by the ever-growing menace of tobacco. She soon quit her teaching job to devote full time to the monumental task of freeing America's cigarette slaves.

Realizing that the best way to battle the cigarette was through legislation, she haunted state capitols and city halls, buttonholing luckless lawmakers and demanding sweeping anti-cigarette statutes. Her program aroused public opinion, secured wealthy and influential sponsors, and forced balky legislators to outlaw the cigarette, not only for minors but for everybody.

After a few patient years of vigorous campaigning, Gaston's crusade caught on. Sponsored by the Chicago Board of Education, Lucy and a corps of recruited lecturers invaded Chicago schools and delivered words of reform in an ongoing program.

Eager ears, already attuned by the W.C.T.U., heard her pleas to organize leagues against the cigarette. Recruits wearing pins and badges took to the streets, singing songs and marching in parades. Before long, leagues were being formed throughout the Middle West.

Gaston's persistent lecturing outside Illinois began to bear fruit. Newspapers took up the hue and cry, some praising, some criticizing but all publicizing. Finally, just before Christmas in 1899, Gaston, with the financial backing of local businessmen, founded the Anti-Cigarette League in Chicago.

Within a week the new organization boasted a 100,000-plus membership, most of whom were prior converts, and branches of the organization sprang up from coast to coast. In two years, the number of members had swelled to a figure in excess of 300,000.

WORKING THE STREETS

Lucy Gaston became a familiar sight in Chicago police courts where she hauled in scores of dishonest tobacco dealers, guilty of selling cigarettes to minors, and had them prosecuted. Within six weeks, cigarette sales of one chain of tobacco stores in the Loop district fell off by an average of 8,500 cigarettes a day.

The gaunt Miss Gaston, wearing spectacles and rustling black dresses, patrolled Chicago's dingier streets and alleys in search of the boy with a cigarette. Spotting one, she accosted him with the words, "You're just the boy I'm looking for."

Swiftly and in graphic detail, she informed him where he was headed with his cigarette habit. Other boys gathered around. Pamphlets and tracts popped from her bulging handbag. The boys were invited to think things over but she refused to let them swear off on the spot.

After a boy was enticed to A.C.L. headquarters, memorized and signed the Clean Life Pledge and received the Clean Life button, he was saved. For, said Miss Gaston, "a boy is a great stickler for honor. Once he has signed the pledge, he would cut off his hand before he would break it."

Anti-tobacco pledge cards *were handed out to youngsters of all ages in church and in school.*

Through their nearest Sunday school, boys might also join the League and wear the A.C.L. pin. Many did. Buttons and pins appeared all over the country. Children loved them. They also loved jeering, with immunity, adult smokers on the streets, chasing them into sheltering trolley cars. Bolder spirits even snatched the defiling cylinders from the mouths of elderly men.

Miss Gaston spread the word. From her cluttered desk she edited "The Boy," the League's monthly house publication which reviewed the anti-tobacco field. She reported legislative progress and combined pep talks, sermons, anecdotes, children's features, and once a live dialogue between a cigarette and a bottle of whiskey, with much thought-provoking data gathered from the daily press, such as:

Daffy: "John Jones, aged 19, is very sick and at times acts very queer, caused by the excessive use of cigarettes." –Denver Post

Murderer: "Charles Burton, aged 17, is to be hanged for murder. He was a cigarette fiend." –New York Telegram

Jumped: "Elizabeth Scott, an inveterate cigarette smoker, jumped from a three-story window." –Boston Globe

In 1907, she carried her gospel to New York City, stating publicly that "American womanhood and childhood must be rescued from the cigarette peril." Gaston implored members of women's clubs to sign pledges that they would "with the help of God" cast off the cigarette habit.

By now, Gaston's purse had become legendary. The large black bag slung over her shoulder, like her career, was a jumbled mass of pamphlets, papers, loose change, graham crackers, and gentian root. She was incapable of keeping records or files. Money flowed through her fingers like water and the cause kept her constantly in debt.

Wherever she went, Lucy distributed the pamphlets which contained the organization's songs and yells, and the gentian root to chew on when the craving for cigarettes grew unbearable. "Remember gentian root," she would say, and then spell it out, letter by letter.

DISAPPOINTMENT AND DESPAIR

In the peak of her career, Lucy Gaston busied herself throughout the Midwest, carrying on a successful campaign of education and agitating for legislative reform against the cigarette. Directly or indirectly through her efforts, anti-cigarette laws were passed in 11 states by 1913.

In spite of her efforts and by her own admission, however, smoking in these same states where cigarettes were banned went on as usual and, in some cases, increased. While the anti-cigarette movement caused a temporary falling off in national consumption of cigarettes between 1897 and 1901, every legislative triumph and every bit of adverse publicity Gaston and her coworkers were able to score, seemed to act as a stimulant to cigarette sales. Record numbers were posted with each passing year.

The tobacco industry was curiously feasting on Gaston's hard work.

And then came the War. Crushed by the overwhelming response of the American public in sending tobacco and cigarettes to the fighting troops in France, Miss Gaston did her best to staunch the rapid loss of support her cause had once enjoyed.

Doggedly she drove on. The cigarette was a double menace in the trenches, she claimed, the glowing ash furnished the enemy with a target.

By the time the conflict ended, Gaston, heavily relieved, declared that "the War is over now, and the cigarette is once more a poison." But this time few were listening. Soldiers came home confirmed cigarette smokers. Women, too, were becoming more emancipated and jacking up the demand for cigarettes.

Several states, admitting that their prohibitory cigarette laws weren't working, repealed them, substituting statutes forbidding sales to minors. Miss Gaston had all her work to do over again.

"GASTONIZING" KANSAS

The devastating aftermath of World War I left little public support for Lucy Gaston's League. Although it looked like a hopeless cause, the gallant campaigner carried on. The old Carrie Nation-style of reform tactics, however, no longer worked. The post-war generation laughed off Gaston as a harmless old crank.

Seeing that new methods were in order, Gaston turned her attention away from adults and back to saving boys and girls from cigarettes. But she caused a host of trouble along the way.

Kansas was a good example. The reformers in that state had scored a major victory in 1917 when a previous law of 1909 was broadened to prohibit not only the sale of cigarettes, but the advertising of them as well. It had been sustained by the Kansas Supreme Court but was haphazardly enforced, a chronic problem facing anti-tobacco activists.

Gaston received reports that the Attorney General planned to investigate violations of the anti-cigarette law. A group of scofflaws in Atchison had each contributed a dime toward a fund to buy a carton of cigarettes which were sent to President-elect Harding.

That wasn't all. Some prominent women in Topeka and a local American Legion post had sent cigarettes to disabled soldiers in state hospitals. Both the gift and sale of cigarettes were technically illegal in Kansas.

Miss Gaston swept into the state in November, 1920, with the scope and might of a Great Plains tornado, immediately stirring up a hornet's nest as she moved swiftly to attend to the law's enforcement ("gastonizing," editors put it).

"We have put the ban on in Wichita, and it's going to be clamped down here," she announced upon her arrival in the state capitol, promising that there wouldn't be one cigarette for sale in town after she was through.

Her first move was to organize a branch of the Anti-Cigarette League in Topeka. Field workers pushed the organization in every county in the state.

"Down with cigarettes!" "Up with the A.C.L.!" came their battle cries.

Rallying support, Lucy caused the quick death of a proposed amendment seeking to revoke an existing anti-cigarette law. It came about as the result of pressure exerted by the American Legion on behalf of ex-service men who said they "would like the privilege as men to buy a package of cigarettes."

Gaston's vigorous and flamboyant work, however, was not appreciated by the local press who viewed the crusader's efforts as meddlesome and unwanted. They attacked her unmercifully.

Her work finished, Gaston left Kansas and headed for Iowa, leaving behind a storm of discord and controversy. Lucy was 60 years old now, set and demanding in her ways, and her methods were considered too drastic by many fellow workers.

The ax fell swiftly.

The Kansas chapter of the Anti-Cigarette League refused to pay Gaston any further salary ($25 per week), or pay bills incurred during her whirlwind campaign. The falling out was traced to a stink that arose over the publication of "Coffin Nails," Gaston's newly conceived official magazine which she planned to print in Topeka.

The Battle is On.
- From "The Boy," the official organ of the Anti-Cigarette League.

The Cigarette Must Go!

Kansas People Say So!

The Kansas Division of the International Anti-Cigarette League, Incorporated, wants

100,000 Members By Jan. 1st, 1921

And invites all in sympathy with the fight on the cigarette to enrol as members. Fee One Dollar, entitling the member to a year's free subscription to "The Smokeless Day", official organ of the International Anti-Cigarette League. If you are interested in stamping out this insidious menace to the Youth of America, send your membership today to the Treasurer---

Miss Lucy Page Gaston of Chicago, Founder and Superintendent of the International Anti-Cigarette League, is now in Kansas leading the fight. Miss Gaston is Editor of The Smokeless Day.

Kansas Anti-Cigarette League

918 Kansas Avenue, Topeka, Kansas

Do You Know?

That a Determined effort is being made to repeal the Kansas Anti-Cigarette law?

A call to arms. Gaston ran this newspaper ad to rally statewide support against a bill seeking to repeal Kansas' anti-cigarette law in effect since 1909. The League's new publication, "The Smokeless Day," never got off the ground; its title was considered "too weak" by W.C.T.U. leaders in Chicago.

The national headquarters in Chicago, catching wind of her latest brainstorm and fast growing intolerant of her headstrong ways, refused to approve the new magazine and also cut off her funds.

In short, Lucy Gaston was canned.

THE LAST ROUND

The indefatigable warhorse, however, was not down and out yet. She resigned from the head of the Anti-Cigarette League on August 26, 1921, and set up a new one, the *National* Anti-Cigarette League. With "Save the Girl" as her slogan, and "Abolition of the Cigarette in America by 1925" as her goal, she again pressed the battle of reform forward.

But Lucy's time was growing short. Deprived of income and dependent on the aid of relatives, she lived from hand to mouth. Money was now hard to come by and every cent was spent on the cause. Her mother, in her nineties, continued to applaud her daughter's spirit and encourage her militant methods.

In August, 1924, the reformer was struck by a streetcar in Chicago. She was admitted to a hospital, gravely ill. During her stay, doctors discovered that she had terminal cancer of the throat.

Gaston died on August 20, 1924. Her will stipulated that no flowers be sent to her funeral. Instead, she asked her mourners to make donations to the Anti-Cigarette League. Lucy was faithful to the end.

Only a handful of people attended her funeral. Four children were present who, in the middle of the service, stood up and, pointing at Gaston's coffin, said, "Miss Gaston, we thank you for what you have done for us." Then they recited the Clean Life Pledge.

Lucy Gaston, the tireless campaigner, was gone.

The consumption of cigarettes in the United States in 1924, the year of her death, had increased fifty-fold since 1899, the year Miss Gaston founded the Anti-Cigarette League.

LOSING POWER
SUPPORT FADES FOR THE ANTI-CIGARETTE MOVEMENT

World War I loaded and sealed the coffin of the anti-cigarette movement in America. A roll of drums, the strains of "Over There," the tramp of marching feet, and the patient work of nearly two decades of reform went swiftly down the drain. Enemies of nicotine were trampled in the public's mad rush to prepare cigarettes for shipment overseas while the nation was singing, "While you've a lucifer to light your fag, smile, boys, that's the style."

But not all were silenced. Dr. Clarence True Wilson, head of the Methodist church's Temperance and Moral Board, charged that the tobacco industry had taken advantage of American patriotism and supplied cigarettes so full of dope that soldiers were becoming drug addicts.

Frances Beauchamp, a prohibitionist, attacked the Red Cross and the federal government for sending smokes to soldiers, claiming the agencies were "unwittingly the tools of the American Tobacco Company."

Feelings grew so strong that, in retaliation, one champion of tobacco wondered if the Espionage Act was broad enough to apply to anyone who had the audacity to suggest that cigarettes were "bad" for soldiers.

THE TOBACCO WAR THAT NEVER CAME

"Prohibition Won – Now for Tobacco!" shouted evangelist Billy Sunday in 1919. His words rang out loud and clear as temperance groups across the country rejoiced with the passage of the Nineteenth Amendment, imposing prohibition of liquor on an unwilling nation.

These words came as good news to the anti-tobacco crusaders whose campaign had ground to a virtual halt while the United States helped fight the war in Europe. Prohibition signaled the possibility of resuming the battle against the other evil in America, cigarettes.

Strong evidence of a renewed fight took form immediately. Anti-smoking literature hit the mails with greater regularity; so did a rush of advertised tobacco "cures."

Newspaper headlines rang with the words: "Nicotine Next!" or "A Tobaccoless World by 1925!"

Prohibition of liquor was now an accomplished fact. The vast amounts of reform energy dumped on the sociological market by temperance activists led everyone to fully expect the momentum gained by the prohibitionists to shift over and join the drive on tobacco.

It was a natural thing to expect. Tobacco shared many of the same arguments raised with alcohol. Liquor did no one any good; neither did tobacco. The human labor expended in the making of liquor served no useful purpose; the same was true with tobacco. Liquor was not healthy for the human body; tobacco, it was generally assumed, posed the same dangers, especially in women and children.

Many people believed that eliminating tobacco would be easier than it had been with alcohol. But the fight against liquor had apparently sapped the strength of the reformers and the public. Both parties were exhausted and needed a break – and certainly smokers were not interested in being reformed.

The first sign of trouble in the reform ranks began when the powerful Anti-Saloon League announced in May, 1919, that it "would not make any campaign against tobacco." Andrew Volstead, author of the liquor prohibition amendment, later added: "I am not interested in any anti-smoking movement." The departure of the saloon-fighters proved a powerful blow to the anti-tobacco cause.

"MOTHER" LEADS THE FIGHT

Opposition to cigarettes and smoking in the 1920s was largely shouldered by the Women's Christian Temperance Union. "Mother," the Anti-Saloon League nicknamed this group which it had served so faithfully in the fight against liquor. From its bitter experiences fighting Lady Nicotine, the W.C.T.U. had become street-smart and battle-wise. They had learned all too well the futility and anguish of orchestrating passage of anti-cigarette laws only to watch them fail. Tactics had to be changed.

Overriding a small but vocal minority within their ranks, the temperance leaders now stressed education, not legislation. This change in battle strategy was carefully calculated. A better informed American public no longer considered tobacco a "demon" as it had with liquor. Those hysterical days were over. Even at its worst, tobacco did not "sharpen the parricidal axe" or "start the orphan's tears."

Consequently, the W.C.T.U.'s headquarters in Frances Willard's cozy little cottage in Evanston, Illinois, became the nation's center of anti-tobacco propaganda as thousands upon thousands of pieces of literature were mailed out daily denouncing the evils of tobacco.

To boost waning public interest, temperance leaders dispelled longstanding rumors that it was seeking another constitutional amendment, the so-called "Twentieth Amendment." They knew better. Neither did they make war against smoking by men, nor did they express disapproval of tobacco chewing.

Soft-peddling demands, the temperance group continued to support legislation banning the sale of tobacco to minors, secured no-smoking pledges from youngsters, sponsored anti-tobacco essay contests in high schools, condemned cigarette smoking by women, and hammered away at the physical dangers of smoking. Scouring the streets, W.C.T.U. members picked up and crushed to pieces discarded cigarette and cigar butts (they proudly kept track of the numbers) to remove temptation from the paths of the young.

Still joined in the anti-tobacco fight were the now-thinned ranks of church, civic and women's clubs, as well as the shattered remains of Lucy Gaston's old legion of followers. This once

A well-known cigar-smoking figure on Capitol Hill was "Uncle Joe" Cannon, *longtime Speaker of the House. He is shown here doing what he liked best at the age of 86 and, tobacco proponents were proud to report, in robust health.*

mammoth organization was renamed the Anti-Cigarette Alliance and was nursed along in Washington, D.C., by Dr. Kress, the untiring physician who took over the reins following Gaston's fall from grace.

Following the example set by the Governor of Arkansas who proclaimed March 22, 1922, as "No-Tobacco Day," Dr. Kress staged "Clean Life Week" the next month in the nation's capitol and asked for abstinence from cigarettes.

But the reformers' efforts were wasted. World War I had done much to break down the prejudice against cigarettes, and the well-publicized vices of the "Roaring Twenties" finished off the job. Many youngsters in their teens at the dawn of Prohibition remembered well the imploring words of their parents: "You can smoke cigarettes if you don't touch bootleg booze."

That sentence epitomized the cigarette's ascent to virtue. Enjoying the economic boom of the '20s, Americans took to cigarettes in ever-increasing numbers, driving up consumption to record highs each year.

MR. BLOCH SPEAKS OUT

Those who enjoyed smoking did not take the campaign against them laying down. In 1919, the Allied Tobacco League of America was formed in Cincinnati by tobacco manufacturers and public supporters. This militant group made no bones about their purpose. "We are not going to sit idly by and see a wonderful industry destroyed by meddling women," a spokesman proclaimed in response to continued threats posed by the W.C.T.U. He added that speakers would soon tour the country and pass out tons of pro-smoking literature.

Jesse Bloch, prominent tobacco manufacturer of Wheeling, West Virginia, addressed a meeting of the Tobacco Merchants Association in May, 1923. He warned the congregation of the dangerous influence being spread by anti-tobacco crusaders who Bloch stated planned on "burying tobacco in the same grave as John Barleycorn."

He went on to say: "Every attack on tobacco brings forth an additional flood of scientific authority testifying to the harmlessness of tobacco. But while our victory in the recent anti-tobacco war has been almost complete, the menace has not yet passed, and it is not likely to pass so long as professional agitators are able to pass their hats and collect the coin."

THE 1920S

THE ANTI-CIGARETTE MARCH GRINDS TO A HALT

In 1921, an industry tally sheet showed that 92 measures affecting smokers were pending in the legislatures of 28 states. But now, for the anti-tobacco reformers, things were different. They had just entered a new age of rapidly declining public support and sympathy.

Soldiers returning home from the war opened a powerful attack on anti-cigarette laws. Their lobbying was credited with the repeal of a statewide ban on cigarettes in Iowa in 1921.

There were other problems, too. Moderate elements of society, notably the press, found the voices of anti-cigaretters too strident and too exaggerated to believe, driving credibility of the crusaders to an all-time low.

The situation was not helped when scientists remained in a medical muddle over the cigarette's threat to health. Researchers were unsure and lacked agreement. Trying to distinguish smokers from non-smokers on the basis of mental efficiency and physical coordination, they came up with conflicting and meaningless results.

Credibility grew worse when, in 1927, medical extremists in Michigan claimed that 60% of all babies born of cigarette-smoking mothers died before the age of two, presumably due to "nicotine poisoning." Such outlandish reports were ignored, even by medical peers.

NO SMOKING IN THE NATION'S CAPITOL

In 1921, two legislative salvoes against cigarettes were fired off in Washington, D.C. First to attack was Reed Smoot. In January, the Republican senator from Utah introduced a bill prohibiting smoking in all buildings belonging to the executive branch of the government (judicial and legislative offices were oddly exempted).

Smoot's action was prompted by a fire caused by a cigarette that destroyed some census records. The proposed law meant, among other things, that President Harding, a confirmed cigarette puffer, would not be permitted to light up in the White House.

The no-smoking ordinance was roundly defeated in the House, the majority of the representatives being smokers.

Later that year, Representative Paul Johnson of Mississippi, offended at the sight of a young woman taking a drag off her boyfriend's cigarette, sponsored a bill fining women who smoked on the streets of the nation's capitol. "Worse than whiskey," Johnson called the vile habit and added that Washington women smoked too much anyway.

The self-righteous lawmaker found little support and his bill, too, ended up on the Congressional scrap heap.

ROUNDUP AT THE HOTEL UTAH

A celebratory confrontation between the cigarette and its foes took place on the shores of the Great Salt Lake in 1921. It started in March when the state legislature, upon the urging of the Utah Anti-Cigarette League and church officials, passed a law prohibiting the sale of tobacco and smoking in public places. A 90-day grace period was granted for dealers to dispose of their wicked wares.

The law, however, was poorly enforced; trade in tobacco went on as usual. One enterprising cigar store owner in Salt Lake City stocked his smoking supplies in a nearby laundry and conducted business there by special arrangement.

All ran smoothly until trouble was stirred up in 1923 by a Salt Lake City sheriff who happened to be head of the No-Tobacco League of Utah. The crusading lawman led a series of raids on cigar stores, confiscated smoking stocks and arrested scores of guilty proprietors.

On February 21, 1923, the sheriff, heading a posse of deputies, swooped down on the grill room of the fashionable Hotel Utah. There he arrested a handful of local luminaries including the city's war hero and manager of a city newspaper. Anti-tobacco activists rejoiced as the malefactors were hauled off to jail.

The furor caused by this highly unpopular act was so strong that the Governor, two months later, signed into law a bill repealing the anti-cigarette statute.

FINAL SHOWDOWN IN KANSAS

The last bastion of national tobacco reform came tumbling down in 1927. Kansas, for twenty years, possessed one of the most stringent anti-cigarette laws in the nation, but its enforcement was haphazard.

Although the sale of cigarettes (their advertising, too) was outlawed, they were readily available. The smokes were not sold openly but many drug stores and pool halls hid cartons under their counters.

William Allen White, passing through Topeka in 1924, chided local police officials for failing to uphold the cigarette ban.

Veterans of the war, returning home to Kansas, complained vehemently about the anti-cigarette law. They tried in 1920 and again in 1923 to force its repeal, but failed. Responding to the crises, the W.C.T.U. and church groups sounded a call to arms and flooded state legislators with petitions and, on roll calls, successfully defeated repeal measures.

In 1927, the stage was set once more for another showdown between the warring parties. In response to angry demands of the American Legion, a new bill was introduced, calling for repeal of the old law. It advocated the licensing of dealers, prohibition of sales of cigarettes to minors and a special rider calling for a two-cents-a-package surtax to finance the state road building fund.

"Bait for the unwary!" anti-tobacco forces cried out as they rankled at the true intent of the rider. The bill passed, however, and was signed into law on February 3, 1927, and, with it, the anti-cigarette movement in America essentially passed into history.

There was widespread rejoicing in the Sunflower State as newspaper editors rushed to apply their personal epitaphs to the nicotinophobic era in Kansas.

"Cigarets, for twenty years outlawed in Kansas," one editor crowed, "are now a perfectly legitimate solace for adults, and papers outside that State satirically congratulate Kansas grown-ups on their new freedom. In Kansas itself, to judge from a telegraphic poll of leading State papers, there is considerable relief over the repeal of a law that made cigaret smokers statute breakers and patrons of bootleggers."

THE GAY DECEIVER

From the Topeka State Journal (1927)

AN ORGY OF BUNCOMBE

Reed Smoot, senator from Utah, kept up his sniping attacks on the U. S. cigarette industry. In 1929, he proposed legislation placing tobacco under the supervision of the Pure Food & Drug Act, and asked that all tobacco advertising be subject to the same regulations as patent medicines. He also had strong words for the cigarette marketeers:

"Not since the days when the vendor of harmful nostrums was swept from our streets has this country witnessed such an orgy of buncombe, quackery and downright falsehood and fraud as now marks the current campaign promoted by certain cigarette manufacturers to create a vast women and child market for the use of their product. I try to denounce the insidious cigarette campaigns now being promoted by those tobacco interests whose only god is profit, whose only bible is the balance sheet, whose only principle is greed."

Utah's enemy of the cigarette, Senator Reed Smoot.

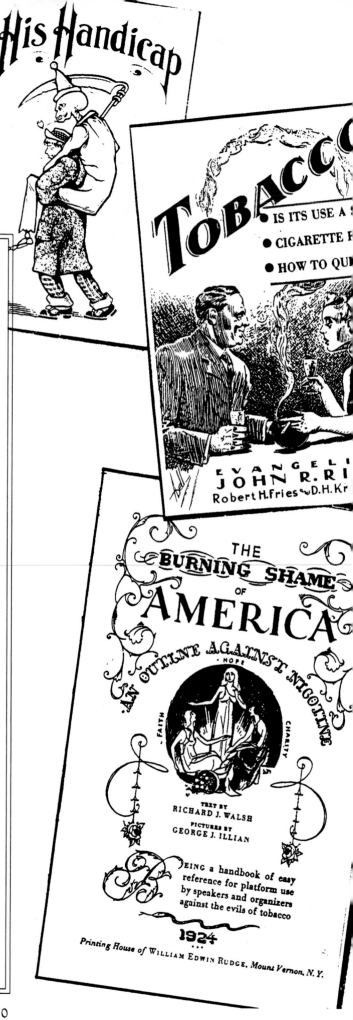

TOBACCO REFORM GOES OUT OF STYLE

Although reduced to ineffectual levels of social and political clout, tobacco reform never went out of style. From the 1920s through the 1950s, nihilistic evangelists could be found around the country preaching anti-tobacco gospel.

For a short time, some groups held out great hope. Dr. Charles Pease, a feisty reformer and head of the Non-Smokers Protective League in New York City, enjoyed good press in 1923 as he readied his mighty 3,000 member army for a national assault calling for "legislation that will prohibit the growth, importation, and sale of tobacco." The attack never materialized.

Dr. Kress' Anti-Cigarette Alliance continued to wage a feeble but valiant battle against smoking well into the 1940s. The organization advocated the abolishment of coffin nails and offered smokers a choice of "cures" which included swallowing doses of Rochelle salts and cream of tartar, taking frequent Turkish baths or, Lucy Gaston's favorite, chewing gentian root.

The group also cited lurid medical "facts." Dr. Raymond Smith, vice-president of the Alliance, told in 1929 how three leeches dropped dead when attached to the arm of a cigarette smoker.

The No-Nicotine Alliance of Illyria, Illinois, churned out tons of anti-smoking literature. Founded in 1924, the association grew to 23 national chapters and their principal tract, The Burning Shame of America, attacked the usual evils of tobacco and proposed a constitutional amendment outlawing its manufacture and use.

The No-Tobacco League, headquartered in Indianapolis, achieved widespread membership. In 1925, the group made national headlines when it wired Vice President Dawes in Washington, D.C., and urged him to quit his pipe habit as a New Year's resolution and set a good example for America's youth. General Dawes, whose underslung briar had become famous during the presidential campaign, responded to the telegram with a grin, described as "expansive but not responsive."

HOW WOMEN CAME TO SMOKE

Catherine Medici, 16th century wife of Henry II and Queen of France, was the first documented female smoker in Europe. She enjoyed a pipeful of tobacco presented her by the ambassador to England, Jean Nicot (whose name became the source of the word, nicotine), and then proclaimed, "From hence, it shall be known as the queen's herb-nay, the sovereign herb."

Catherine Medici would not be the last female to enjoy the "herbe de la reine."

No one knows just when grandma laid aside her pipe and took up cigarettes but the fad obviously originated in Europe. The credit, however, was shared.

American females placed the blame on their "gentle English cousins with blushing cheeks and soft, mild voices." English ladies, on the other hand, claimed they were merely copying the habits of "independent American girls and women who are confirmed smokers."

It was customary, well into the 1800s, for grandma, after the day's haying was done, to sit in front of the fire and break out her short, black pipe or seamed nosewarmer and enjoy a bowlful of crushed shag.

THE CONTINENTAL FAD

English women of title and position were the first to smoke cigarettes at public dinners. It was around 1885 that cables first brought news to America of a dinner given by Mona Caird, a prominent socialite of London.

Among her guests were more than a dozen noted women. Cigarettes were handed out with coffee and when the news spread abroad, there was a lot of talk and criticism. Then many women copied the idea and smoking after dinner grew as a fad.

The cigarette habit among women in this country did not attract undue public attention or social comment until the 1880s. A reporter on the staff of the New York Herald was one of the first to identify this new class of smoker. He wrote in 1885:

"They were women – but not ordinary ones. They were well bred and well dressed. They frequented the music halls and beer gardens from Fourteenth Street to 33rd, between Third and Sixth Avenues, holding the slender white rolls saucily in their mouths."

American correspondent Elizabeth Banks, on a visit to England in 1895, was surprised to see so many women smoking cigarettes. In London, women of means frequented smoking rooms fitted with Oriental draperies in swank, exclusive clubs. There they enjoyed puffing smokes while reclining on overstuffed couches and divans.

It had long been an open secret that the women of rank in many foreign countries smoked cigarettes. Princess Eulalia of Spain, while visiting the World's Fair in Chicago in 1893, thought nothing of lighting up after dinner, shocking her guests.

It was also rumored that many women of fashion in New York City maintained well-appointed smoking dens and Turkish boudoirs in their homes. However, it was generally held that this form of moral dissipation and bourgeois indulgence was limited to just a few who had a preference for the "Bohemian style."

The same class of woman ventured out in public and enjoyed a few cigarettes at the dinner table, or with a small select group of friends in permissive restaurants (or in ladies' dens at certain hotels).

The cigarette had, by the turn of the century, found a place in the affections of proper American womanhood, exploding the myth that no one but those with peroxided pasts and skirts that showed ankles smoked.

A REAL NEW WOMAN FROM LO[N]

A shocking example. Some free-spirited European women visiting this country caused heads to turn and tongues to wag when they wore knickerbocker costumes in public – and puffed perfumed Turkish cigarettes with absolute nonchalance. Such was the case with Miss Dorothy Chestie, a London actress, sketched here upon her arrival in New York City in 1895.

The Polite Smoke of Society.

Many respectable women showed more than a passing interest for the slender rolls of tobacco and took them to their lips, not publicly, of course, but in the privacy of their homes.

In many households of social prominence, the feminine contingent joined their husbands or brothers in taking cigarettes after dinner – and the presence of guests was not allowed to interfere with this tradition.

Women had advanced from the days of tight laces and sudden fainting. They had learned that the hour when they strode solemnly as a group to the drawing room, leaving the men at the dinner table, was the best hour of a dinner party.

And there they remained. That is how the cigarette gained its first feminine foothold.

Three adventuresome Victorian damsels enjoy a round of smokes within the sanctity and privacy of a parlor. It was not yet safe or smart to take their cigarette habit outdoors.

MRS. THAW'S DESSERT

By 1900, old guard patrons and matrons of society began to take offense at the appalling scenes of unescorted females who openly lit up cigarettes in the smartest hotels and finest restaurants. It was all so shameful.

Female members of New York City's Sunrise Club met one evening in 1903 and, upon hearing that popular young actress Mrs. Evelyn Nesbit Thaw was having dinner downstairs, forgot their meeting and rushed down to the dining room. There they caught a glimpse of the notorious young woman who bore their scrutiny without embarrassment as she naughtily lit up cigarette after cigarette while enjoying after-dinner coffee and a lengthy chat with friends.

In 1905, word again reached America that English club women were now smoking in after-dinner drawing rooms. The next year, English railroad officials adopted special smoking cars for women.

This new spirit of liberation spread to the United States. Upper class women puffed cigarettes when reading the newspaper at the breakfast table, when

SOME HUSBANDS ENCOURAGE THEIR WIVES TO SMOKE!

giving instructions to the kitchen help, in idle moments when writing notes to friends, and when receiving dinner guests.

"Unhappily, women have now become so demoralized as to imitate men in this the most serious of all vices," cried Mrs. John A. Logan in 1906 on the pages of the American Journal Examiner. "Every self-respecting woman should resent this reflection upon the morals of their countrywomen,' she added with bitter emphasis. The outrage expressed by Mrs.

A GIRL'S SMOKING CLUB.

Logan would soon be picked up and amplified in many social circles over the next few years.

Society matrons warned young women of the dangers of being a "jolly girl," or a "good old girl." Mannish types like these, they said, inclined to talk slang and smoke cigarettes, were almost certain to never find a husband in life.

The Y.W.C.A. in the nation's capitol also made it clear that female smokers were not welcome on its premises.

The walls crumbled slowly. When Mrs. Patrick Campbell lit up a cigarette in the tearoom of the Plaza Hotel in New York City in 1908, she was curtly asked by the head waiter to extinguish her smoke. The same rude admonishment was given a cigarette-puffing female visitor from London at the posh St. Regis Hotel, who had the audacity to touch a match to her gold-tipped Egyptian cigarette in the dining room.

But once again, Great Britain struck a blow for the freedom of women. Hotels in London posted "Ladies May Smoke" signs in their cafes. Women were permitted to smoke their cigarettes after lunch and dinner, but not during tea time.

By 1907, cigarettes had become quite the rage with many young privileged women of society. Legends surrounding the new fad were built at resorts of the rich and famous. Female socialites smoking at the beachside colony in Newport, for instance, made juicy headlines in gossip columns that summer.

Shocked society leaders were at their wits' end as to what action to take when cigarettes were fired up by women during and after dinner parties. Before the social season was half over, the cigarette habit had become so commonplace that a woman smoking a cigarette was no longer an object of special notice – or scorn.

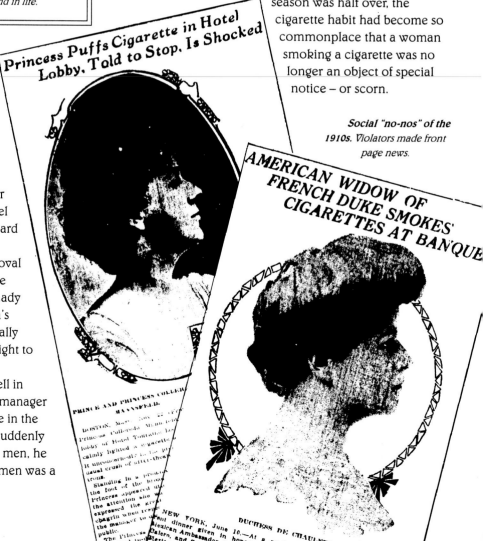

Social "no-nos" of the 1910s. Violators made front page news.

BREAKING THE SOCIAL BARRIER

Women continued to show their independence by lighting up in hotel lobbies, restaurants and parlors aboard steamships.

An official stamp of social approval was given by certain members of the British female aristocracy, notably Lady Juliet Duff, one of Queen Alexandra's maids of honor. Said Ms. Duff, "Morally and legally, women have as much right to smoke as men."

This kind of news did not set well in America. A Washington, D.C., hotel manager who, preparing to let women smoke in the public rooms of his establishment, suddenly changed his mind. Like many other men, he was convinced that smoking by women was a passing fad.

THE LAW AND KATIE MULCAHY

Shortly after midnight, January 23, 1908, Katie Mulcahy, out for a late evening stroll, paused in the cold night air near the Bowery, struck a match against a wall and lit a cigarette. Much to her surprise, she was arrested.

Hauled protesting into night court, she indignantly refused to pay a five-dollar fine and was taken to jail, clutching her package of cigarettes.

What Katie did not know was that earlier that day the local board of aldermen had passed an ordinance prohibiting public smoking by women. Spearheading the law was an alderman named Sullivan ("Little Tim" to his friends and constituents). Sullivan believed that the sight of a woman smoking sullied the respect she deserved and he, as an elected official, felt obligated to correct the matter with the power at his hand.

The board's public hearing on the proposed law, held two days earlier, was nothing short of a theatrical farce. First, Dr. Charles Pease, head of a local nonsmokers' league, demanded an amendment making it a crime for anyone to smoke in a public place where women were present, lest they be forced to inhale the poisonous fumes of tobacco.

Next, Alderman Brown stood up and announced his opposition to the law. Shaking his fist at Sullivan, Brown claimed that it would be better for the board to concern itself with the hardships of the poor than "such nonsensical things" as a few women smoking in a restaurant. Why don't we prohibit everybody from smoking, he asked in seriousness, if the board was going to take up the subject of public smoking?

Alderman Doull claimed the new law was unconstitutional. He recalled old William Kleft, governor of New Amsterdam, who tried to outlaw smoking in the Dutch community but it backfired. Angered burghers gathered around his house, lit up their pipes and smoked him out. And then there was old Peter Stuyvesant. He tried to regulate the way women dressed and danced only to have the wrath of all the women brought down on his head. It was folly, Doull warned, to expect women to follow such a regulation.

Bringing the house down was the testimony of a group of showgirls bussed in by a press agent from Wallack's, a nearby theater. One, Bobbie Roberts, said that the board should stop automobiles from going so fast because they make the girls hop, skip and jump across the street instead of passing anti-smoking ordinances. Anyway, she asserted: "We girls from Chicago don't smoke."

Notwithstanding the opposition, Sullivan's motion was voted into law the next day. Reporters had a field day. They aimed a sarcastic blast at Sullivan who, in their minds, had applied a heavy-handed solution to a delicate problem. The newsmen pointed out that "the surest way to make a woman do anything is to forbid her to do it." Referring sarcastically to the diminutive alderman as "Sullivan the Lesser," the press concluded that he was "morally superior to his time."

Two weeks later, peace was restored when the mayor, no doubt feeling the heat of unwanted publicity, vetoed the ordinance by explaining that the board had overstepped its authority.

"Little Tim" was not available for comment. He had skipped to Hot Springs, Arkansas, for a quick vacation, the climate there being more to his liking. Five years later, Sullivan was committed to an insane asylum.

Of all communities enacting no-smoking legislation after the turn of the century, New York City appeared conspicuously negligent. At any point in time, the smoking population of the nation's largest city alone exceeded that of all states with anti-cigarettes laws on the books. Finally, in 1908, an abortive effort was made.

The Woman Who Smokes Cigarettes in Public Places

THE WASHINGTON POST: SUNDAY, OCTOBER 12, 1912.

Feminine Bad Taste One of the Crying Wrongs of Today

WOMEN IN TROUSERS SMOKED AT BIG GO

PUT OUT LIGHT OF HER CIGARETTE

Woman Smoking in Dining Room at

WOMEN NOT TO SMOKE

Washington Hotel Managers Declare

SMOKE CLOUD CAUSED BY PRETTY VISITOR

Women of Artists' Guild Did n Her in Use igarettes.

NEW HAVEN WOMEN MUST STOP SMOKI' WOMEN SMOKE AT BIG PEACE DINNER

SOCIETY WOMEN IN WASHINGTON SMOKE AT BALL

MOKING IS BARRED EXCEPT ON STREET

shington Women Warned ot to Vitiate Atmosphere of Favorite Cafes

SMOKES IN STREET, SHE GOES TO JAIL

Denver Woman, Protesting Equal Rights, Prefers Cell to Quitting Her Cigarette.

A SEETHING CAULDRON OF DISSIPATION

Women contributed more and more to the tobacco consumption in America. Several prominent tobacconists in St. Louis admitted in 1909 that were it not for their female customers, they would have trouble paying the rent. They also were of the opinion that women would be smoking in public before long.

"For the past year, Washington society has been a seething cauldron of dissipation," the Washington Post hissed in 1912. It seems that cigarette smoking and new dances like the turkey trot and the jelly wobble had combined to "undermine the mental and moral character and stamina of Washington society women."

High-profile party goers such as Alice Longworth were watched disapprovingly by the stunned older crowd as she wantonly danced with a cigarette dangling precariously from her lips.

"The sight of a woman smoking in public is enough to make angels weep and men sigh over the memory of their mothers," lamented the San Francisco Examiner in 1912.

The next year, Miss Amy Lowell, the wealthiest bachelorette in New England and owner of some of the finest bred dogs in America, startled staid Bostonians when she declared, "It is just as natural for a woman to smoke a cigarette as it is for her to drink a cup of coffee."

Ms. Lowell admitted that she enjoyed a smoke now and then and expressed confidence that the day was not far off when women would commonly be seen smoking in cafes, theater smoking rooms, and other public places. She added diplomatically, though: "When a women smokes now, she has to do it very quietly, as I believe she should, because the prejudices of the people should always be regarded very carefully."

A Self-Made Man. From Life magazine (1895).

CIGARETTE HABIT GROWING AMONG ST. LOUIS WOMEN

Girls Are Rapidly Adopting Continental Fad and Tobacconists Are Doing Thriving Business.

HER FIRST ATTEMPT

THE ONLY CHANCE SHE HAD TO SMOKE

THE PRESIDENT'S DAUGHTER CAUGHT IN A FIB

Y. AUGUST 13, 1910.

MRS. LONGWORTH CRITICISED FOR ALLEGED SMOKING OF CIGARETTES

Society watchdogs of the W.C.T.U. were not intimidated when it came to confronting prominent women with smoking cigarettes in public. And so, in 1910, when Alice Roosevelt Longworth, married daughter of ex-President Theodore Roosevelt, was caught red-handed, she got her picture splashed on the front page of "The Woman's Daily," accused of the dastardly act. "Too ridiculous to be answered," snorted Mrs. Longworth. It came as no surprise to many, however, when, in 1927, she posed for an advertisement for Lucky Strike cigarettes.

FEMININE SMOKING ACCESSORIES

One of the most reliable indications that cigarette smoking by women was on the rise was found in the various trades that catered to female smokers. Sales of feminine smoking accessories had become big business. Faddists were spending over $1 million a year on fancy inlaid smoking taborets and other trinkets.

By the 1920s, cigarettes had become as much a part of women's personal trappings as their vanity cases. In New York City alone, women were smoking up over $1.5 million worth of cigarettes every year. The habit was on the increase, observers noted, with more and more older women taking it up.

A well stocked jewelry counter carried a wide display of articles in precious metals, cloisonne, tortoise shell, and fine leather. They were worn everywhere, from the wrist to special carrying cases on women's stockings.

The practice of adorning cigarettes with personalized names became passe. Fancy monograms, hand-somely embossed in gold or silver foil, became the latest rage.

The young swain at the turn of the century planning on a Christmas gift for his sweetheart had little reason to hesitate. There was something newer and naughtier than garter buckles, and all the jewelers in town had laid in big stocks of them for the holiday trade – the feminine cigarette case.

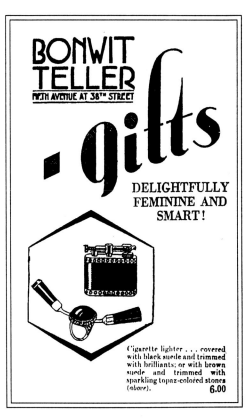
A Society Woman WHO Makes and Sells CIGARETTES for Society Women

An unusual situation developed in the mid-1910s when a prominent New York City socialite, Mrs. Frederick Coudert-Brennig, entered the cigarette-making business. Her brand, Brennig's Own, was a pricey Turkish smoke, hand-rolled on the Fifth Avenue premises. Although most of her business was mail order, Mrs. Brennig also maintained a well-appointed salon for walk-in clientele. In the 1920s, she ran ads in Vanity Fair magazine.

And Here She Tells Why She Went Into the Business.

THERE is no reason why all women should not smoke cigarettes if they want to. Cigarettes can be made as harmless as sterilized milk!

Cigarette smoking is not injurious to any woman. It aids digestion, soothes her nerves and keeps her temper.

I began to make cigarettes because I wanted to do something unusual to make money.

Nowadays, when a woman wants to make a fortune, not a mere living, she must do the unusual thing.

And so I made cigarettes.
—*Mrs. Frederick Coudert Brennig.*

No finer gift for the modern young woman who smoked could be purchased than a dainty gold or silver case, jewelled, monogrammed or richly engraved with a personal sentiment or a special date. The New Woman openly sneered at flowers or bonbons as gifts, and thumbed her nose at jewelry unless it was some article which could be added to the smoking table in her private boudoir.

The naghali, or water pipe, was a special favorite with female Victorian smokers, and was available in a wide variety of Eastern designs. Traditionally it sat on a low table, octagonal in shape and inlaid with mother-of-pearl. Rose water was used exclusively with the naghali.

No detail of smoking comfort was left unattended. Telltale yellow nicotine stains on the fingers was a vexing problem with fastidious or self-conscious female users of the weed until cigarette tongs came along. They were the prettiest little toys one could imagine, made exactly like miniature sugar tongs except that the ends were flat, not curved, and were made of blue enamel on silver.

SMOKING TOGS AND OTHER FASHIONS

At their spring opening in 1913, Macy's department store in Kensington Gardens, New York City, displayed feminine smoking fashions for the first time. Live models strolled through elaborate stage settings, showing off a wide selection of imported French and domestic smoking gowns, all quite chic in their soft colors, skirts draping to the rear and high frilled lace collars.

Smoking jackets, cut in shape like men's, were among the latest luxuries for the woman who used cigarettes. Of soft silk and interlined with cotton, they were quilted like Japanese dressing gowns and also doubled as negligee garments. Those seen in finer shops were pink and blue and yellow, all rendered in delicate shades, and complemented with dangling cords in matching hues. A fetching point was the two thoroughly masculine pockets, one above the other, on the left side.

Smoking suits became high fashion with women – red velvet robes trimmed in skunk and worn with silk Turkish pants embroidered with silver thread.

The smoking cap most favored by women was the Turkish fez which was always becoming to a pretty face. Set rakishly on the side with the long tassel falling toward the front, it imparted a particularly jaunty appearance to the wearer, especially when worn with a smoking jacket along the lines of a Japanese kimono.

CHANGING TASTES

In 1923, celebrated opera singer Frieda Hempel warned that smoking ruined the singing voice. But fellow artists Alla Nazimova, who had a brand of Turkish cigarettes named after her, and Pauline Frederick, both disagreed. So did Caruso who was also a devoted smoker of cigars and cigarettes.

For a time, medical fears of "tobacco heart" drove some women away from cigarettes and into an earlier generation's habit of smoking clay pipes. While most females agreed that pulling on one was like inhaling a brush fire, the modern woman smoked pipes not so much to look smart (which it wasn't) but because she had truly become addicted.

It wasn't long before pipes took on a stylish look. The most unpipelike creations soon appeared on the market, small ones with wood or porcelain bowls set on long, slender stems and inset with jewels. Some were overlaid with strips of platinum, gold and silver and ranged in price from a few dollars to several hundreds.

-Newspaper ads (1920s)

FOR THE
GIRL OR
BOY FRIEND

Smart cigarette cases of moire will reveal good taste anywhere. These have four 14-kt. gold corners...**6.50**

A Chinese Treasure For Cigarettes
4.95
Lined with heavenly blue and patterned with magnificent dahlias is this handsome cloisonne cigarette box!

Cloisonne is the magic material of which no end of lovely gifts are made. Rose jars, covered urns, bowls and vases of every shape and size. The smoking set above is modestly priced at $5.50.

TARGETING WOMEN WITH CIGARETTES

The first cigarettes designed for women appeared briefly in the 1880s. The Kimball Tobacco Company of Rochester perfumed a cigarette brand, Satin Straight Cuts, and tantalized adventuresome young ladies by packing a few loosely in cute little satin drawstring bags suitable for carrying in a purse.

The same company also distributed trade cards depicting gowned seductresses languishing on divans and blowing out wisps of smoke from hand-held cigarettes. The images were considered racy for the time.

But the rigid Victorian taboo against women smoking was so strong and pervasive that, even as the popularity of cigarettes grew, most manufacturers of last century refrained from marketing cigarettes exclusively for feminine tastes.

Companies that advertised cigarettes with women in mind risked adverse publicity. While the feminine face and form constituted the backbone of tobacco advertising imagery since the 1860s, it was a completely different matter to show a woman actually smoking a cigarette...or even suggesting it. To do so was in utterly poor taste.

The nearest anybody dared to get to the subject was to portray women casting approving eyes on gentlemen at their side who were enjoying a cigar or cigarette, or even a pipe, but the ladies themselves were never seen indulging in the habit.

While it could scarcely be said that cigarette manufacturers were stricken with a moral or social conscience, it remains a fact that for decades they avoided promoting cigarettes aimed at women. It was strangely out of character for the tobacco men, considering the industry's penchant for aggressive and exploitative merchandising. The unwritten law seemed to stand in their way.

And so it was that this odd paradox of marketing ethics went forward as the new century dawned. Beginning around 1905, however, cigarette makers grew bolder. Slowly and subtly, the public was introduced to scantily clad Oriental females in filmy veils and gossamer pantaloons casually holding cigarettes and blowing smoke.

The American public was gradually introduced to the sight of cigarette-wielding females in advertisements for various Turkish cigarettes between 1900 and 1915. The marketing of brands such as Ladies' Astrons, Ulissa and Gold Tip helped break the social barrier. Prize Cup cigarettes were truly feminine–small, gold-tipped and scented–and built along the lines of a matchstick, about an eighth of an inch thick and two inches long.

It was at this time that women took a shine to expensive imported cigarettes made of Turkish tobacco. Although catering to the well-heeled dilettantes of society, these specialty smokes also carried a distinctive feminine appeal. A few Turkish smokes were perfumed but all came packaged in pretty cardboard boxes with alluring labels and enticing brand names such as Milo, Mogul, Egyptian Deities, Fatima, and Turkish Trophies.

Other cigarettes were made smaller and lighter, and packaged in attractive satin-lined boxes with puffed sides which, when emptied, doubled as jewelry cases.

Some cigarette boxes were large affairs, looking like wedding cake boxes, and displayed ornate monograms or initials on the lids. A few of the satin boxes were tinted a delicate cream color and inside the cigarettes were covered with a sheet of pale yellow Russian maize paper.

By the mid-1910s, ads plugging Turkish cigarettes began to appear in Vanity Fair and Theater magazines, mandatory reading fare for female socialites in the know.

From there, things grew easier.

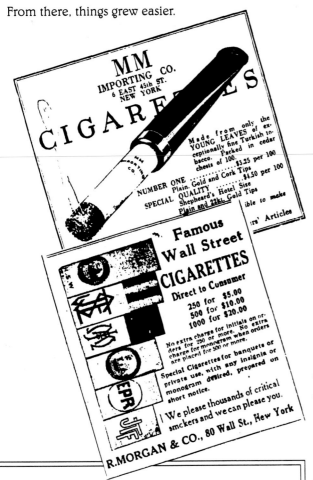

By 1918, women in America were well on their way to achieving smoking freedom. This was the year perfumed, gold-tipped Milo Violets were introduced, clearly catering to an established feminine trade.

"*The general use of tobacco* is perpetuated from generation to generation, by the desire, common to children and young people, to act and appear like older persons. Few ever begin the use of this nauseous weed because it is agreeable to the senses to which it is applied; but because they fancy, in their childish simplicity, that it confers upon them some additional importance." From *Every Man's Book, Philadelphia (1837).*

HIS FIRST PIPE

From Harper's Weekly (1879)

THE BOY WHO SMOKES

Juvenile use of tobacco has been a vexing social problem in America for well over a century. Starting in the 1880s, readers of newspapers and magazines could find editors making reference to the alarming numbers of boys and girls who had taken up the tobacco habit.

A New York Times editorial of 1879 makes the point:

"Unquestionably one of the most lamentable evils which afflict the rising generation flows from the early use of tobacco. Street boys who are not yet out of child's clothes snatch the discarded stubs of cigars of grown

The experiences of youth first meeting tobacco *were generally unpleasant ones. Preliminary to the pleasures of the real stuff still forbidden by tongue lashings, stern warnings of stunted growth, and even the strap, young lads secretly lit up corn silk or rattan pulled from old buggy whips, wrapped in tissue paper and twisted at the ends. Others preferred smoking pipes stuffed with dried leaves of sweet fern or pulverized coffee. If the kids were flush, they bought a paper package of Sweet Caporals and got a handsome picture of Della Fox or John L. Sullivan to boot.*

men and smoke them in apish imitation of their elders. Lads at school acquire a taste for tobacco by surreptitiously smoking cigarettes – cigarettes which have done more to demoralize and vitiate youth than all the dram-shops of the land. What manner of men shall they be, when this generation is grown, if lads of every degree shall be taught to use tobacco? What hope for posterity when the children of today are poisoned and dwarfed by a pernicious habit?"

THE ROAD TO OBLIVION

Youths who smoked gave themselves away by yellow-stained fingers and clothes that reeked of tobacco smoke. Their gloves often displayed ash burns. Some folks felt that it was just a matter of time before these hoodlums ended up in juvenile court, bound for reform school.

Cigarettes put them there, of that there was little doubt. The youngsters all looked alike – sallow complexions, sunken eyes and vacant stares. They called it "cigarette face."

Nicotine destroyed red blood corpuscles, robbed the body of its vitality and the mind of its keenness, shattered the nerves, dimmed the vision, impaired the memory, weakened the will, and ruined the prospects of success in life, "experts" stated with absolute authority.

And that wasn't all. When cigarettes got a boy down, they jumped on him. They led to drink, delinquency, disease, and vice. They also led to petty larceny, divorce, insanity, and death.

Everywhere the menace was in existence, especially behind the barn where tough boys taught young innocents the manly art of lighting up and inhaling. Chubby hands salvaged discarded cigar and cigarette butts from the streets. Street urchins stopped strangers with a cocky, "Gimme a light, mister?"

Worst of all, unscrupulous cigarette dealers in the very shadows of the school house broke down packages of cigarettes and sold them to minors, two or three for a penny.

This was the shocking scenario presented to America at the turn of the century. Tobacco reformers crowded the offices of state legislators and city councils and demanded strict anti-cigarette laws. The youth of this country was on the line, they said, and only the prohibition of the cigarette could save them from oblivion and ruin.

The harm done by cigarettes was too horrible to comprehend. In 1902, the San Francisco Examiner summed it up: "Cigarettes always mean destruction to young children; they very often mean failure in life and an unnecessary early death to adults. They are unmanly, obnoxious, nerve and mind-destroying. It is unbelievable that any human being in his right mind should deliberately encourage their hold on his nervous system and his success in life."

More radical opinions also prevailed. A professor at Hahnemann Medical College in Philadelphia, delivering an address in 1906 to a medical congress, said that the free use of cigarettes by boys made thieves and liars of them, because the majority of those brought before juvenile courts were liberal users of tobacco.

BOYS WHO SMOKE CIGARETTES CAN NOT BE TRUSTED

INNOCENT YOUTH

"Say, mister, give us a match, will yer!"

s Weekly

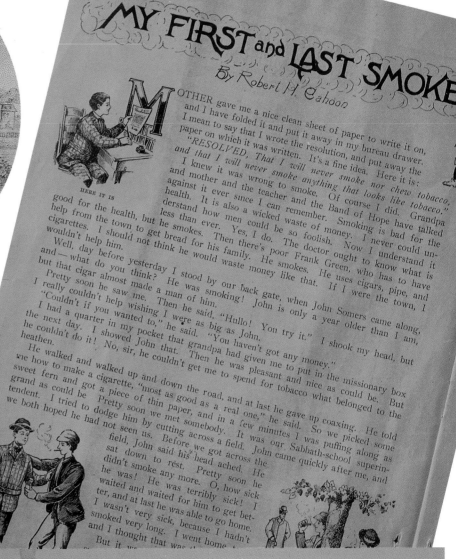

MY FIRST and LAST SMOKE

By Robert H. Cahoon

MOTHER gave me a nice clean sheet of paper to write it on, and I have folded it and put it away in my bureau drawer. I mean to say that I wrote the resolution, and put away the paper on which it was written. It's a fine idea. Here it is:

"RESOLVED, That I will never smoke nor chew tobacco, and that I will never smoke anything that looks like tobacco."

I knew it was wrong to smoke. Of course I did. Grandpa and mother and the teacher and the Band of Hope have talked against it ever since I can remember. Smoking is bad for the health. It is also a wicked waste of money. I never could understand how men could be so foolish. Now I understand it less than ever. Yes, I do. The doctor ought to know what is good for the health, but he smokes. Then there's poor Frank Green, who has to have help from the town to get bread for his family. He smokes. He uses cigars, pipe, and cigarettes. I should not think he would waste money like that. If I were the town, I wouldn't help him.

Well, day before yesterday I stood by our back gate, when John Somers came along, and — what do you think? He was smoking! John is only a year older than I am, but that cigar almost made a man of him. Then he said, "Hullo! You try it." I shook my head, but Pretty soon he saw me. Then he said, "Hullo! You try it." I shook my head, but I really couldn't help wishing I were as big as John.

"Couldn't if you wanted to," he said. "You haven't got any money."

I had a quarter in my pocket that grandpa had given me to put in the missionary box the next day. I showed John that. Then he was pleasant and nice as could be. But he couldn't do it! No, sir, he couldn't get me to spend for tobacco what belonged to the heathen.

He walked and walked up and down the road, and at last he gave up coaxing. He told me how to make a cigarette, "most as good as a real one," he said. So we picked some sweet fern and got a piece of thin paper, and in a few minutes I was puffing along as grand as could be. Pretty soon we met somebody. It was our Sabbath-school superintendent. I tried to dodge him by cutting across a field. John came quickly after me, and we both hoped he had not seen us. Before we got across the field, John said his head ached. He sat down to rest. Pretty soon he didn't smoke any more. O, how sick he was! He was terribly sick! I waited and waited for him to get better, and at last he was able to go home. I wasn't very sick, because I hadn't smoked very long. I went home too, and I thought that was all.

But it w——

Victorian publications aimed at juvenile audiences frequently preached temperance. Tobacco always made a handy subject for anti-smoking stories set to lurid type in the hope of saving a few more youthful souls from the clutches of Lady Nicotine.

WORMY APPLES

Condemnation and castigation of the schoolboy who smoked was a fixation of educators around the turn of the century. They painted him in the same picture as a modern-day Jack the Ripper, a completely immoral degenerate with little hope of salvation. Some school officials made unofficial and amateurish observations on the "personality profile" of juvenile smokers that reached truly outlandish proportions. It resulted in a high state of hysteria.

The experiences of the Chicago Board of Education in 1897 were typical of many large-city school districts in the United States dealing with the cigarette problem.

A principal in Chicago revealed the appalling fact that, in his career, he only graduated two students who smoked cigarettes. Another teacher said that few users of the weed ever reached high school. Boys in her school smoked from two to twenty cigarettes daily, she went on to state, and not more than ten of them were able to keep pace with their classmates, yet most came from "good" families. Of the 125, nearly all were from two to five years older than their classmates. Most were hard to discipline and all were in the habit of playing truant.

From frank interviews, 25 of these boys admitted that they failed to learn their lessons because they were too sleepy to study; several "felt shaky" when they walked. A large number were unable to run any distance. Nearly all had constant headaches. They were unable to fulfill class assignments although kept at school night after night for that purpose.

In 1907, a school superintendent in Malden, Massachusetts, announced the results of a personally conducted study of 40 students, aged 7 to 15, who were using tobacco, chiefly cigarettes. He was motivated because of the "hysterical persuasion and violent denunciation" that commonly surrounded the subject.

"He is after the little ones now." - From "The Boy," a monthly publication of the Anti-Cigarette League (ca 1915).

The educator wished to provide cold, hard facts.

While making it clear that nonsmoking children were not necessarily paragons of virtue, he enumerated a long list of undesirable qualities present in the majority of smokers studied, among which were: "undersized, weazen, unkempt, sallow, weak, often sick, lazy, nervous, dull-witted, unable to think at times, mentally dwarfed, incapable of sustained attention, poor memory, poor reasoning powers, weak of will, cowardly, liars, vulgar, disobedient, disrespectful, truant," and so on.

The schoolmaster concluded that a close connection existed between low mentality, physical weakness and moral delinquency, and cigarette smoking. If this be true, Hervey stressed, then "the cigarette, far from being the sign of manliness and of superior intelligence, should be regarded as the badge of the physical weakling, the mentally incompetent, and the morally unsound."

In 1912, a superintendent of schools in Red Bluff, California, carefully observed tobacco-using students from 1902 to 1908 and was terribly dismayed by their poor performance.

"Tobacco, worse than any other factor, is responsible for those boys who fall by the wayside," the educator said. "Wormy apples," he called them because "they drop long before the harvest time." Never in his 18 years of teaching experience had he ever graduated a "tobacco boy" with enough credit to gain entrance to the state university.

THE ST. LOUIS REPUBLIC.
EIGHTY-EIGHTH YEAR.
SUNDAY MORNING, JANUARY 26, 1896.
CIGARETTES RETARD DEVELOPMENT, SAY TWO NOTED SPECIALISTS.
Statistics Prove That Among College Students Who Smoke the Percentage of ... Is Lower Than It Is Among ... Not. ... Mental and Phys-... by the Use

THE NEW YORK TIMES, SUNDAY, FEBRUARY 27, 1916.
TESTING THE BOY WHO SMOKES CIGARETTES

Bad Results of Habit Shown in Records by Prof. McKeever.

MORE NAILS IN THE COFFIN

Educators were not the only persons raising an alarm. Men with scientific credentials took turns at evaluating the boy who smoked and found him to be as advertised: physically, morally and scholastically a hopeless case.

In 1897, physicians in St. Louis were convinced that cigarettes produced moral degradation. "The boy who smokes at 7 will drink whisky at 14, take to morphine at 20 or 25, and wind up with cocaine and the rest of the narcotics at 30," a neurologist claimed, adding that the evolution was a pathological version of Hogarth's "The Rake's Progress."

There were more horrors. Habitual tobacco use led to imbecility, lying, cheating, and stealing. Physiologically, the smoking of tobacco produced "all sorts of heart disturbances" and, if excessively indulged in, eventually caused insanity.

School children were not the only victims. By profession, bootblacks and newsboys, followed by hotel clerks and elevator boys, seemed particularly vulnerable to the cigarette vice.

Dr. William McKeever, a professor at Kansas State Agricultural College, released the results of a study in 1910. It received widespread press coverage, including the New York Times. After examining 2,500 "cigarette smoking schoolboys," the doctor described them in pathetic terms: "pale faces, bleary eyes, trembling fingers, and the foul stench of cigarette fumes" about them. Their electrocardiograms showed a slow heart rate and other minor abnormalities.

Constitutional symptoms blamed on cigarette smoking were "sore throat, weak eyes, pain in the chest, short wind, stomach trouble, and pain in the heart." Overall, the juvenile smokers appeared "very sickly."

Dr. McKeever also remarked that trying to cure youngsters of the cigarette habit was a futile task. He would know. His own son was a confirmed cigarette addict, a fact well known to residents of Lawrence, Kansas, McKeever's home town.

STAMPING OUT
THE CIGARETTE EVIL

Discouraging teen-age smoking has exhausted the patience of tobacco reformers for well over a century. Early day methods were blunt and heavy-handed, not unlike the time-honored "country cure," a switch administered to a lad's bottom behind the woodshed.

A student anti-cigarette badge worn in New York City schools in 1894.

In 1889, the Pennsylvania State Legislature put a law on the books making it a misdemeanor for anyone selling tobacco to minors. The mayor of Pittsburgh, zealously proclaiming "the cigarette is next door to suicide," favored arresting boys caught smoking and throwing them in jail. This was how they did it in New York City, he said, where police were empowered to arrest boys under 16 found using tobacco in any form. Jailing as a "solution" was tried for a decade or two, but failed miserably.

In 1897, concerned citizens in Chicago, frantically trying to help educators fight the smoking problem, suggested opening up schools in the evening and making sports facilities available to bored youths with excess energy to burn. Soup kitchens and free coffee were also offered as remedies under the assumption that children smoked because they were hungry.

A principal of a public school in New York City took matters into his own hand in 1904. After turning in four of his students who smoked to the police, he then swore out complaints against four neighborhood dealers in tobacco and candy whom he accused of selling cigarettes to minors.

A minor degree of success was scored by the formation of anti-smoking leagues within school bodies. Any boy wishing to join had to pledge on his honor not to smoke cigarettes until he reached the age of 21.

> *"The girls of Detroit are here to stay;*
> *Hear what we say,*
> *This very day;*
> *The cigarette we're bound to down,*
> *For naught like that we'll have in town."*

That was the yell adopted in Detroit in 1909 by schoolgirls enrolled in an anti-cigarette crusade sponsored by a local women's group.

Local school anti-cigarette leagues gathered momentum in towns and cities and led to the formation of similar organizations on a larger, national level, guided by experienced anti-tobacco campaigners and temperance leaders.

Counselling and anti-smoking lectures by teachers usually paid poor dividends. As a group, juvenile smokers proved to be recalcitrant and resistant to reform.

In 1911, the California State Superintendent of Public Instruction issued "The Cigarette Boy," a pamphlet designed to aid teachers in curbing cigarette use among their pupils. As one cynical teacher put it: "What's the use of telling the children about the effect of tobacco? We can talk to them all day and they go home at night to see the very people they think most of in all the world smoking like a house afire! They see people hale and hearty who have been using tobacco every day for 50 or 60 years. We waste our time and get nowhere in that way."

Suspension or expulsion from school – or a one-way ticket to reform school – were standard punishments meted out to cigarette-smoking boys well into the 1910s.

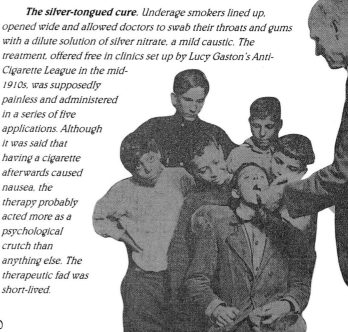

The silver-tongued cure. Underage smokers lined up, opened wide and allowed doctors to swab their throats and gums with a dilute solution of silver nitrate, a mild caustic. The treatment, offered free in clinics set up by Lucy Gaston's Anti-Cigarette League in the mid-1910s, was supposedly painless and administered in a series of five applications. Although it was said that having a cigarette afterwards caused nausea, the therapy probably acted more as a psychological crutch than anything else. The therapeutic fad was short-lived.

FOULING THE AIR:
SECOND-HAND SMOKE

A major factor in the decline of social manners over the last century was the insidious use of tobacco, especially cigarettes. The supreme test of a "gentleman" was his willingness to forego a habit which could only be practiced at the discomfort of others. It took a thoroughly well-bred man to resist the temptation.

The first battle between smokers and nonsmokers in America was fought on the public conveyances that plied the streets and waterways. The tight, crowded interiors of streetcars, electric trains, subways, elevated trains, railroad cars, ferry boats, and steamers often hung blue with the choking haze of tobacco smoke.

Early complaints of second-hand smoke are a matter of public record. While it was generally assumed that inhaling the fumes of tobacco combustion were not healthy, the exact nature of medical consequences were not known.

People were sure of one thing, though; how offensive it was to be trapped in a room full of tobacco puffers. Smoke burned the nonsmokers' eyes, made them cough and, with cruel irony, followed them home by clinging to their clothes.

Outraged citizens demanded action. In the late 1860s, special smoking compartments were set aside on horsedrawn streetcars in large cities. Railroads followed suit. However, stubborn smokers disregarded no-smoking signs and crowded into the places reserved for those who would escape them, claiming the right to fumigate, sicken and half-strangle those who shunned the weed.

Bad manners won out. Politeness and consideration became rare qualities among the ranks of the nation's smokers.

MS. FERGUSON'S WILD RIDE

Edward Henriques of New York City was a man of means, one of the "Old Guard," a member of Company I of the Seventy-First Regiment and a special deputy sheriff. He waited patiently one December day in 1879 for a horsedrawn streetcar on Third Avenue. He was neatly dressed and, being fond of smoking, carried a supply of cigars in his coat pocket. Having business downtown, he lit up a cigar and waited patiently for a smoking car. He boarded one and passed the time contentedly smoking and reading his newspaper.

All went well until the conductor stopped to take on a lady, Ms. Frances Ferguson, secretary of the Woman's Employment Society, who was on her way to the mayor's office. She went to the rear of the car and sat down.

Soon Ms. Ferguson began to show signs of distress (and rising temper). She arose and walked forward, carefully avoiding Mr. Henriques' outstretched legs in the aisle. Approaching the conductor, she informed him that she did not know that she had boarded a smoking car and the awful fumes were making her quite ill. The conductor listened with politeness but told her that, although sometimes gentlemen extinguished their cigars in the presence of ladies, they still retained the right to smoke because it was a special smoking car.

Resignedly, Ms. Ferguson took a seat, refusing to ask the men to stop smoking, figuring they weren't gentlemen anyway because if they were, they would have done so by now. She soon asked the conductor to open her window but was told that it couldn't be done because it was nailed shut.

By this time, the male passengers were becoming amused at the lady's predicament. At length she got up again and walked to the rear platform, holding on to the door handle to keep from falling off the car. The conductor asked her if she wished to get off. No, she replied, she had gone there to escape the overpowering odor of cigars and smoke.

Then the attack began in earnest. A man who was smoking dropped into her vacated seat and added his smoke to the cloud being wafted into her face by a draft. Ms. Ferguson inquired if they were near Chambers Street. Mr. Henriques, who was now standing close by, repeated the question, accompanied by whiffs of smoke carried directly into her face.

That did it. Ms. Ferguson, losing control of herself, aimed a blow with her muff at her tormentor. It crashed into Henriques' cigar, smashing it into the face of its much surprised owner.

Recovering from his astonishment and now angry, the old soldier promised that he would have her put off the car and arrested. This added fuel to the fire. Ms. Ferguson argued that this would not be the case and a minor scuffling match ensued, culminating in another clout to Henriques' face.

Excitement reigned in the car. Catching sight of a policeman on the street, Henriques summoned him and ordered the removal of the obstreperous Ms. Ferguson. Another round of loud arguments followed after which she finally agreed to descend from the tram, assisted by the officer of the law, but not before she turned and delivered the third and final blow to Mr. Henriques who was standing behind her.

Ms. Ferguson was subsequently arrested and appeared before a judge. She was defiantly unrepentant. She was only sorry in that the blows were not hard enough to leave a permanent mark upon Henriques face. The judge determined that she had not acted in a ladylike manner and fined her $5.

She refused to pay the fine, stating firmly that she would rather go to prison. Her lawyer, exhausted by his pleading and her steadfast refusal, finally paid the fine out of his own pocket. Ms. Ferguson was released.

A GROWING MENACE IS RECOGNIZED

As the country approached the turn of the century, smoking manners grew even more deplorable. A gentleman wishing to light his cigar in the presence of a woman no longer asked her permission.

In hotels, restaurants, public buildings, on the rails, steamboats, and in bank lobbies it became the rule and not the exception to see the smoker of cigars or cigarettes indulge his pleasures without a passing thought of whether it was agreeable or comfortable to those about him.

Public signs and private requests to smokers were universally ignored. "No smoking allowed", "Gentlemen will please not smoke in this elevator", "Smoking or carrying lighted cigars in this car is forbidden," "No smoking abaft this notice" were familiar signs deliberately defied every day by men whose appearance otherwise indicated good breeding and intelligence.

Reformers clamored for relief and some efforts were successful. In the early 1900s, the city of New Orleans adopted an ordinance prohibiting smoking in streetcars, classifying it as "a most vile and objectionable custom to a majority of our citizens," and at the same time set a legal precedence that swept like wildfire throughout America.

In spite of moneyed opposition, the Louisiana State Supreme Court upheld the law, declaring that it violated "no private right either of person or property," and added that it was the duty of municipal authorities to require proper ventilation in "public places, theaters, halls, etc., that there may be a supply of fresh and pure air."

The Court made a distinction between the private right of the smoker and his public right, and in so doing, clearly pointed out the line of demarcation in the following language:

"ANOTHER CIVIL-SERVICE OUTRAGE."
Less Smoke and More Fire.

SLAVES TO THE WEED—
Forget that they can't serve two masters

Political cartoonist Thomas Nast, in the 1880s, helped focus public attention on the problem of smoking in the workplace.

"Smoking, in itself, is not to be condemned for any reason of public policy; it is agreeable and pleasant, almost indispensable, to those who have acquired the habit, but it is distasteful and offensive and sometimes hurtful to those who are compelled to breathe the atmosphere impregnated with tobacco in close and confined spaces."

In Alabama a tobacco curing house was declared a public nuisance. Odors of the burning fire, wafted by the wind, polluted the air and inflicted "headaches and other nervous disorders" on the occupants of an adjoining building.

Outlook Magazine, in 1910, lent its editorial weight to the fight:

"So indiscriminate public smoking not only ought to be, but is a legal nuisance. There is no vice which is more persistently annoying to a large part of the community. That it can be regulated and its evils removed without any interference with the smokers' rights is beyond question. Where he persists in disregarding the welfare of the community and the rights of the non-smoker, he should be restrained by public sentiment backed up by proper laws.

"In this manner, the public smoker may be educated to a proper understanding of his relations to the rest of the community, and he will learn how to enjoy himself without involving so much suffering, inconvenience, and danger to others."

WAR ON THE RAILS

The smoking car, once a bleak and uncomfortable means of travel on the rails, had reached new heights of luxury and service by the 1890s, especially on limiteds plying between Chicago and New York.

The traveller, while covering ground at the rate of forty miles an hour, could take a bath, get a shave and have his hair shampooed as if he had never left home. Chairs were comfortably upholstered in which he could sit and enjoy his favorite form of tobacco while he perused a wide variety of books, magazines and weekly newspapers. To the passenger who smoked, the extra 10 percent fare for smoking car accommodations was well worth it.

However, more concerns were now being raised by nonsmokers. Health authorities claimed that the smoke of cigars and cigarettes in the confined spaces of streetcars and other vehicles contributed to the spread of tuberculosis, provoked attacks of asthma and bronchitis and was responsible for rare instances of sudden death.

In 1907, a young lady's dress on a Philadelphia streetcar was ignited by a carelessly dropped cigar ash. Her clothes burst into flames and she was burned extensively, later dying in a hospital.

Something had to be done.

Railroad smoking car (ca 1905).

He Gives Him a Seat By
The Best Dressed Woman
in The Car.

Smoking car on the Los Angeles Limited (1911).

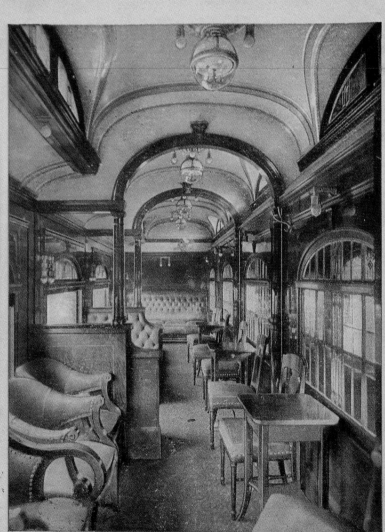

The Buffet-Smoking Car on The Los Angeles Limited

NO-SMOKERS SCORE A BIG VICTORY

To Smoke Is to Walk.

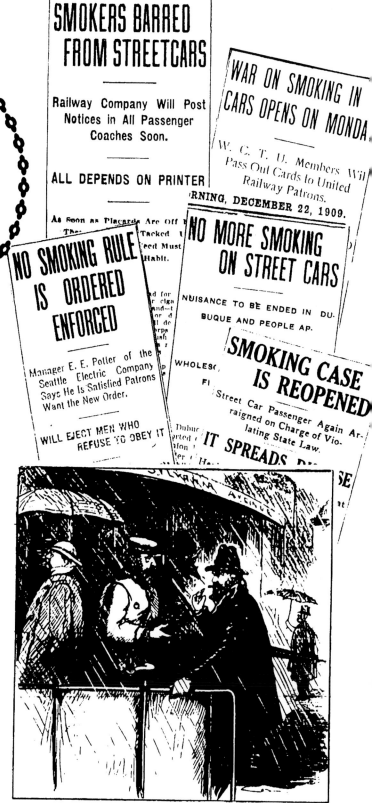

As the new century dawned, so did prospects for victory by the no-smoking-in-public activists. City after city legislated ordinances designating specific smoking and non-smoking sections on board public conveyances.

In 1901, a law was passed in St. Louis that reserved the last three rows of seats on streetcars for smokers and specified that identifying signs be posted in prominent places.

"Gentlemen will not smoke on closed cars, and others will be prohibited," announced a sign placed on electric street cars in Seattle in 1908. Previously smoking was confined to the three rear seats but the fourth and fifth were also usually occupied by puffers of pipes, cigars and cigarettes. The rule was not enforced and signs were frequently torn down or ignored. Violators were now put off the train.

In 1912, street traffic became snarled one day in Kansas City as several men passed out cigars to patrons of the city's streetcars. It was the parting shot in a brief but bitter battle waged between smoking passengers and railway officials. A city ordinance already in effect allowed passengers to smoke but streetcar authorities said no.

The battle raged on for a week as streetcar employees were ordered to stop all cars on which passengers smoked, bringing traffic to a complete halt on downtown streets. The streetcar company won the showdown.

Baseball fans in Portland, Oregon, found a happy compromise with city laws in 1913. Prohibited from smoking on streetcars, they deposited their well-chewed cigars on the car's rear bumper. Each stogie was identified by a colored thread and when the streetcar reached the ball park, there was a mad scramble to retrieve the butts.

Ulysses S. Grant (to conductor of street car): "Stop at the Capitol, will you?"

Conductor: "Yes, I'll take your fare first, please–and you've got to throw away that cigar! Smoking not allowed in the cars, you know."
- From Leslie's Weekly (1869)

DO UNTO OTHERS...

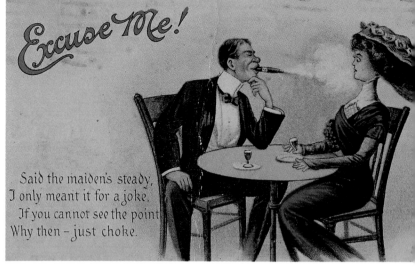

"The paper cylinder makes quick and safe conduct through crowds."

THE LIBRARY.

SMOKING ALLOWED ON SATURDAYS.

"**Mrs. Russell Sage, a lady highly respected** and of mature years, complains that she must give up her habit of attending a certain annual dinner because the men, in spite of her protests, insist upon smoking. She would like to listen to the speeches made at these dinners, but she cannot endure the clouds of smoke and must stay away."
- From the San Francisco Examiner (1912)

LIVING ON THE EDGE
THE MEDICAL DANGERS OF SMOKING

Ever since tobacco was introduced in England, it was considered good for almost anything that ailed you. "What is a more noble medicine, or more readie at hand than tobacco?" asked Edmund Gardiner in his "Trial of Tobacco" in 1610.

Physicians prescribed it and, notwithstanding the opposition of King James I and a few others, tobacco's role as a medicine quickly spread to all levels of society. It was new and novelty always has its attractions in both medicine and art.

Tobacco found use at one time or another as an emetic, expectorant, diuretic, narcotic, anesthetic, aphrodisiac, stimulant, and as an antiparasitic agent. It was said that dropsy sometimes responded to treatment with tobacco and that the drug could also induce childbirth. When injected into the bowel, tobacco had been used with success in some cases of strangulated hernia.

But as the weed grew old and familiar, some of its ancient illusions were dispelled, thus narrowing its range of medicinal usefulness.

Scientific studies on tobacco's therapeutic benefits were nonexistent. Instead, holding sway for many years were the uncontested opinions of prominent, non-medical laymen.

By the late 1800s in America, a few benefits attributable to tobacco were still in vogue. Tobacco, it was argued, aided digestion, quieted the nerves, preserved the teeth, stimulated the mind, and prevented the wasting away of tissues.

The prevailing opinion in America for many years, both in the public's mind and in medicine, was that excessive smoking was bad, but that the moderate use of tobacco did no particular harm. Even if the effects of smoking could be proven as bad, the chances were poor that healthy smokers could be induced to abandon what they regarded as one of greatest pleasures of modern times. This attitude still persists, despite overwhelming medical evidence that the likelihood of physical harm caused by tobacco is no longer remote, but only a matter of time.

The king of tobacco-based nostrums in the 1880s was Thomas Clingman, former U. S. Senator and Confederate general. After self-administering tobacco poultices to his wounded leg during the siege of Petersburg and saving it from amputation, the popular Southerner sold tobacco in various medicinal forms–ointment, cake, or plaster, take your pick–and praised its miraculous healing properties for a long list of maladies ranging from hemorrhoids to mosquito bites.

HORRORS OF NICOTINE

Nicotine had been identified and accepted as the cause of tobacco's toxic properties as early as the 1860s. Laboratory experiments had graphically proven its poisonous qualities: A few drops of pure nicotine injected into a small animal was enough to kill it, and as an insecticide, nicotine had few equals.

But embarrassing and baffling inconsistencies existed. If nicotine is so deadly, medical experts were asked, how can a smoker survive after taking into his system an apparently lethal dose of nicotine with each cigar, quid or pipeful of tobacco?

"Most of the poison is passed off in the smoke or in the saliva," was the stock answer, "and the human system, in some way, slowly adapts itself to nicotine after prolonged exposure, much as an arsenic-eater can ingest a dose lethal to a man unaccustomed to its use."

A similar question was asked: How is it that some tobacco users live a long time?

Again, the inexplicable ability of the body to somehow ward off the toxins of tobacco was offered as a weak explanation. But the "best" answer came from the anti-tobacco evangelist of old, George Trask.

Of a smoker, aged 104, who was still alive and brought to Trask's attention for an explanation, Trask inquired: "In a word, did he love anybody or hate anybody, dead or alive, in this world, or in any world?"

"I think not," came the reply.

"Well, well," Trask pronounced triumphantly, "your old man died fifty years ago and your only mistake was that you didn't bury him!"

Vexing questions and incomplete, illogical answers would haunt the medical community for many years to come.

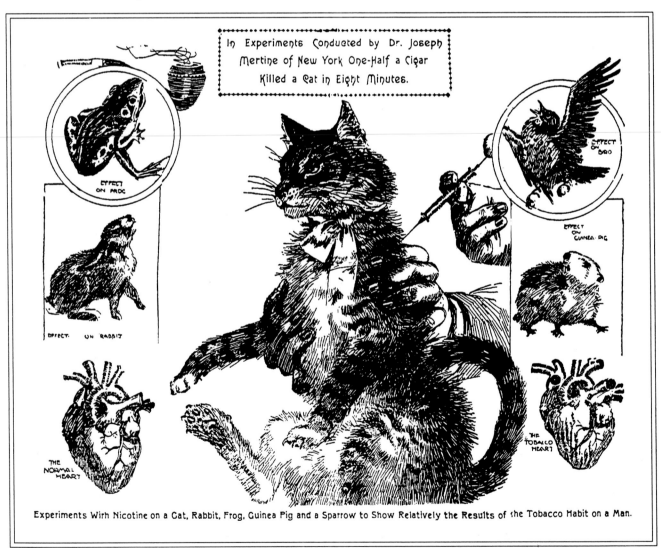

Experiments With Nicotine on a Cat, Rabbit, Frog, Guinea Pig and a Sparrow to Show Relatively the Results of the Tobacco Habit on a Man.

From the San Francisco Examiner (1897)

CIGARETTES ARE BAD

Cigarettes, as opposed to other forms of tobacco, always raised medical concerns, even from the start.

Prevailing scientific opinion in the 1870s and 1880s, for instance, held that smoking seriously affected digestive function, especially in the young, and increased heart action, causing palpitations. The tobacco also produced "catarrh in the head," flared asthma and made smokers more susceptible to pneumonia and bouts of bronchitis.

Cigarette smoking had a particularly deleterious effect on the nervous system, experts maintained, and dulled appetite for solid food. It destroyed nerves of the eyes and, as a result of constant expectoration, led to a morbid craving for drink.

In 1877, a little tract entitled Disease in Cigarettes was published and, through the efforts of various anti-tobacco groups, attained a very wide distribution. In common with most publications of this type, an attempt was made to impress readers by drawing on imaginary evils and by picturing the terrible fate that awaited all smokers.

The fateful destiny of a young man in whom physical decline was induced by excessive use of cigarettes was made the text of a fierce attack on tobacco. The author charged that the filling of cigarettes were mostly made up of discarded cigar butts and contained disease-causing germs. Even finer tobacco, such as that used in Turkish cigarettes, was not safe "because it is generally laced with opium, a known fact." As if this were not enough, "cigarette paper held white lead which, everyone knows, is a deadly poison."

So when the young man or young woman (the writer assured readers that the latter were fast becoming slaves to the habit) lit up this little roll of drugged or contagious poison, certain effects were produced in internal organs which "eminent physicians" (the names of whom were omitted) classified as the "cigarette disease."

Now, with these possible horrors staring

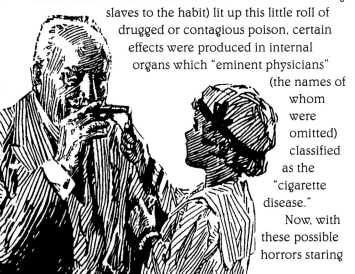

one in the face, it was a bold reader who would not rather keep his money in his or her pocket than make so perilous an investment as a package of cigarettes.

Cigarette smoking was popular enough in 1875 to merit a full page in William Demuth's wholesale catalog for tobacconists. Formerly it had been difficult to purchase cigarettes; few dealers kept them in stock. But that changed and soon every tobacconist's window was filled with a profusion of different brands in gleaming, colorful packages.

The reason for the popularity of cigarettes was due in part to imitation, in part to economy.

Americans were great imitators of the habits of foreign visitors, and if they happened to see an exotic lady or gentleman lighting up a dainty cigarette made in Havana or Turkey, then the American had to try it. Besides, cigarettes were cheaper than cigars.

For the minority of smokers (who actually inhaled) cigarettes were a necessity. Not counting the gross exaggerations and falsities contained in the tract, the known hazards of cigarette smoking in 1877 boiled down to this: the use of adulterated tobacco was dangerous; the aroma of burning rag paper did not add to the pleasure of smoking; and the possible health hazards of inhaling tobacco smoke were unknown.

The first two points were brushed aside by devoted smokers who felt that smoking cabbage leaves or a cheap "long nine" cigar wrapped in brown wrapping paper was better than smoking nothing at all.

Inhaling tobacco smoke was a special matter; nothing was known about its effects on the body. Foreigners routinely inhaled. To them it seemed ridiculous to draw smoke into the mouth and puff it out again. It was the same as trying to quench thirst by holding water in the mouth and then spitting it out.

Inhaling smoke, they said, eased the nervous system. This goal was readily obtained from a cigarette in minutes instead of an hour with an expensive Cuban cigar.

It was felt that the real danger lay in the excessive use of tobacco, or to "weaknesses" in the body which predisposed smokers to health problems.

In summary, the tract reflected the ignorance of tobacco and its effects on health at the time. To one in good health and who was willing to smoke moderately and make his cigarettes from light Turkish or latakia tobaccos, there seemed to be little danger.

THE AGE OF
MEDICAL NONSENSE

The period, 1890 through 1915, marked the high point of medical propaganda concerning the health dangers of tobacco. Unlike well-founded medical attacks that would come in the 1950s, this condemnation of the weed was largely based on fanciful notions.

Statements of eminent scientists formed the substance of the war against tobacco. Embellished and distorted, this information found its way into inflammatory tracts of the period and saturated the public mind.

Credibility and reason were swept aside by the fervor of the anti-tobacco movement. Fanaticism ran to paranoia as the extensive physical, mental and moral harm and degradation inflicted by tobacco was religiously chronicled.

By 1910, the full range of bodily trauma wrought by tobacco ran into volumes. In fact, if the tobacco activists were to be believed, it seemed that there were few human diseases which were **not** caused by the weed.

No organ, no physiological function was spared from the insidious effect of tobacco's poison. Eyes were weakened and made blind. The loss of "manly courage" and male libido were common side effects. Mental power was diminished; the brain could no longer do normal "work."

Tobacco injured the heart. Medical authorities were convinced that chronic tobacco use produced a weak and fluttering pulse, spasm of the heart muscle, chest pain, and, if the effect was severe enough, sudden death.

The term, "tobacco heart," lingered in the medical and public literature for decades. It probably scared more smokers into abstention than any anti-smoking device ever invented.

Oral cancer due to tobacco was known as early as the 1880s. Physicians correctly surmised that prolonged heat and chemical irritation of pipes and cigars caused cancer of the lip. Rubberized cigar holders, peddled in the 1890s, enjoyed brief popularity as a cancer preventive by keeping the "poisonous irritation" of nicotine away from mucosal surfaces. Lung cancer was an extremely rare disease at this time.

In 1913, the government issued a health statement, warning smokers to stop using community cigar cutters present in practically every tobacco shop in the country. Smokers habitually licked the ends of cigars before inserting them which made the cutters a health danger; communicable diseases like tuberculosis could be spread this way.

CIGARETTES ARE PROBABLY GOOD

Medical concerns over the dangers of nicotine and the smoking of cigarettes were temporarily sidetracked in 1901 when an article appeared in Lancet, England's prestigious medical journal. Scientists there exonerated nicotine as the harmful agent in tobacco and placed the blame instead on pyridine and its derivatives for the headaches, trembling and giddiness that were associated with smoking.

These experts went on to state that the toxicity of tobacco depended on the completeness of combustion, being more so in cigarettes than in cigars or pipe tobacco. Pipes acted as condensers of combustion products and tended to prevent the passage of harmful tars and oils into the oral cavity and eventual absorption by smokers. This was not the case with cigars where these toxic compounds passed directly into the mouths of smokers.

The bottom line, medically speaking, was to pronounce cigarettes as the least potentially harmful means of smoking, followed in turn by pipes and lastly, cigars, the most dangerous form of all.

HOW LITTLE DELL DE FORREST WAS MADE INSANE BY SMOKING CIGARETTES.

BEFORE THE FOOTLIGHTS

HER FAMOUS WHIRL DANCE

IN THE INSANE WARD

NOTICE SMOKING STRICTLY PROHIBITED BY ORDER

The Whirlwind Dancer Now in an Asylum.

She Smoked and Smoked Cigarettes Night and Day Until at Last the Poison Reached Her Brain.

The story of pretty Dell Forrest as told below is even more pathetic than that of the terrible sufferings of Robert Rodes, the California dandy died from the effects of cigarette poison, etc. Dumb can illustrations of the deadly effects of these evils.

To the Editor of "The Examiner:"

DRIVEN MAD BY CIGARETTES

A ludicrous assertion made by men of medicine long ago was that excessive cigarette smoking caused insanity. The superintendent of the New York Insane Asylum claimed: "Tobacco has done more than spirituous liquors to precipitate the mind into the vortex of insanity." This notion flourished for many years. Headlines often announced the sudden death, suicide or some senseless act of violence perpetrated by a helpless victim of "cigarette intoxication."

SUICIDE FROM CIGARETTES.

A Fine Young Indianian Deliberately Blows Out His Brains.

Special to The Republic.

TERRE HAUTE, Ind., Dec. 29.—This city was furnished with a sensation to-night by the suicide of James A. Byrns, the 20-year-old grandson of Theodore Hudnut, the wealthy miller of this city. The young man went to his room in the story of Mr. Hudnut's block this evening and, or, fired a bullet into his head on the floor. He the doctors arrived, ng for him and he ning unconscious all

n for the act. The etorate cigarette believed that this He was a clerk Milling Co. and andfather. Both oung man occu and was a boxes. He was the Lotus club, ht young man. service at St. lord the fam hom he com ly. Nothing duct to-day. ed to-night

CRAZED BY CIGARETTES.

HOMER STRICKLAND, AGED 16, LIES STRAPPED TO HIS BED.

Excessive Use of Narcotics and Domestic Troubles Upset His Nervous System— He Develops Strange Psychic Power in Delirium.

How Strickland, the 16-year-old son of Mrs. M. C. Strickland, a professional nurse, who lives at 407 Landis court, became insane last Sunday from cigarette smoking. For a year or more Homer has been smoking the little "coffin nails," and for the last six months he has been a confirmed cigarette fiend. without one to derable, smoke, the cravin but as soon as he lifted he would b and contented un arette. After it overcome the hal he began to sh chewed tobacco Saturday, the da when he sudder bacco altogether Sunday morni that her son v

150 CIGARETTES A DAY FATAL.

Newark Man Falls Dead at His Desk in Express Office.

REPUBLIC SPECIAL.

Newark, N. J., Sept. 9.—William Werner dropped dead at his desk in the office of Reinhardt's Express Company, Newark, from heart failure. A doctor who was lan's death was prob excessive cigarette y friends of 1 about 160 low and sh in the to hold nt. At the au

DRIVEN TO DEATH BY CIGARETTES.

Crazed by Incessant Smoking Young Smith Poured Poison Down His Own Throat.

UNCONSCIOUS WHEN FOUND.

shattered by the

CIGARETS, SAY POLICE, INCITE BOY TO SHOOT FATHER, DR. WEINSBERG

Physician Rallies, Though Four Bullet Wounds Give Him Slimmest Sort of Recovery Chance.

AD PROUD OF DEED AND LOVES THE PUBLICITY

TTITUDE TO PARENT CHANGED WHEN HE LEARNED THAT SUPPOSED MOTHER IS REALLY STEP RELATIVE.

In St. Anthony's hospital Tuesday it was stated that Dr. Julius Weins berg, shot four times by his son, Os car J. at his home, 2015 Russell av Monday evening, had rallied nicely from the operation performed by Dr and other surgeons fairly good night but his

CIGARETTE SMOKING DROVE HIM CRAZY.

YOUNG MARIE SANCHE AT TEMPTED SUICIDE.

Slave to the Nicotine Habit for Fifteen Years—Used 500 a Day.

REPUBLIC SPECIAL
New York, July 11.—Marie Sanche, years old, a victim of cigarette smoking, was taken from the home of his father, a well-known Fifth avenue physician, to-day to Bellevue Hospital.

CREDIBILITY GAP

On the eve of World War I, the American public was beginning to take a hard look at extreme medical claims made against tobacco; reformers were no longer reliable sources of information. Backlash was inevitable.

An editor for American Medicine magazine, bothered by the movement's extravagant denunciations of smoking, wrote in 1916: "The good that might be accomplished by antitobacco reformers is largely nullified by the ridiculous, ill-founded conclusions to which many of them are led by their processes of thought."

True scientific information, he said, was more or less neglected by those whose earnestness compels them to view things in an abnormal way. As an illustration, he cited the following quotation from a recent article on tobacco smoking disseminated by anti-smoking sources:

"I repeat, hot nicotine fumes inflame membranes, thereby increasing temperature constantly above normal, a low fever, destroying tissue of the human flesh, baking the roots of the hairs, causing baldness and premature grayness, spreading the pupil, impairing the eyesight, also impairing the hearing. This is not all by half, directly and indirectly, that tobacco-smoking does to human health."

Upon this the editor commented:

"Arguments based upon such theories are hardly provocative of faith in the integrity of the antismoking crusade...When will those who seek to correct personal habits realize that it is in the abuse of most things that the evil is found, not in their reasonable use?"

CIGARETTE HYSTERIA

But old notions lingered on. On the eve of World War I, England's military leaders claimed the average British recruit was physically weak and intellectually feeble, owing to his addiction to cigarettes.

General Lyttleton, in referring to the status of recruits of the Army and Navy, remarked: "They are physically immature and of an exceedingly low order of intelligence."

Surgeon General of the British army, Sir W.D. Cubbins, added his words of warning: "In the interest of the Army as well as the individual soldier, this habit must be greatly checked."

SMOKED TO DEATH

"In the cold routine of daily news, there came the other day a short story from Syracuse, New York. It told of the death of William S. Strauss in a hospital in that city. According to the doctors and the facts, Strauss was killed by smoking cigarettes.

"He managed to smoke himself to death in five years, and this in spite of the fact that he was 34 years old when he took up the habit. He died at 39. He died a death of atrocious suffering, calling for cigarettes when he was too weak to hold them between his lips. A few days before his death, he became paralyzed in his legs and lost the power of speech. He died three days after he was taken to the hospital.

"HE DIED BECAUSE CIGARETTES HAD POISONED AND DESTROYED THE NERVES IN HIS BODY."

–San Francisco Examiner (1900)

Newspaper reports detailing the horrible deaths suffered by cigarette smokers were not uncommon, supported in large part by medical "facts" too outlandish to really be believed.

An alarming cable message from London was received by the Chicago Tribune:. "The cigaret is playing havoc with the British Army, and if something is not done soon, Great Britain will be defended, or rather left undefended, by a collection of weak-minded and weak-bodied youths, capable of no real effort of any kind. The chief disposition (of most recruits) seems to be to hunt some place to lie down and rest."

The flames of controversy were fanned by Dr. D. H. Kress, medical spokesperson for the Anti-Cigarette League. Seizing the moment, he warned that tobacco would be a decisive factor in the European War. He was right, but in a way he would never suspect.

Skeptical editors in America laughed, pointing out: "Dr. Kress fails to tell us how the Germans and Turks take their tobacco. That would be as valuable to know as the brand of whisky consumed by General Grant with which Lincoln desired to acquaint his other generals."

CHOOSING YOUR POISON
THE CHEMICAL DOCTORING OF TOBACCO

In the old days, consumers were not always certain that the weed they were smoking or chewing was safe; sometimes they were better off not knowing. Tobacco tends to naturally improve with age and it is not necessary to add chemicals to help it, but its adulteration, for better or worse, is as old as the industry itself.

Fears of unsafe tobacco were periodically raised whenever news of disgusting schemes came to light, like the one reported in 1882: A gang of street urchins were arrested in New York City for picking up discarded cigar butts from gutters and sidewalks and selling them to unscrupulous tobacco dealers who "recycled" the used tobacco into inexpensive cigars and cigarettes.

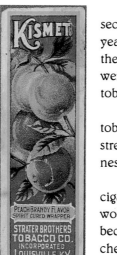

In the manufacture of chewing tobacco, the addition of flavoring agents to produce distinctive tastes, hence brand preferences, was not only a tradition but a widely advertised fact. The majority of plug brands were flavored and sweetened with a variety of substances, chiefly licorice, molasses, maple sugar, rum, denatured alcohol, and even champagne.

Recipes for these flavoring concoctions were well-guarded trade secrets. Flavorings were not used with any intent to deceive but were employed to kill the natural taste of the tobacco which, to many customers, was not particularly palatable. Most people would rather chew candy.

Smoking tobacco typically depended on the spicy nature of the leaf itself for flavor and aroma, but at times traces of tonka bean, cinnamon, rum, maple sugar, and other substances were added. Chocolate, for example, was a well publicized additive to Tuxedo pipe tobacco in 1919.

Old-time tobacco shop proprietors, preparing custom-made tobacco mixtures, often sprinkled piles of the weed with cognac, brandy and other strong liquors with a grand flourish of their hands as a final touch. Maccoboy snuff was traditionally scented with attar of roses.

Formulas for preparing cigarette tobacco were also secrets in the industry...and still are. In the very early years, it was common knowledge that glycerine (later in the '30s, diethylene glycol) and other simple chemicals were added to improve moisture retention and make the tobacco "smooth."

Other trade formulas employed in the treatment of tobacco were: spraying leaf with citric acid to cut the strength, steeping tobacco in vinegar to combat mustiness and applying saltpeter to improve the burn.

Danger awaited those who liked to smoke cheap cigars. Of all tobacco products made, cigars had the worst reputation. They drew considerable suspicion because in the old days chemical doctoring of cigar leaf tobacco was a common practice in the cigar-rolling trade.

In 1882, for example, 15 cigar factories in New York City employed chemists whose only job was to develop flavoring agents for cigar leaf. Tincture of vanilla was favored to impart aroma to the filler tobacco. Tonka beans, balsam of fir, cedar oil, and valerian were also utilized, as well as potato leaves, potash, tamarind, anise seed, gum, and a host of aromatic oils.

For a while in the 1880s, a New York City cigar-maker found success in selling cigars rolled from brown wrapping paper saturated with a solution of nicotine. Surprisingly, the smoking qualities of the bogus paper cigars, sold deceitfully as fine imported Havanas, were close to the genuine article. They fooled many a veteran smoker.

"Good Tobacco never harmed anyone"

One of the biggest dangers came from treating the weed with sulfuric acid or potassium bromide which, it was claimed, "produced an injurious effect akin to alcohol intoxication."

Disturbing reports came from New York City's cigar factories where cigar-rollers were in the filthy habit of wetting leaf wrappers with saliva, and biting the ends of cigars into shape. Health authorities claimed that tuberculosis and syphilis were spread in this manner and, in San Francisco, it was said that cases of leprosy were traced to cigars and cigarettes made by Chinese workers.

ONE POISON AT A TIME

Cigarette paper, it was rumored in the late 19th Century, contained arsenic and the tobacco filler was laced with opium. The cigarette habit, it was believed, was really an opium habit. Later, there were allegations that tobacco leaf was sprayed with arsenic, lead and other chemical poisons to make it cure faster.

In the days of dangerous patent medicines, such allegations were not always unfounded. Most folks, however, took them with a grain of salt. The anti-tobacco crusaders were obviously making up or distorting the facts, they figured. Authorities were caught napping, however, when truly addictive brands like Cocarettes (next page, below) showed up in the marketplace.

On occasion, chemical laboratories alarmed the public by reporting that many cigarettes actually contained traces of opium, further muddying the waters.

However, these accusations were put to final rest in 1897, when, at the request of several state legislatures on the verge of proposing anti-cigarette laws, government scientists in Washington, D.C. examined the contents of a number of American-made cigarettes. They found no traces of arsenic, opium or other toxic substances.

It was a defensive but smart tobacco company which quickly countered this sort of damaging gossip by assuring the public of the safety of its products:

Allen & Ginter, in 1879, claimed Pet cigarettes were "absolutely without adulteration or drugs."

James Duke got right to the point when he advertised his new Duke of Durham brand of cigarettes in 1881 thusly: "If you like a DOCTORED cigarette, or want to learn the habit of using opium, don't buy the 'Duke'..."

Henceforth, the terms "pure" and "safe" became vital buzz words in tobacco advertising copy.

Makers of "Bull" Durham *tobacco and Select Society cigarettes ensured consumers of product purity in the 1880s and 1890s. "Pure" tobacco is "safe" tobacco, they said, even rosy-cheeked cherubs would dare to smoke it.*

SETTING THE RECORD STRAIGHT

The Goodwin company let people know in the 1880s that the paper used in the rolling of Old Judge cigarettes was perfectly safe from the "injurious effect of the oil of creosote," thanks to a special patented process (a thin coating of shellac on the mouthpiece). Popular at the time was the notion that arsenic was used in the bleaching process of cigarette paper and, during combustion of the paper, threw off oil of creosote.

TRY A LITTLE DOPE IN YOUR CIGARETTE

A passing but dangerous smoking fad of the 1880s was Cocarettes, a product of the Cocabacco Tobacco Company of St. Louis. These lethal smokes contained shredded leaves of the Bolivian coca plant, the source of cocaine. Preposterous and inaccurate statements filled the wordy advertising pamphlet extolling the safety and virtues of this new and exciting smoking adventure. The same company also marketed a companion product, Coca Plug, for those who preferred to get their kicks from chewing, not smoking. Products like these lent credence to tobacco opponents who claimed that American-made cigarettes contained opium and were addicting. They weren't wrong with this one. Courtesy Strong Museum, Rochester, New York.

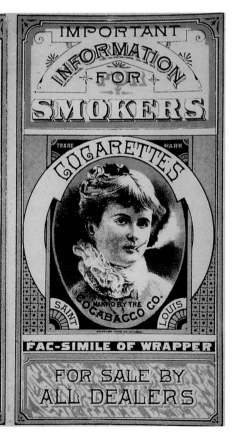

TAKING NICOTINE OUT OF TOBACCO: MAKING TOBACCO "SAFE"

After the turn of the century, scientists isolated a list of chemicals such as acrolein, carbon monoxide and furfural which were identified as being dangerous ingredients in, or thrown off from, burning tobacco. These chemicals received brief showers of publicity and notoriety.

But the focus always returned to the well known toxic agent present in all tobaccos, nicotine. This poisonous alkaloid was considered responsible for nearly all the harmful physiological effects of tobacco.

Scientists years ago did not consider nicotine a physically addictive substance like opium or cocaine. That it could be mentally addicting was perhaps a different matter. Many medical experts, however, agreed on one point, namely, that smoking was bad for the heart and the "nerves."

It seemed only reasonable then that the production of tobacco free of nicotine would be a boon to smokers and the medical community alike. This obsession occupied the minds of countless men who, like medieval alchemists trying to turn base metal into gold, searched for the magic formula.

The result was a plethora of "nicotineless" tobacco products that glutted the market as early as the 1880s, but particularly between 1900 and 1920.

Early on, it was relatively easy for companies to make their tobacco products free of nicotine; they simply declared it so. In 1884, for instance, the Globe Tobacco Company of Detroit advertised Gold Flake smoking tobacco as made by "a new and original process through which the rank nicotine is extracted." The power of the printed (but not necessarily proven) word set the stage for future promotional slogans as manufacturers joined the rush to bring "safe" products to market.

Scores of patents for "nicotineless" tobacco were issued to laboratory tinkerers and garage chemists, but efforts to remove nicotine from tobacco through chemical treatments and still make it palatable never proved successful.

The summary of an 1876 article in Scientific American entitled "Detoxicated Tobacco" always came back to haunt those who tried: "It is the combination of poisons...which produce the agreeable taste and smell, and to remove any of the ingredients seems simply to render the tobacco unpalatable."

Some tobacco companies made the ultimate claim: every bit of nicotine had been removed. No further assurance was needed. Such claims, of course, were false.

Experiments continued in Europe and America. All claimed to have succeeded in finding a way to neutralize tobacco's "injurious principles."

Dr. Ambialet's secret in 1914 was mixing tobacco with the dried leaves of an indigenous plant called "asse's foot." It removed all the dangerous ingredients of tobacco, according to the French scientist.

In the 1930s, low-nicotine cigarettes such as O-Nic-O and Sano were introduced but proved unprofitable. Their failure was blamed on tight advertising budgets, consumer disinterest and domination of the market by major cigarette brands.

TOBACCO IS GOOD FOR NERVES

Nicotineless cigars and pipes, and absolutely safe-to-smoke-or-chew tobacco, were readily available to America's consumers as early as 1910. One cigar firm in New York City carried the heartening name, the Health Tobacco Company.

When nerve and daring were required, so was tobacco. This is Barney Oldfield, the famous race driver.

JOEL HILLMAN
proprietor "Harvey's" Washington, D.C.

"*Tuxedo is a good, wholesome tobacco, with a mildness and fragrance all its own. It adds many degrees to my pipe pleasure.*"

Joel Hillman

L. S. BROWN
General Agent of the Southern Railway at Washington

"*Tuxedo has gained and maintained a high reputation for superiority. Its coolness, mildness, and genuine soothing qualities are unrivalled.*"

L S Brown

Tobacco That is Good For Your Nerves

TUXEDO actually *soothes* the nerves. It is just mild enough to keep your nervous system in poise, your muscles in tone. Unlike other tobaccos, Tuxedo *burns cool* and *slow*. There cannot be a speck of irritation in a pound of Tuxedo.

Great singers smoke Tuxedo just before a performance. Public speakers testify as to its soothing influence. Doctors recommend it to smokers whose throats are delicate.

Tuxedo
The Perfect Tobacco for Pipe and Cigarette

The secret of its superiority is the unique "Tuxedo Process" by which all the unpleasant features are eliminated from tobacco.

Another reason is that Tuxedo is made from the *best tobacco grown* — the choicest, mildest, mellowest leaves of the highest grade Burley tobacco.

Tuxedo is widely imitated—but no other manufacturer has succeeded in making a tobacco as good as Tuxedo.

Go to your dealer today and get a tin of Tuxedo. It will give you the greatest pleasure and satisfaction that money will buy.

YOU CAN BUY TUXEDO EVERYWHERE

green tin with gold letters — curved to fit the pocket **10c**

pouch, inner-lined moisture-proof paper . . **5c**

AMERICAN TOBACCO COMPANY

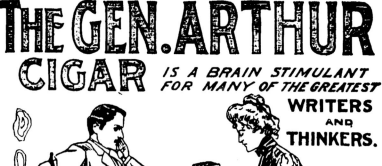

THE GEN. ARTHUR CIGAR
IS A BRAIN STIMULANT FOR MANY OF THE GREATEST WRITERS AND THINKERS.

KERBS, WERTHEIM & SCHIFFER, Makers NEW YORK.

Tobacco's sedative action on "jangled nerves" was a common medical misconception that was played up heavily in advertisements for cigars, cigarettes and smoking tobacco. Eventually, the Federal Trade Commission, in the late 1920s, forced tobacco companies to remove such statements.

In 1901, when this ad appeared, the idea of tobacco being brain food was not disputed.

THE MEDICAL STAMP APPROVAL

In the advertising days of old, tobacco companies often applied liberal endorsements of their products by the medical profession. It looked good.

It was standard practice, for instance, to portray the good doctor (nameless, of course) in early twentieth century advertisements attesting to the purity or safety of certain brands of smoking and chewing products.

He was also quoted as recommending cigars and cigarettes for "nervous" people, lending his advertising weight with a look of utmost confidence and reassurance. And why not? Didn't he use the same tobacco himself?

The family physician was an important member of the long list of professionals whose testimonies were incorporated in tobacco advertising copy.

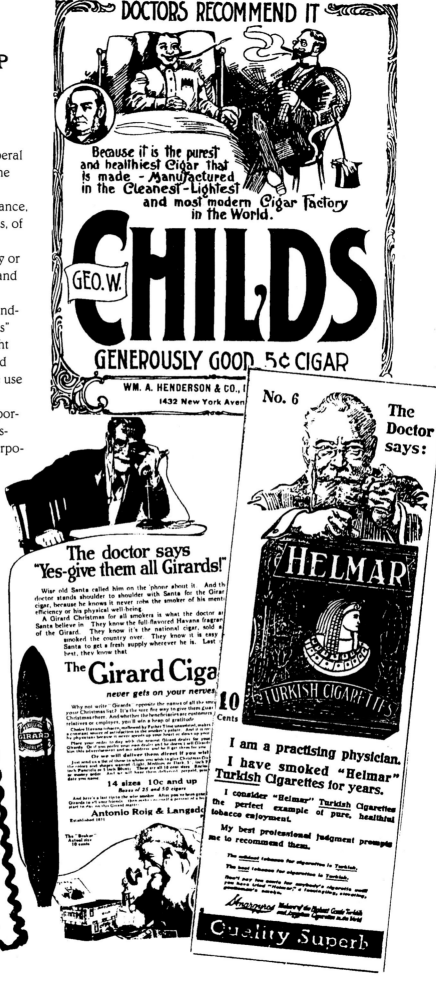

DOCTORS RECOMMEND IT

Because it is the purest and healthiest Cigar that is made - Manufactured in the Cleanest - Lightest and most modern Cigar Factory in the World.

GEO. W. CHILDS

GENEROUSLY GOOD 5¢ CIGAR

WM. A. HENDERSON & CO.,
1432 New York Aven

The doctor says "Yes–give them all Girards!"

Wise old Santa called him on the 'phone about it. And th doctor stands shoulder to shoulder with Santa for the Girar cigar, because he knows it never robs the smoker of his ment efficiency or his physical well-being.

A Girard Christmas for all smokers is what the doctor an Santa believe in. They know the full-flavored Havana fragran of the Girard. They know it's the national cigar, sold a smoked the country over. They know it is easy Santa to get a fresh supply wherever he is. Last best, they know that

The Girard Ciga

never gets on your nerves

14 sizes 10c and up
Boxes of 25 and 50 cigars

Antonio Roig & Langsdo

No. 6   The Doctor says:

HELMAR

TURKISH CIGARETTES

10 Cents

I am a practising physician. I have smoked "Helmar" Turkish Cigarettes for years.

I consider "Helmar" Turkish Cigarettes the perfect example of pure, healthful tobacco enjoyment.

My best professional judgment prompts me to recommend them.

Quality Superb

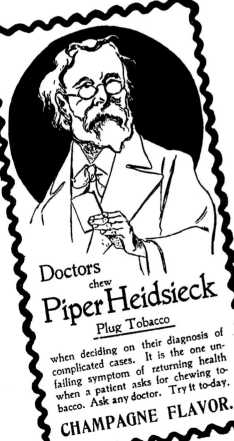

Doctors chew **Piper Heidsieck** Plug Tobacco

when deciding on their diagnosis of complicated cases. It is the one unfailing symptom of returning health when a patient asks for chewing tobacco. Ask any doctor. Try it to-day.

CHAMPAGNE FLAVOR.

"TOBACCO is a FILTHY WEED says LITTLE ROBERT REED"

But Uncle Sam's experts are making a science of its cultivation and learning how to produce definite percentages of nicotine so as to suit all tastes.

FLOWERS OF THE TOBACCO PLANT.

TRANSPORTING TOBACCO BY WAGON.

THE U. S. GOVERNMENT GROWS "SAFE" TOBACCO

Beginning in 1908, the U. S. Department of Agriculture attempted to grow strains of tobacco with a range of uniform and predictable nicotine levels, low to high. The goal was to propagate a hybrid entirely free of nicotine for consumers with "weak nerves" or "heart trouble."

By altering soil conditions, federal researchers were able to reduce the nicotine content of Cuban leaf tobacco at a field station in Texas to levels as low as 0.12% by inbreeding low-nicotine strains. They proved, theoretically at least, that a true nicotine-free tobacco could be produced by further selective breeding.

Samples of certain cross-bred tobacco were further treated with chemicals during the fermentation process to neutralize the free nicotine and reduce its percentage.

This low-nicotine tobacco was then rolled into cigars. While a cigar made of low nicotine content possessed a mild taste and barely passable aroma, smoking one lacked what researchers called "a fully physiological reaction." Without a jolt of nicotine, it became clear to the scientists that a "safe" cigar was not a "good" cigar, from a commercial standpoint, that is.

The project, after ten years of experimentation, had run into a dead end and was discontinued.

HOW THE FRENCH DID IT

In 1907, "nicotineless" tobacco was introduced by the French government. Referred to as caporal doux, it was "ordinary caporal" tobacco washed with water until the standard 2.5% nicotine content had been reduced to 1%. In this form, it was used by consumers who were "nervous" or had "cardiac weakness" or were just plain leery of nicotine.

Ordinary caporal tobacco was a mixture of French, American and Oriental tobaccos, prepared by the regie, the governmental agency which controlled the manufacture of all tobacco, cigars and cigarettes in France. The mixture produced a rank, but not unpleasant, aroma and flavor and was the cheapest, most popular, form of tobacco used in France.

To smokers accustomed to full-flavored tobacco, the smoke of caporal doux was somewhat insipid. Its only advantage was the low nicotine level.

TOBACCO CURES
HOPE FOR THE HOOKED

A hundred years ago, tobacco "cures" were selling like weight-loss programs today. For the countless users struggling to shed tobacco's death grip on their souls, there appeared to be help – plenty of it.

The marketing of tobacco cures peaked with the patent medicine craze in America. Turn-of-the-century magazines and newspapers were awash in a sea of advertisements for nonprescription medicinals and universal panaceas guaranteed to cure everything from tapeworms to sick headaches, insanity and fits, to opium and tobacco addiction.

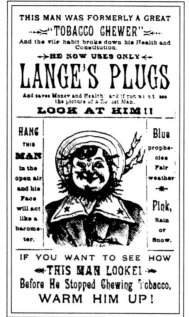

THIS MAN WAS FORMERLY A GREAT
"TOBACCO CHEWER"
And the vile habit broke down his Health and Constitution.
HE NOW USES ONLY
LANGE'S PLUGS
And saves Money and Health: and if you want see the picture of a Robust Man.
LOOK AT HIM!!

HANG THIS MAN in the open air and his Face will act like a barometer.

Blue prophecies Fair weather

Pink, Rain or Snow.

IF YOU WANT TO SEE HOW
THIS MAN LOOKED
Before He Stopped Chewing Tobacco,
WARM HIM UP!

EASY WAYS OUT

One of America's first commercial cures appeared in 1867. For five dollars, H.S. Ballou of New York City sped a package of his magic bullet, the "Tobacco Disinclinator," through the mails to those in need. "An effectual cure to the most inveterate," Ballou confidently promised the public.

Lange's Plugs, patented in 1869 and costing only a dime, was a remedy that beckoned to chewers of the weed. Small cubes were masticated and the saliva swallowed which eliminated the desire for tobacco in every form.

Nationally advertised cures for the tobacco habit first made their appearance in the 1890s and picked up steam after 1900. Pitching an endless stream of hope and salvation, they were enthusiastically embraced by thousands of smokers and chewers of the weed who rushed to buy a quick and easy antidote in the form of a pill or "secret method" disclosed in a book or a pamphlet.

Some concoctions were odorless and tasteless. These were ideally suited for long-suffering family members who wished to slip them into the food and drink of unsuspecting fathers addicted to Lady Nicotine. Personal testimonials abounded and the products were "guaranteed," most with money refunded. It was heady stuff.

Two basic formulations were offered to the public, those that required the user to stop tobacco when the treatment started, and those that didn't. This fundamental difference was emphasized when the makers of Baco-Curo prevailed in a lawsuit brought against them by the makers of rival, No-To-Bac, in 1895.

No-To-Bac directed clients: "Stop first and then take our cure." Baco-Curo said: "Don't stop tobacco until the cure makes you stop." The latter company saw its product as a true cure, not a substitute for tobacco, and promptly declared Baco-Curo as the only scientific treatment on the market.

Chemical cures were the most popular form of therapy, chiefly pills of double chloride of gold. These tablets not only "cured" the tobacco habit but also opium and alcohol addiction, according to the Keeley Institute which peddled the medication through a nationwide chain of offices.

Hill's Gold Tablets, made by the Ohio Chemical Company of Lima, Ohio, claimed to "completely destroy the desire for tobacco in from 3 to 5 days."

There were "natural cures," too. They included vegetable compounds like Baco-Curo imported from Germany, oil of tobacco, and "Double Shot," an herbal tea made in Akron, Ohio, but most contained secret ingredients.

"Tobaceen," an imported English herbal formulation, was the tobacco slave's dream. It allegedly purged the system of poisonous nicotine while still allowing the smoker to use tobacco with perfect safety and impunity.

Hypnotism, a vaunted remedy of the 1890s that produced hit-or-miss results, still remains a viable therapeutic option today.

Despite impressive and confident advertising claims, none of the so-called cures stood the test of time. After being hot sellers for nearly two decades, sales dropped off precipitously following the passage of the Pure Food Act in 1906. By 1920, the market had virtually dried up, but compounds could still be found advertised well into the 1950s.

FREEING TOBACCO SLAVES

The best publicized, best known patent remedy of the 1890s was "No-To-Bac," a product sold by the Sterling Remedy Company with offices in Chicago, New York, and Montreal.

The company's alarming battlecry, "DON'T TO-BACCO SPIT AND SMOKE YOUR LIFE AWAY!," appeared regularly in magazine and newspaper advertisements for a number of years and provoked many nicotine addicts into action.

An impressive 37-page booklet, mailed free for the asking, was an advertising marvel and a veritable cornucopia of medical misinformation. It included six pages of testimonials followed by a $5,000 reward for proving any claims to be false.

The text explained how the use of tobacco was a disease of the nervous system and how nicotine, absorbed through the mouth and throat, soaked nerves, sapped manliness, led to "liquor-drinking," poisoned the heart and other vital organs, and resulted in complete debility. "Cigarette insanity" was a particular dread complication of smoking which was manifested by hollow eyes, parchment-like skin, tobacco-stained lips and teeth, and other horrible physical and mental infirmities.

No problem. "No-To-Bac" stopped the craving for all forms of tobacco – permanently. The brochure said so. It cured 99 out of 100 cases – guaranteed!

Action of the product, the purveyors said, was enhanced by taking laxatives which hastened the elimination of nicotine from the body. Two bowel movements a day was sufficient. For this step the company recommended another of their products, "Cascarets, the candy cathartic," whose market life far surpassed that of No-To-Bac which fell out of favor by 1900.

THE 1920S:
THE FINAL CHAPTER

A NATION HOOKED ON CIGARETTES

Tobacco, by 1924, had become a billion-dollar industry. More than 450,000 farms were growing the weed on two million acres of American soil, making the United States the leading producer of tobacco in the world.

After a long and honorable career as the aristocrat of smokes, the cigar fell into consumer disfavor, its lofty position usurped by the despised and lowly cigarette and leaving a generation of young men uninitiated into the long brown roll's joys and mystique.

Cigarettes had become clearly established as the number one form of tobacco enjoyed in America. Their production, 52 billion in 1921, broke through the 100-billion mark by 1928, setting an industry record. Tobacco taxes paid in 1927 poured $387 million into the federal treasury.

The runaway market success enjoyed by Reynolds' Camel cigarettes forced rival companies into action. American Tobacco Company dug out one of its previously acquired but long defunct chewing tobacco labels, Lucky Strike, and turned it into a cigarette brand in 1917.

Liggett & Myers dusted off Chesterfield cigarettes, briefly marketed in 1912 in a cardboard slide-and-shell box, and re-introduced them in a soft pack in 1915.

The fourth industrial giant, the Lorillard company, took an old chewing brand of 1884, Old Gold, and used it for its late entry in the cigarette field; the brand first appeared in 1926.

In 1923, Luckies took to the air. City dwellers were astonished to look skyward and find floating above them at 10,000 feet, the name "Lucky Strike" formed in letters one mile high and 6-1/2 miles long. It was the first aerial tobacco advertisement in history, the result of a $1 million deal swung by the American Tobacco Company

with a New York City-based skywriting firm and calling for 350 such flights across the country. It was billed as the "advertising sensation of 1923."

Ads of the four major cigarette companies – the "Big Four" – dominated the marketplace. Cigarette companies, by 1927, were investing $60 million a year on promotion and had become the third largest advertiser in American newspapers. Tobacco, as an industry, was spending more money on advertising than any other business in the United States.

Declaring that "newspapers offer the most effective medium of appeal," George Washington Hill, president of the American Tobacco Company, announced that over $12 million had been allocated to promote Lucky Strike cigarettes in 1929, the largest appropriation ever devoted to a single product in American history. Newspapers were earmarked for the bulk of advertising expenditures, followed by magazines, billboards and radio.

Nickel cigars staged a spectacular market comeback during the 1920s despite an industry-wide slump in business. By 1928, they accounted for almost 50 percent of all cigar sales. Consumption of five-centers had taken a steep dive when, during a temporary period of post-war inflation, cheaper cigars, along with their makers, were forced out of business, unable to compete with larger firms.

This resurgence of popularity was spurred by nationwide advertising campaigns and the installation of automatic cigar-making machines in factories. In 1924, the General Cigar Company presented a complimentary box of 25 Robert Burns cigars to every male golfer in the country who scored a hole-in-one.

Society Premiere!
Tomorrow at 9·P·M.
GLORIA
SWANSON
in her long-awaited picture
"SADIE THOMPSON"
United Artists Picture

preceded by
"Debutante's Parade"
a motion picture

Proceeds to charity—
Reserved seats now on sale

Regular popular price performances
begin Saturday at 10:15 A. M.
RIVOLI-UNITED ARTISTS
Broadway at 49th

RIALTO
"HOUSE of HITS"
Times Square

Truly—
The Sensation
of New York!

EMIL
JANNINGS
in
"The LAST COMMAND"

A Paramount Picture
Directed by Von Sternberg, maker of "Underworld"

The Hollywood screen and American stage did
much to spread the glamour and appeal of cigarette
smoking. Talkies of the '20s and New York stage sets
teemed with screen stars and matinee idols of both sexes
enveloped in clouds of cigarette smoke.

MOGUL
EGYPTIAN CIGARETTES
STAGELAND'S FAVORITE

My favorites are Moguls—
they always register
with a big O.K. for me.

Bryant Washburn

Bryant Washburn
POPULAR PARAMOUNT STAR

MOGULS are made of the most delicate
Egyptian tobaccos. Exclusively
refreshing and of charming flavor. They
are deliciously mild, the correct size and
Cork Tip.

20¢

MOGUL

255

MODERN CIGARETTE ADVERTISING STRATEGY

Cigarettes were advertised during the 1920s to improve the quality of the singing voice, lose weight, relieve fatigue, calm nerves, and clear the mind. The promotional methods of cigarette manufacturers irritated a magazine editor. "What this country needs is not a good five-cent cigar but a good cigarette, sensibly priced and sensibly advertised," Commonweal magazine said in 1929. The editor even offered advertising advice: "Manufacturers could say this is just a cigarette. It is neither a tonic nor a cough drop. If you smoke too much, it will result in a loss of weight and nervousness. For the sake of health, it is best not to smoke at all. But if you must smoke, and you want a cigarette, here it is!"

For tobacco manufacturers, finding a market winner with a new cigarette brand was much like picking a lucky number at roulette. While some brands made it, many others fell by the wayside. In the end, it was advertising (and particularly slogans) that offered the best chances of success.

No matter how skillful the blending of tobaccos, or how pretty the package, it was the competency and originality of the advertising agency that really counted. By 1930, the budget needed for introductory promotional campaigns for new cigarettes now stood at about $10 million.

Cigarette advertising slogans were brief: a few words about taste, flavor, smoking enjoyment, or low cost and that was it. There was really little else to say about a cigarette.

But it was the associated imagery, lots of it in vivid, inviting colors, that conveyed the real message. The strategy of cigarette manufacturers was to build pleasant associations of a brand through frequent and consistent visual images that tempted a non-user into trying cigarettes for the first time or, at the least, reinforced the brand preference of the user. There was little chance, however, of inducing smokers to switch brands; they were the most loyal of all consumers.

There is no other cigarette like Tareyton because Tareyton has *something* no other cigarette has ~ ~ ~ *Something* that just puts Tareyton in a class all by itself

"There's *something* about them you'll like"

Herbert **Tareyton**
CIGARETTES
TWENTY FOR A QUARTER

The UNION TOBACCO COMPANY-*Purveyors of Better Cigarettes*

Helping to push the popularity of cigarettes in the 1920s were chain operations such as A&P grocery stores and Liggett drugstores which began selling them at cut-rate prices. Camels, Luckies and Chesterfields went for a dime a pack instead of the usual 15 cents. Old Golds were more expensive; two packs sold for a quarter.

Cigarette advertising of the 1920s primarily focused on major brands–plus a few new ones. In 1928, Babe Ruth picked up a check from the Lorillard company for declaring it possible to recognize Old Gold cigarettes while smoking blindfolded. Endorsements for Lucky Strike cigarettes always seemed to be at the center of controversy, if not with the U. S. government then with endorsers, such as aviatrix Amelia Earhart. She was not a smoker and denied the ad's suggestion that she was. While it was true that Luckies had been carried on her trans-Atlantic flight, it was never proven that anyone smoked them.

Retired opera singer Madame Schuman-Heink was another celebrity angered at the inference that she smoked Luckies. The diva (who never used tobacco) insisted that her signature was obtained under false pretenses.

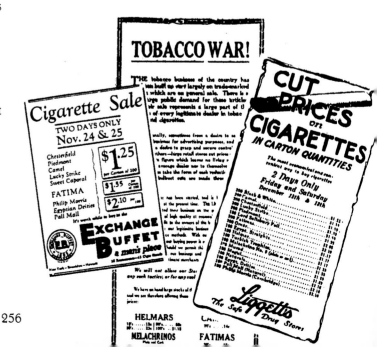

RECRUITING WOMEN SMOKERS

Women took to cigarettes in staggering numbers following World War I. While it was impossible to determine the exact number of cigarettes consumed by women, by 1927, of the 88 billion that went up in smoke that year, the female population was responsible for nearly half, estimates said.

Various explanations were offered for the explosion of feminine smoking. Some observers charged it to the freedom now exercised by the Emancipated Woman of post-war America; others said ladies did it to look smart. A few blamed the stage and movies where actresses were shown in the midst of rapture as they pulled at their cigarettes.

Manufacturers were quick to deny charges that the gentle sex was being lured into smoking. On the contrary, cigarette makers voiced alarm at the rapidly spreading fad fearful that it would lead to a resurgence of agitation by anti-tobacco reformers.

Many people agreed that smoking by women was not a question of personal rights, but of what was best for them. Prominent medical men of the 1920s were of the opinion that cigarette smoking was more harmful to women than men; it induced a faster pulse rate, increased blood pressure and, in general, made the heart "irritable."

Notwithstanding these objections, the conspicuous torch of progress borne aloft during the 1920s was that of the feminine cigarette. The time was gone when the glow of the slender cylinders was known only in shaded boudoirs. The army of female smokers marched right out in public with their habit.

Feminine preferences for cigarettes changed in the 1920s. The stage had passed when women stepped into tobacco shops and politely asked for "ladies' cigarettes." They were now smoking the same brands as men. Scented Turkish articles were dumped in favor of domestic blend Camels, Chesterfields and Lucky Strikes.

Special Prize "New Yorker"—Marlboro Contest for Distinguished Handwriting,

A Cigarette for Those Who Can Afford 20¢ for the Best

H. P., Portsmouth, N. H.

MARLBORO
Featured by Best Dealers

PHILIP MORRIS & Co., LTD INC.

The Philip Morris company, makers of Marlboro cigarettes, sponsored a snobbish "distinguished handwriting contest" in 1929, inviting women who could afford their cigarettes to submit handwritten samples of advertising slogans. The Depression brought a swift end to this promotion.

"The smoking car is the last of the old masculine institutions that the higher sex type has reached out for and said: 'This, too, is ...mine.'" New York Times (1925)

For female members of high society who liked a really long after-dinner smoke, there was the Longfellow brand, a well-named 5.5-inch-long cigarette.

WOMEN JOIN THE ADVERTISING RANKS

The year, 1927, marked the beginning of a new and radical departure from conventional tobacco advertising; women were now shown smoking in advertisements.

The story started one year previously. One afternoon, Albert D. Lasker, advertising genius of the Lord & Thomas agency and responsible for the Lucky Strike account, dined at the Tip Top Inn in Chicago. After lunch, his wife, Flora, lit up a cigarette. This act promptly brought the manager to Lasker's table who apologetically informed Mrs. Lasker that she was not permitted to smoke in the restaurant. Albert flew into a rage and vowed to make it possible for women to smoke in public.

The event set into motion one of the greatest cigarette advertising coups ever witnessed in the industry.

It was Lasker's idea to have female celebrities not only provide testimonials for Luckies, but also to show them smoking them as well.

The result was a series of magazine and newspaper ads run in 1927. The impact on American womanhood was devastating. Ladies started smoking cigarettes in record numbers.

Lasker's next step was even more diabolical and cunning. Learning that candy manufacturers were ready to mount an advertising campaign against cigarettes by claiming that eating candy lessened the desire to smoke, Lasker turned the tables on them. In collaboration with George Washington Hill, president of the American Tobacco Company, the two hatched the famous "Reach for a Lucky Instead of a Sweet" promotion in 1928.

This campaign, too, produced staggering results. Lucky Strike sales tripled within a year.

In 1928, the American Tobacco Company broke the taboo by urging women to "reach for a Luckie instead of a sweet." In promoting the association of a slim figure with cigarette smoking, still a prominent advertising gimmick today, the makers of Lucky Strike were the first to make a strong pitch for female smokers, and to tap a vast, growing market. Backed by almost limitless funds and testimonials by the score, the cigarette campaign was launched amidst a storm of protest by the confectionery industry, prompting a warning from poet Carl Sandburg that a misconducted tobacco business could result in a ban on cigarettes. Lorillard took advantage of the war of words passing between the American Tobacco Company and candy manufacturers by sneaking in a quick plug for Old Golds, brazenly labelled a "healthful treat." By 1930, sales of Luckies passed Camels, the market leader, for the first time. Boldness and innovation paid off.

THE TWENTIETH CENTURY WOMAN

The last step in hooking a nation on cigarettes was accomplished in the 1920s when women reached smoking equality with men. The time had finally arrived when women could light up anywhere (even the street) without suffering fear of reproach or blush of shame.

Gone were the long, wicked glances that came their way in restaurants when they chose to enjoy an after-dinner smoke. Henrici's, one of Chicago's oldest and finest restaurants, finally broke with tradition in 1925 and set out ashtrays for female guests.

Gone also were the days when enterprising taxi drivers in New York City made a thriving business of driving female office workers around town during the noon hour while the ladies puffed a few quick cigarettes before returning to work. Cabs were one of the few safe smoking havens available for women; smoking at the office was quite out of the question.

Cigarette smoking by females spread to college campuses. At all the exclusive schools cigarettes smoked on the sly were common pastimes indulged in by venturesome dormitory dwellers. The smoking habit, once acquired in college, was rarely dropped when the young ladies left campus and entered business or domestic life. Women of the twentieth century, mothers of the next generation, would smoke.

Women's smoking rights were now fiercely defended. Whenever lawmakers attempted to discriminate against females through fines or prohibitory decrees, they were accused of archaic thinking and showing a lack of respect for a woman's right to smoke.

"Class" or "sex" legislation, was how one feminine columnist put it. "Conventions aren't morals," she said, "and the prejudice against women smoking is one of those conventions grown rigid...having its start in the

clinging vine days when it wasn't considered attractive for women to be mannish."

Yes, women were now full-fledged members of the cigarette-smoking elite of America, entitled to all the rights and privileges accorded thereto, including the late-stage medical complications of smoking – pulmonary emphysema and lung cancer – and a shortened life.

Women had truly come a long way.

A joke now. Women smoking in public no longer raised eyebrows. The entire matter, by the late 1920s was largely treated as a joke.

"I've sworn off smoking.
"Why?
"It's getting to be too ladylike."

CLASHING WITH THE FEDS: A PERMANENT STATE OF WAR

The bold wording of tobacco advertisements eventually led to confrontation with the federal government.

In 1930, the Federal Trade Commission, the government's official watchdog for the American consumer, forced the American Tobacco Company to rid their Lucky Strike ads of false and misleading statements, particularly those used in the "Reach for a Lucky Instead of a Sweet" campaign.

At specific issue were the manufacturer's claims that "women retain slender figures" and "overweight is banished" made in newspaper, magazine and radio advertising. The ads strongly suggested that smoking Lucky Strike cigarettes prevented obesity, an obsession with the American public.

Cited as proof of the F.T.C.'s allegations were the declarations of unnamed actresses in a musical show who were quoted as saying that, by smoking Lucky Strike cigarettes, "that's how we stay slender." The truth was that none of the actresses were smokers, and it was abundantly clear that some of them were not "slender," either.

As additional evidence in this case, the F.T.C. discovered that a well-known musical comedy star who had endorsed Luckies had, in fact, been paid a sum of money for such a statement which "he did not prepare or see prior to its use, or sign," the agency claimed.

Also banned from advertising were endorsements made by famous people who smoked Lucky Strikes and found that the cigarettes "protected their throats from irritation."

In 1928, the F.T.C. rapped the knuckles of the Bayuk cigar company of Philadelphia for suggesting that its domestic cigars were made of Cuban leaf tobacco, which they were not. As a result, the federal commission ordered the cigar makers to stop using the misleading brand names, Havana Ribbon and Mapacuba.

The Bayuk company filed a lawsuit in protest. Eventually a settlement was reached that allowed Bayuk to use its trademark names provided all labels and containers carried statements clearly revealing the exact type of leaf tobacco used in the cigar manufacture.

From showdowns like these arose a never-ending battle between tobacco manufacturers and the F.T.C. The federal agency struck for truth in advertising while cigarette companies engaged in what tobacco opponents labelled as camouflage tactics designed to cloud, confuse or draw away from the real issues. At stake were billions of dollars in cigarette sales.

"Luckies Do Not Affect My Wind,"
Says Paul Waner, Voted National League's Most Valuable Player In 1927

"When I first started to smoke I was anxious to find a cigarette that would give me pleasure without taxing my wind or irritating my throat. I soon discovered Lucky Strikes. I am very fond of the excellent flavor of these cigarettes and they keep my throat clear and do not affect my wind in the least."

Paul Waner

LUCKY STRIKE "IT'S TOASTED" CIGARETTES

The Cream of the Tobacco Crop

"Buy the best Cigarette tobacco sold on your market.' These are my only instructions in buying tobacco for LUCKY STRIKE Cigarettes. As a buyer, it gives me a thrill to know that I am getting the 'Cream of the Crop.'"

"It's toasted"
No Throat Irritation–No Cough.

©1928, The American Tobacco Co., Inc.

While manufacturers were anxious to assure smokers that cigarettes were safe, they had little to worry about. The smoking habits of the average American consumer were so strong that he or she puffed blithely on, despite swirling storms of charge and countercharge passing between government and tobacco company, even when the smoker's health was at stake. Few really cared, anyway.

Any lingering doubts about the safety of cigarettes vanished in 1928. English medical experts, writing in Lancet medical magazine, assured smokers that cigarette smoking did not cause lung cancer, quieting a rumor currently circulating.

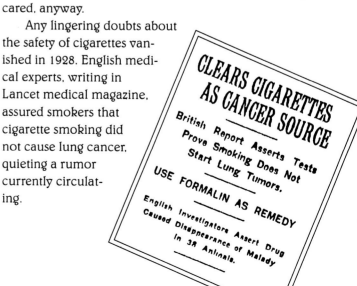

CLEARS CIGARETTES AS CANCER SOURCE
British Report Asserts Tests Prove Smoking Does Not Start Lung Tumors.
USE FORMALIN AS REMEDY
English Investigators Assert Drug Caused Disappearance of Malady in 38 Animals.

EPILOGUE

Few obstacles now stood in the way of cigarette manufacturers as America moved into the economic uncertainties of the 1930s. Despite being in the throes of the worst national depression in history, nationwide sales of cigarettes climbed steadily upward and an additional $180 million worth were sold abroad in 1930, boosting tobacco into third place among all U.S. exports.

Cigarettes had become the nation's largest revenue producer and brought in three times as much income to manufacturers than all other forms of tobacco.

Looking back on the past century, the tobacco industry had pulled off one of the greatest selling jobs in modern U.S. history, ironically, as it turned out, with unsafe goods. Senator Smoot was right. Cigarettes, born in the wild and uncontrolled age of snake oils, medical "cures" and other dangerous nostrums, were driven in demand by nicotine's addictive property and stand today as a curious leftover relic of our patent medicine past.

No unhealthy habit had ever invaded American society and the civilized world so swiftly and remained so triumphantly rooted as the paper-wrapped rolls of tobacco. The indulgence may have been wasteful, but cigarettes tasted good and smokers liked the buzz, making the ritual of "lighting up" one of the most constant and ubiquitous social habits in the world today.

> *"Tobacco is a dirty weed. I like it.*
> *It satisfies no normal need. I like it.*
> *It makes you thin, it makes you lean,*
> *It takes the hair right off your bean.*
> *It's the worst darn stuff I've ever seen.*
> *I like it."*
> –G.L. Hemminger

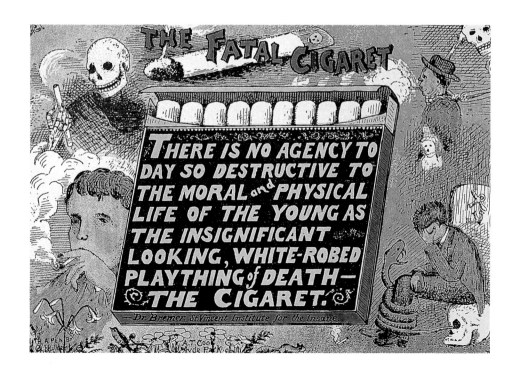

263

PRICE GUIDE

PAGE	DESCRIPTION	PRICE	PAGE	DESCRIPTION	PRICE
8		150	78	Cutter	75
20	R	250-300	78	Trays	35-75 ea.
21		500	78	Busts	50-75 ea.
25-31		10,000-75,000	79	Cutters & lighters	150-300 ea.
32	BL	50-75	79	Posters	200-1,500 ea.
33	TR	50-75	85	Tax lic.	5-10
33	B	25-40	85	Match bks	5-10 ea.
36-38		50-150 ea.	85	Pocket holders	10-15 ea.
39	Trade cards	20-30 ea.	85	Ply'g Cards	5 ea.
39	Bus. cards	5-10 ea.	85	Bus. card	10
40	TL	25-50 ea.	86	TR	1,500
41	TR	10-25 ea.	87	Chargers	100-400 ea.
42-43	5-50 ea.		87	Clock	400
44	T	75	88	T	175
44	B	15	89	First Nines	1,000
45	Posters	150-200 ea.	89	BC	20 ea.
45	Buckets	50-75 ea.	91	YHP	125
45	Chips	5-10 ea.	91	Ashley	10
46-47		25-75 ea.	91	Elsie	10
48	BR	150	91	Sunset Club	65
49		150	91	Round-Up	5
54-55		5-20 ea.	91	Amer. League	15
56		5-25 ea.	91	Honey Girls	125
57	TC	9,000 (auction, 1995)	92	Golf Links	500
57	BL	125-150 ea.	92	Far West	1,000
57	C	75-100 ea.	92	Seaside Dudes	850
57	BR	50-150 ea.	92	Speed King	300
58	T	100-150	93	Champions	2,500
58	B	15-20 ea.	93	Klondike	750
59		100-150 ea.	93	On Time	800
60		10-20 ea.	93	Rail Birds	1,000
61	Fast Mail	150	94	Great Chief	7,000
61	Banner	1000	94	Champions	2,500
61	Diadem	150	94	Bully	700
61	Old Abe	750	94	Cool Smoke	1,000
61	Hess	750	95	Ken'l Club	25
61	North Star	750	95	Just Good	5
61	Florida	750	95	James Lewis	15
61	Lock unit	50	95	Jockey	50
61	May Queen	750	96		5-15 ea.
61	Century	750	97	Almeda	10
62	B	15	97	Monkey	75
63	BL	50	97	Vaud. Sports	40
65	CL	100	97	Geraldine	25
65	B	150	97	Yellow Hornet	25
66	Trade cards	35-50 ea.	97	Spider	25
66	Chair	200	97	Indra	35
66	Paperwt.	35	97	Alrg't	20
66	Poster	400	97	Uncle Sam	125
68-69		200-400 ea.	98		5-35 ea.
78	Slugs	5-15 ea.	99	Touchstone	40
78	Machine	150	99	Hummer	40
78	Mat	25	99	Uncle Jake's	10
78	Tools	10-25 ea.	100		5-30 ea.

PAGE	DESCRIPTION	PRICE	PAGE	DESCRIPTION	PRICE
101	Cgr Bd Book	100	129	Fountain	125
102		1,000	129	Uncle Daniel	125
103	TR	50	129	Hiawatha	125
103	CR	50	129	Old Abe	750
103	BR	100	129	Express	500
111	TL	50	129	Tiger	350
115	BL	500 ea.	129	Plow Boy	600
117	C	75	129	Sure Shot	325
122	BL	l:15; r: 25	129	Nic Nac	1,200
122	BR	50	129	Sweet Mist	125
123	Cigar Box	125	129	Sweet Burley	100
123	Cig. Packs	20-125 ea.	129	Sweet Loma	1,200
124	Bags	50-100 ea.	130	Virgin	500
125	Packages	50-125 ea.	130	Plow Boy	35
126	Bro. Jonthn	3,000	130	Eagle	150
126	Boston Slice	125	130	Gold Leaf	75
126	Dixie	125	130	Tip Top	125
126	Surbrg Purse	150	130	Eight Bros.	50
126	Pig Skin	750	130	Full Dress	85
126	Gail & Ax	1,500	130	City Club	100
126	Good Cheer	75	130	Miners & Pud.	125
126	Whip	350	130	Hand Made	75
126	Qboid	75	130	Pedro	500
126	Twin Oaks	50	130	Fast Mail	500
126	Union Leader	150	130	Uniform	1,000
126	Calif. Nugget	100	130	Dixie Queen	250
126	Eutopia	150	131	Every Day	250
127	Cavalier	75	131	Gold Medal	100
127	Prune Nugget	75	131	Madeira	225
127	Virg. Creeper	175	131	Pride of Turkey	100
127	Island Hash	350	131	L.A.W.	500
127	Princeton	125	131	Yacht Club	125
127	Cameron's	75	131	Scroll Cut	125
127	Jule Carr	175	131	Motley's Finest	500
127	Engl. Pug	200	131	My Swtht	100
127	Handsome Dan	150	131	La Belle Creole	125
127	Constellation	75	131	Amer. Girl	750
127	Clover Club	200	131	Exquisite	1,250
127	Virginity	150	131	Idle Hour	225
127	Raleigh	225	131	3 Aces	750
127	Post Office	325	131	Hiawatha	50
127	Fox's	175	131	Virginians	400
127	Berta Grav'ly	1,000	132	Durham	4,000 (auction)
127	Club Room	2,500	132	Detr't Club	1,000 (auction)
127	Poker Club	2,500	132	Four Roses	400
127	Golden Wed'g	100	132	Bull Dog	225
127	Richmond Belle	500	132	Bagdad	150
127	Winner	75	132	Cont. Cubes	400
127	Hand Bag	100	132	Honey Moon	125
127	Elctc Mixt	450	132	Luxura	900 (auction)
128	Friends	150	132	Hindoo	350
128	Dixie Kid	225	132	Gravly's Spec.	400
128	Winner	125	132	High Grade	1,000 (auction)
128	U.S. Marine	250	132	Rock Castle	500
128	Fash'n	125	132	Trout Line	300
128	Green Turtle	100	132	Three Fthrs	175
128	Chas. Denby	75	132	Yacht Club	500
128	Burley Boy	800	132	Whip	500
128	Commander	200	132	Orchid	700
128	Red Indian	850	133	Stetson	8,250 (auction)
129	Mellow Sweet	150	133	Ty Cobb	Ext.Rare

PAGE	DESCRIPTION	PRICE
175	Hassan	100
175	Mogul (B&W)	1,500 (auction)
176	Turk. Trophs	250
176	Tiger	250
176	Star	150
176	Egypt.Luxury	150
176	Fatima	300
176	London Life	150
176	Ramleh	600
176	Admiration	3,000 (auction)
176	Mayo's	150
177		75-250 ea.
179		75-150 ea.
203	CL	15
218	L	25
221	BR	50-75 ea.
236	TR	15
237	TR	25
243	TL	15
244	CR	45
246	TC	50
252	CR	35
253	BL	25
263	BC	15

INDEX